The
Fast Forward
MBA in
Business Math

THE FAST FORWARD MBA SERIES

The Fast Forward MBA Series provides time-pressed business professionals and students with concise, one-stop information to help them solve business problems and make smart, informed business decisions. All of the volumes, written by industry leaders, contain "tough ideas made easy." The published books in this series are:

The Fast Forward MBA in Business Math

PETER GARRITY

John Wiley & Sons, Inc.

New York • Chichester • Weinheim • Brisbane • Singapore • Toronto

To those wonderful Garrity girls,
Delia, Maura, and Patricia
And my dad, Joe

Published by John Wiley & Sons, Inc.
Published simultaneously in Canada.

Forbes is a registered trademark. Its use is pursuant to a license
agreement with Forbes Inc.

This publication is designed to provide accurate and authoritative
information in regard to the subject matter covered. It is sold
with the understanding that the publisher is not engaged in
rendering professional services. If legal, accounting, medical,
psychological or any other expert assistance is required, the
services of a competent professional person should be sought.

ISBN   0-471-31503-6

Printed in the United States of America.

10 9 8 7 6 5 4 3 2 1

Peter Garrity is an adjunct professor at Columbia University's Graduate School of Business, where he teaches Management Information Systems and MathCamp, a very successful math and technology program. He has taught at the Columbia Business School for more than 25 years and has a reputation for delivering lively interactive lectures focused on the practical. His Math-Camp program has been adopted by a number of financial institutions to support product training.

Professor Garrity is an expert in systems implementation and training for the financial services sector. He is the founder and president of HeurisTech Solutions, a training consulting firm specializing in implementing technology. His love of math and his views on technology have influenced his work at Columbia, where he has made a career of studying both areas. He brings his real-world consulting experience in implementing enterprisewide systems to his Information Systems for Today's Manager course. He has written more than 20 applications-oriented computer manuals that have been adopted by many of the New York financial institutions where he also consults.

But his real love is mathematics, or, more specifically, the applications of mathematics. "Mathematics makes business concepts come alive," he says in Math-Camp, "because the applications from economics, finance, or statistics are exciting and so much easier to understand when math leads the way."

Professor Garrity can be contacted at mathcamp.com.

ACKNOWLEDGMENTS

In the 25 years I have been teaching at Columbia University, there have been a number of people who have shaped my directions in education, my philosophy of instruction, and my interests in the teaching of mathematics. Bruce Vogeli, the esteemed chair in the Department of Mathematics Education, has been a mentor to me, and a source of encouragement. The faculty of the Graduate School of Business has supported my efforts in developing an exciting applications-oriented math program, upon which this book is based. Many of its members have supplied me with wonderful examples that help make my efforts come alive for students. In particular, I thank Tom Ference, the first Dean of the Executive M.B.A. program, for hiring me 25 years ago, and Dean Safwan Masri for his support in my current efforts.

I could not have done the statistics section without the advice and observations of Paul Thurman. Thanks to my many teaching assistants, who have supported MathCamp and encouraged me to write this book. In particular, my thanks to Frank Pometti, the major model TA, for his reviews and feedback.

Thanks to my close friends, Don Pardew, a gifted statistics professor, and Lloyd Sherman, an innovative science educator, for all their wisdom, insight, and support in my professional accomplishments. A special thank-you to Renana Meyers, my editor at Wiley, for her guidance throughout this process.

And thanks to my wife, Delia, whose infinite patience, love, and understanding have always been there for me. I am truly appreciative.

CONTENTS

PART 1

Making Decisions with Time Value of Money

It Makes Cents

CHAPTER 1

The Basics of Time Value of Money

Why is it that this book on the mathematics of business should start with time value of money? Because a basic understanding of how you value an opportunity is a necessary skill, whether in business, determining the cost of financing a new truck or computer system, or personally, in planning a retirement package or the cost of a child's college education. In either situation the results could prove disastrous if you do not know how to evaluate your options. The fact is, the need to know how money works is key to understanding—and *solving*—life's, as well as business's, major problems. Not to be too dramatic, but many of the important decisions in business, as well as in life, are financial in nature. As a consequence we need to know the tools that help us in analyzing these decisions—hence, time value of money.

Part 1 explains how money grows over time and defines key financial tools that help you make business decisions. We demonstrate how to determine the return on the purchase of a new computer system, how a product will grow in the market, and the projected units of production or revenue. These are all part of a large family of business problems that behave in a similar way to that of the growth of money. That is, if you need to know what your projected sales will be based upon a 5 percent increase in sales each year, then you will be using the exact same mathematics as for time value of money. We also examine the first stages of education and retirement planning—for example, determining how much you need today, to fund a year of college education for your oldest child in 10 years. You will find more on all these exciting topics in the applications section of this chapter.

A SIMPLER TIME: THE BASIC DEFINITIONS

As you have gathered by now in life, this entire topic of the time value of money is based on the principle that when you borrow, lend, or invest money there is a fee for this opportunity. Let's go back in time for an example. Recall your fifteenth birthday, when you received the grand total of $100 from all your relatives. Your mom and dad took you down to the local bank, impressed upon you the importance of savings, and helped you start a savings account with that $100. "Remember," they said, "from little acorns big oaks grow." Such a familiar phrase—just how does it apply to your money?

When you place that $100 into a savings account at your local bank, the bank pays you for the use of your money—that is, when you return a year later to withdraw funds or check on your balance, you expect to see more than $100 in the account. That's the beauty of investing, your money makes money. Unlike hiding your money on the top shelf of your bookcase, where, although it's close to you (and easily spent!), it will not grow beyond what you hide. This is mathematically, as well as personally, a very rich topic! Let's introduce some key terms.

CONCEPT   Present value + Interest = Future value

or Money now + Interest = More money later

Present Value

Before you can get or pay interest, you have to deposit money into the account (or, on the other side of the transaction, borrow an amount). *Present value* (PV) is another name for principal; it refers to the value of the amount of money today—in the *present*. For example, as you walk into the bank with your $100, the amount of the deposit is your present value. It refers to the worth of money—that is, your investment—today.

Interest

Whenever money is borrowed, there is a fee for the use of the funds. Likewise, when funds are invested or deposited in a savings account, you are paid for the use of your funds. *Interest (I)* refers to the amount of money gained or charged for the use of money. Sometimes you get it, as in a savings account, and sometimes you pay it, as in a car loan or mortgage. The amount of the interest is determined by the rate the bank uses in its calculation. And with mathematics we will be able to determine the amount of interest.

Future Value

But time marches on, and so begins the growth in interest. *Future value* (FV) is the term used to define the sum of the principal *P* and the amount of interest accrued over the time period. *Accrue* is a term used to describe the cumulating value of interest. Two factors influence the amount of the future value:

- *Time.* The longer the money is left in the account, the more interest it gains.
- *Rate.* The greater the rate, the larger the interest, and as a result, the future value.

MATHEMATICALLY SPEAKING

How Money Grows

We will define FV_1 to be the future value of the investment or principal *P* after 1 year of gaining interest *I* at the rate *r*. It can be calculated by using either of the following two methods:

$$FV_1 = P + I$$

$$FV_1 = PV + PVr$$

Or, with just a little factoring

$$FV_1 = PV(1 + r)$$

Trick is, they are both actually the same. Let's demonstrate. Suppose you deposit $100 (PV) in the bank at 8 percent (*r*) for 1 year. Then we ask, "How much is the future value one year later?" We will demonstrate that with either formula you will arrive at the correct amount. (Recall that the use of parentheses is an indication of multiplication.)

$$
\begin{array}{lcl}
FV_1 = PV + PV(r) & \text{or} & FV_1 = PV(1 + r) \\
FV_1 = 100 + 100(0.08) & \text{or} & FV_1 = 100(1 + 0.08) \\
FV_1 = 100 + 8 & \text{or} & FV_1 = 100(1.08) \\
FV_1 = 108 & \text{or} & FV_1 = 108
\end{array}
$$

You try: **Find the Future Value**

Show that $1,000 deposited for 1 year at 5 percent will have a future value of $1,050.

So, determining the future value or worth of the investment after one year is straightforward. Where all this gets very interesting is when we calculate the interest during the second year. Is it another $8 or should it be more? The answer is found by determining if the calculation employs simple interest or compound interest.

Simple Interest: The Linear View

Simple interest refers to the fact that the annual amount of interest is the same for each year of the investment. It is calculated by multiplying the principal and the annual rate. Then this amount is added each additional year for the specified number of years, as follows:

For 1 year	*For t years*
$I_{1\text{ year}} = \text{PV}r$	$I_{t\text{ years}} = \text{PV}rt$
$I_{1\text{ year}} = 100(0.08)$	$I_{t\text{ years}} = 100(0.08)t$
$I_{1\text{ year}} = 8$	$I_{t\text{ years}} = 8t$

Therefore:

$$\text{FV}_{1\text{ year}} = 100 + 8 \qquad \text{FV}_{t\text{ years}} = 100 + 8t$$

$$\text{FV}_{1\text{ year}} = 108 \qquad \text{FV}_{t\text{ years}} = \text{PV} + \text{PV}rt$$

For example, at the end of 1 year, your account will contain not only the principal of $100, but also the interest of $8. If you always received simple interest, then this method of interest accrual would be a linear function. Let's see how.

Linear functions are described in more detail in Chapter 13. At this point we want to show how they apply to interest calculations that accrue for periods longer than one year. The following are examples of first-degree functions in two variables. They are termed *linear* because they produce a line when graphed.

$$y = 2x \qquad f(x) = 0.5x \qquad \text{FV}(x) = 100 + 8x$$

The preceding example of $\text{FV}(x)$ is the calculation of simple interest given an annual rate of 8 percent. Specifically, the question before us is, what does the relationship $\text{FV}(x)$ look like, and how does it relate to the growth of money? Let's take a look at Figure 1.1, which shows how it works by considering your $100 at 8 percent over a few years.

This constantly increasing function is an example of an arithmetic progression in that each sequential unit of time (1 year) corresponds to an $8 increase in interest. You bet it sounds like the slope of a line, and in fact, as the formula and graph show, the slope of the line is 8. This straightforward linear function is used to calculate the total amount of the future value by multiplying the number of years times 8 dollars, and adding it to the principal (or present value), $100.

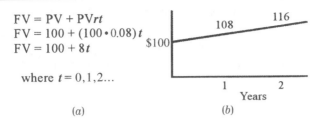

$$FV = PV + PVrt$$
$$FV = 100 + (100 \cdot 0.08)t$$
$$FV = 100 + 8t$$

where $t = 0, 1, 2 \ldots$

(a)

(b)

FIGURE 1.1 *Simple interest as a linear function: (a) the formula, and (b) the graphic representation.*

You try:

Determining Simple Interest

How much simple interest would be generated on a 4-year loan for $25,000 if the interest rate was 10 percent?

Answer: $10,000.

Making Payments with Simple Interest

How is a monthly payment determined? It depends on how interest is calculated. For example, how much should you pay on a monthly basis if you borrow $10,000 from an institution that employs simple interest in its future value calculations? A small number of borrowing situations still employ this method. Suppose you have to pay back the loan over 4 years, and the rate of interest applied to the principal is 5 percent. It is a two-step process to determine the monthly payment, in that you must first determine the future value (the total cost of borrowing) under this scenario, and then divide that number by the total number of payments you must make to pay off the loan.

$$FV_{4\,years} = PV + PVr(4)$$

Make your substitutions.

$$FV_{4\,years} = 10,000 + 10,000(0.05)(4)$$

$$FV_{4\,years} = 10,000 + 2,000$$

$$FV_{4\,years} = 12,000$$

This is your total cost.

$$\text{Monthly payment} = \frac{\text{future value}}{\text{number of payments}} = \frac{12,000}{48}$$

Monthly payment = $250

You try: →

Determine the Monthly Payment

What is the monthly payment on a loan of $18,000, which must be paid on a monthly basis over 5 years to an institution that charges simple interest of 8 percent?

Answer: $420.

THE NATURE OF COMPOUND INTEREST

The previous example does not demonstrate the way money actually accrues interest in most investments— it's really not *simple.* (What a pun!) And that's good news for your savings account, as we shall soon see. So, how then, is it calculated? The interesting point is that during the second year you get interest calculated on the initial principal *and* the interest you made during the first year. Hence, there will be a few extra pennies added to the future value. *Compound interest* is the method whereby interest is calculated on both the principal and interest accrued from previous periods. It's great the way the banks think in our best interest, and realize the injustice of the linear perspective. But before their beneficence overwhelms us, we should not get too excited. Remember, the banks also do this on loans that they make to us.

MATHEMATICALLY SPEAKING

How Compound Interest Is Calculated

Let's see what actually happens in year 2 as the investment accrues more interest on your $100. In the first year you accrued $8 worth of interest and, as a result, you ended up with future value of $108 at the end of the year. Now, here's the trick. The future value at the end of year 1 is exactly the beginning principal for the second year (not the initial $100). The extra $8 that you had earned in interest in the first year becomes part of the principal for the second year.

$$FV_1 = 100(1 + 0.08) \qquad FV_2 = 108(1 + 0.08)$$

Year 1	Year 2
PV = $100	PV = $108
(Present value)	(Same as FV_1)

A little algebra will show us how this process called *compounding* works. As an example, let's determine the future value of $100 invested for 2 years at 8 percent. Remember that you accrued $108 for year 1 ($FV_1$), so it becomes the principal for year 2.

$$FV_2 = FV_1(1 + 0.08) = 108(1 + 0.08)$$
$$FV_2 = 108(1.08) = 116.64$$

Here is an alternative way to perform the same calculation that will give you the key insight to the process.

$$FV_2 = FV_1(1 + 0.08)$$

Substitute $PV(1 + 0.08)$ for FV_1.

$$FV_2 = PV(1 + 0.08)(1 + 0.08)$$

$$FV_2 = 100(1 + 0.08)(1 + 0.08)$$

Note that there are two factors of 1.08.

$$FV_2 = 100(1 + 0.08)^2$$

Now square the 1.08.

$$FV_2 = 100(1.1664)$$

$$FV_2 = 116.64$$

So, as the preceding calculation shows, the future value of $100 after 2 years is actually an exponential function, where the base of the function is $(1 + r)$ and r is the rate specified over the entire period of the investment. Note that the number of years becomes the exponent. The graph in Figure 1.2 shows the difference between the two methods, and why you will gain a little extra in the compounding process, thereby increasing the amount of the future value compared to simple interest. So the future value of $100 over 2 years at 8 percent is determined by the following equation, which is very different from the linear case.

$$FV_{2\ years} = 100(1 + 0.08)^2 = 100(1.08)^2$$

 Compounding Is an Exponential Function

Exponential functions are described in more detail in Chapter 13. At this point we want to define what they are, and how they apply to finance. An *exponential function* is any function where the variable is in the

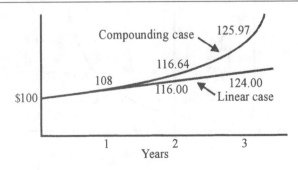

FIGURE 1.2 *Compound interest grows exponentially, not linearly.*

exponent and the base is a given positive number. See the following examples:

$$y = 2^x \qquad f(x) = 0.5^x \qquad F(x) = 1.08^x$$

In each of these examples, you will see that the exponent contains the variable. Specifically, the questions before us are, what does the relationship $F(x)$, the future value, look like, and how does it relate to the growth of money?

As you examine the table and curve in Figure 1.3, you should realize that the values of y are a result of raising 1.08 to a power. The table reveals the values of the exponential function as it ranges over the values $x = 0, 1, 2, \ldots$. Look closely or use your calculator to verify that these values are actually powers of 1.08. But what do these numbers mean? It is important to show in our development of the fundamentals of the time value of money, that these values represent the multipliers that you would use to find the future values of $100, $1,000, and so on, when invested at the rate of 8 percent for x number of years. Table 1.1 shows how the future value of $100 changes as time marches on.

As Table 1.1 demonstrates, by using the values derived from the exponential function whose base is 1.08, we are able to multiply by $100 to determine the future value of a principal that has compounded annually at a rate of 8 percent for the indicated number of years.

Interestingly, how did people solve these problems before there were calculators? In the old days (prior to calculators or Elvis) you had to use lengthy tables in the back of finance and accounting textbooks to determine the financial multiplier. For example, to solve for the future value given 8 percent for 2 years, you multiply 1.1664 times the present value. So, the key to solving for the future value is to know the multiplier, because once it is known, as Table A.1 in the appendix shows, you have the answer. Follow across to the 8.00 percent

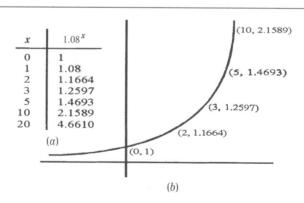

FIGURE 1.3 *Graph of the function y = 1.08ˣ: (a) table, and (b) curve.*

TABLE 1.1 EXPONENTIAL VALUES FOR y = 1.08ˣ

Years x	Multiplier 1.08^x	Future Value $100(1.08)^x$
0	1.0000	$100.0000
1	1.0800	108.0000
2	1.1664	116.6400
3	1.2597	125.9712
4	1.3605	136.0489
5	1.4693	146.9328
10	2.1589	215.8925
20	4.6610	466.0957

column in the table and down 2 rows to find the multiplier for the future value for 2 years. In finance books, you will find tables like these that you would use to look up the required rate (columns) and time (rows represent years or periods). Multiplier values are found in the 8.00 percent column of Table A.1. These multipliers are simply the numbers behind the calculator.

You try:

Determining the Future Value

Show that $100 deposited for 3 years at 8 percent will have a future value of $125.97. Use Table A.1 or cube 1.08. Don't worry, we won't do 5, 10, or 20 years without using the calculator.

$$FV_{3\,years} = 100(1.08)^3 = ?$$

As long as the rate remains at 8 percent you can always determine the future value by performing the following calculation. But what if the rate should change?

$$FV_{t\,years} = 100(?)^t$$

General Compound Interest Formula

KEY CONCEPT

Moving beyond the last example, we need a function that will handle any rate, not just 8 percent. For the general case, the famous compound interest formula, we need to be able to replace the 8 percent with whatever is the new desired rate. Simply, the future value of your investment is determined by the amount you invest (the principal or present value) times the compounding factor $(1 + r)^t$, where r refers to the specified annual rate and t refers to the number of years the investment will accrue interest. Here's the equation:

$$FV = PV\,(1 + r)^t$$

You try: **Future Value at 5 Percent**

Using the general compound interest formula, show that $100 will grow to $115.76 in 3 years with an interest rate of 5 percent. All this multiplying and pencil sharpening means it's time to begin using the calculator.

CALC TIP
Using the Power Key on the Calculator

The Power key, indicated by a caret sign (^), is usually a shift key on your calculator. This key enables you to calculate an exponential statement, such as 5^2 or $36^{1/2}$ or 1.05^3. If you are not sure of these root equivalents, review the exponent section in Chapter 13. Let's try a few examples.

Suppose you wanted to raise 5 to the second power—that is, 5^2:

1. Type in the base, which is 5.
2. Press the Power key, ^.
3. Type in the power, which is 2.
4. Press the equal sign (=) to calculate. There's your answer.

Some older calculators employ the y^x key for doing exponential calculations. It works very similarly to the keystrokes just given.

1. Type in the base y, which is 5.
2. Press the Enter key
3. Type in the power x, which is 2.
4. Press the y^x key to calculate. There's your answer.

The other exponential function you need to perform is taking a root—for example, $\sqrt{36}$, which is the same as $36^{1/2}$:

1. Type in the base, which is 36.
2. Press the Power key, ^.
3. Type in the power using parentheses (1 ÷ 2).
4. Press = to calculate. There's your answer.

You should become adept with the use of parentheses because sometimes the roots will not be so easily performed in your head—for example, a cube root (1 ÷ 3). If your calculator does not employ parentheses, just perform the division calculation after entering the base—from the preceding example, 36—and continue as indicated.

You try: → **Taking a Cube Root**

Using the parenthesis technique with the calculator, verify that the cube root of 21,952 is 28. Note that if you enter 0.33 you will not get the correct answer because 0.33 does not equal 1/3; it would only be an approximation.

TIME VALUE OF MONEY AND YOUR CALCULATOR

The beauty of the calculator is that, just like an automobile, it can get you to where you want to go a whole lot faster than walking. But, you can't drive without the keys, so here we go. As they say at the races, "Start your calculators!" Most calculators have financial functions, which make calculating time value of money problems a lot easier. For example, on the HP 19 or 17 series you can access the Time Value of Money menu by selecting the Finance menu and then selecting TVM. For other calculators, refer to the manual to find how to access these keys. The keys defined in Table 1.2 are used by most calculator manufacturers.

When entering a value into one of these variables, type the number you want to enter, and then press the key assigned to that variable. On some calculators—for example, the HP 12C—the name will actually appear on a key; on others, such as the HP 19 or 17 series, it appears on a display above an assigned entry key.

CALC TIP

Finding Future Value

Now that you know the basic time value of money keys, it's time to exercise them. Lets return to our initial problem (since we know the answer), and demonstrate how to enter the keystrokes for the future value of $100 at 8 percent for 1 year. Since FV is what we are solving for, it will be the last key we press.

1. Type 1 on the keypad, and press N for number of years.
2. Type 100, then press the ± key, which reverses the sign (see note on entering PV).
3. Press PV. This enters the present value amount.
4. Type 8 (not 0.08), and press I% YR for interest rate.
5. Press FV to solve for future value.

The following template shows the key assignments and the entries required of you for this problem. The dark shaded box indicates the variable you are solving

TABLE 1.2 THE TIME VALUE OF MONEY KEYS

Key Name	Purpose
N	The number of years of the investment.
I%YR	The interest rate over the investment period. This entry will assume a percentage, so you should not enter the decimal point.
PV	The principal amount you invest today. This is the amount that will be compounded into the future. In most financial calculators, this amount is entered as a *negative* amount in the sense that it is being taken from you to an investment account, termed *Cash out*.
FV	The future value of your investment.
PMT	This key accepts an entry for an annuity. You will not need to enter any values into this register for our current PV and FV calculations.

for, and will be the last key that you press in this process. Values in the other boxes indicate initial entries required for solving the problem, and may be entered in any order. After pressing the FV key, the display should read 108 as your answer. Whether you got the problem right or wrong, see the next paragraph for advice on calculators.

N	I%YR	PV	PMT	Press FV	OTHER
1	8	−100		to solve for FV.	

The Incorrect Keystroke

The calculator is an amazing piece of technology, which provides a number of ways to do these problems. But sometimes this flexibility can be the source of an incorrect answer. At this point in learning the keystrokes, clarity and exactness come first. Did you get the correct answer of 108?

When using the calculator it is easy to make keystroke errors, so I suggest the following strategy. When looking at the result of a calculation, check it out for correctness. Does it seem reasonable? Make a ballpark estimate in your head and compare. In this case, our result should be a little more than $100. If you got an answer in the thousands, or maybe just the $8, you know something went wrong. When dealing with the calculator, or any technology, it is always best to have an idea of where the calculation is going, of what represents an appropriate answer.

So, if your answer is way off, the best step is to clear the current entries and try again. Usually there is a Clear All key that will perform this function. If you have a negative sign, then you forgot to press the plus/minus (±) key before entering the PV value. When doing these types of problems, you'll never need to make an entry for PMT, which is only used with annuities. When first learning the calculator, it is a common mistake to enter the present value amount as a PMT entry. If you get an incorrect answer you can enter 0 in PMT to make sure it has no entry, then press FV.

CALC TIP
Time-Saving Keystrokes

This tip is very beneficial. Once the values are entered on the calculator, they are stored in their respective registers (PV, N, etc.). This means they remain in those locations (termed *registers*) until either cleared or replaced with another entry. This neat feature allows you to make a change to one of the variables in the problem and recalculate without entering all the other values again. We will demonstrate this important time-saving feature through a few examples. Let's let the fingers do some walking.

You try:

Calculator Dexterity at Its Best

- *Solve for FV.* How much will $100 grow in 10 years if the bank gives a rate of 8 percent? Answer: $215.89.

- *Solve for FV.* How much will $1,000 grow in 10 years if the bank gives a rate of 8 percent? The trick here is that you need only replace the PV entry; other entries remain as entered. Answer: $2,158.93.

- *Solve for FV.* How much will $1,000 grow in 10 years if the bank gives a rate of 10 percent? The trick here is that you need only replace the rate entry. Answer: $2,593.74.

Now that you have the idea, let's use the calculator to help us make an important observation about the behavior of an exponential function. First, show that the future value of $1,000 for 2 years at 8 percent is $1,166.40. So try this variation. How much will $1,000 grow in 2 years if the bank gives a rate of 4 percent? What do you suspect should be the amount of the future value, as you consider a rate that is half of 8 percent? How do these two calculations compare? The following template displays the entries for solving the problem.

N	I%YR	PV	PMT	Press FV	OTHER
2	4	–1,000		to solve for FV.	

What is this problem trying to demonstrate? Did you think the interest would be half? In fact, the amount of interest accrued in the future value at 4 percent (81.60) is not half the amount that you determined for 8 percent (166.40). This is because the function is *exponential,* not linear. That is, for the first year, the return on 4 percent interest will be half of that at 8 percent, but once multiple years are analyzed, you will see that the multiplier no longer maintains this one-half relationship. This important fact is developed in Chapter 2.

APPLICATIONS OF FUTURE VALUE

This section demonstrates how the material you just learned can be applied to projecting sales, calculating the effect of inflation on purchasing power, and retirement planning. Many of these applications are explored more deeply in later chapters.

KEY CONCEPT **Projecting Future Sales**

"How well will your company perform over the next few years?" asked the bank's credit officer. You responded with two observations on the welfare of the company. First, based on all indications (you will get to know what that means after completing the statistics section) sales will be steadily increasing over the next few years at an annual compounded rate of 5 percent. The total revenue (sales) at your company this year was $400,000. Second, any increase in costs by your suppliers will be due to the normal effect of inflation.

In trying to establish a line of credit with your local bank, the lending officer has asked that you submit a pro forma—that is, a projection of your costs and sales for the next few years, along with the assumptions that justify the projections. As manager of Cyber Vineyards, a winery for the new millennium, you need a line of credit so you can purchase software for a website to promote your products as well as to resolve some short-term cash flow problems.

The first task is to project the sales (in terms of dollars) for the next four-year business cycle. To set up the model we will assume that the sales of wine for Cyber Vineyards has increased every year by an average of approximately 5 percent over sales of the preceding year. This model is very typical of business growth, and demonstrates the nature of compounding as explained in this chapter. If the current annual sales for Cyber Vineyards is $400,000, and we assume that sales will increase each year at the 5 percent annual compounded growth rate, then what will be the expected sales over the next four years? Figure 1.4 shows how the sales projection will grow, compared to no growth, which is a line equal to the constant function 400,000. Now that we know what is expected of the analysis, let's determine the solution.

MATHEMATICALLY SPEAKING

Projecting Future Sales

The future value of sales is a compounding function, growing by a factor of 5 percent each year. This translates to the following function, where n represents the number of years in the projection:

$$\text{Sales } (n) = 400,000 \, (1 + .05)^n$$
becomes $\quad \text{Sales } (n) = 400,000 \, (1.05)^n$

So total sales for the next few years will be found by solving our sales function for $n = 2$, 3, and 4.

$$\text{Sales } (1) = 400,000 \, (1.05)^1 = 400,000(1.05) = 420,000$$

$$\text{Sales } (2) = 400,000 \, (1.05)^2 = 400,000(1.1025)^2 = 441,000$$

Or, an alternative way:

$$\text{Sales } (2) = 400,000 \, (1.05)^2 = 420,000(1.05)^1 = 441,000$$

These equations reinforce a very important point about projecting sales: It is a compounding function—that is, it is not 5 percent of the 400,000 units added

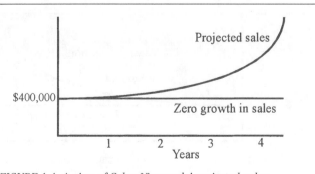

FIGURE 1.4 *A view of Cyber Vineyards' projected sales.*

successively to each year. (Remember the difference between a linear function and an exponential one.) In fact, as the formulas for the first and second years show, each successive year will grow 5 percent over the preceding year. Figure 1.5 shows how the projection will behave over all four years.

Next, we need to know the future value for years 3 and 4. If we want to determine the third-year sales by using the calculator, then we use the following settings for the future value projection.

N	I%YR	PV	PMT	Press FV	OTHER
3	5	−400,000		to solve for FV.	

Verify that the total sales for years 3 and 4 of the projection are \$463,050 and \$486,202.50, respectively.

Determining the Effect of Two Projecting Rates

Suppose you decide to launch the new Cyber Vineyards website with a new advertising campaign called "Got Wine," using Charlie Brown and Snoopy from the *Peanuts* comic strip by Charles Schulz. You anticipate that this marketing arrangement will be continued for the next four years. The marketing consultant who orchestrated the contract anticipates that total sales for your company will increase an additional 4 percent each year due to the increase in software sales. What is the effect on the growth rate of future sales? What would your intuition say regarding the new rate of growth for the four-year period? Good. I hope you simply added the rates; that shows that your intuition is working just fine.

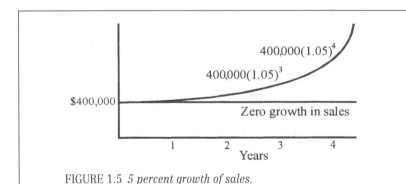

FIGURE 1.5 *5 percent growth of sales.*

How Two Rates Are Added

Recall that we have the forecast; we have just completed the projection for 4 years at 5 percent. The problem now is to determine the effect of an additional 4 percent on that initial forecast. The formula for the projection will change by multiplying the original projection (shown in brackets in the following equation) by the increased rate (1.04). So sales for any year t could be determined by:

$$\text{Sales } (t) = [400{,}000 \ (1.05)^t](1.04)^t$$

For example, for the first year, the advertising campaign will be responsible for adding an additional $16,800 to the total revenue. Let's demonstrate how this works.

$$\text{Sales } (1) = [400{,}000 \ (1.05)^1](1.04)^1$$
$$= 420{,}000 \ (1.04) = 436{,}800$$

Or, an alternative way:

$$\text{Sales } (1) = 400{,}000 \ (1.092) = 436{,}800$$

So, the process of combining the rates actually becomes a multiplication exercise. The rate factors (1.05 and 1.04) could be multiplied, which results in the rate of 1.092 (or 9.2 percent), just a little larger than the sum of the percentages (5 and 4 percent). Certainly as an estimate, you could simply add the two percentages and use the sum as the rate in your future value calculation. But try for the actual rate, as shown in the following steps. Then use your calculator skills to determine the revenue projection after four years of the advertising campaign.

$$\text{Sales } (n) = [400{,}000 \ (1.05)^t](1.04)^t$$

Redistribute rates.

$$\text{Sales } (n) = 400{,}000 \ (1.05)^t(1.04)^t$$

Place rates to same power.

$$\text{Sales } (n) = 400{,}000 \ [(1.05)(1.04)]^t$$

$$\text{Sales } (n) = 400{,}000 \ (1.092)^t \qquad 1.092 = 1.05 \times 1.04$$

Suppose we compared the curve of the revised revenue projection to the original projection of 5 percent. How will the curves be different? The answer is found in Figure 1.6.

We can see from our calculations that the result of the 4 percent increase should be increased sales. The revised projection will be a steeper graph than the original projection of 5 percent, as shown in Figure 1.6. After four years of the advertising campaign, the revised revenue for the fourth year will be $568,788.16. The rate that you should have used is 9.2 percent.

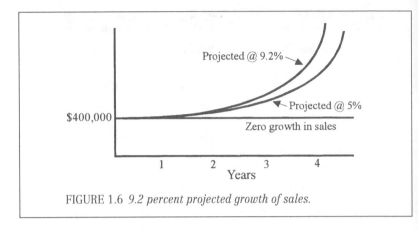

FIGURE 1.6 *9.2 percent projected growth of sales.*

The Effect of Inflation

The annual rate of *inflation* is a statistic that measures the rise in prices of consumer goods and services as determined by the change in the Consumer Price Index (CPI), also known as the *cost-of-living index*. The CPI is determined by prices of goods and services purchased by a typical family of four. Recently, there has been commentary that the CPI no longer tells us the true rate of inflation; in fact, some say it overstates that rate. We show how this percentage affects prices mathematically, and leave the discussion of exactly what it all means to the economists.

As a businessperson, how does inflation affect you? Don't forget that you are a consumer as well. You have suppliers who provide you with product or raw material that goes into your business. Inflation affects the whole supply chain in the delivery of product to the end purchaser; hence, it can have a dramatic compounding effect on price.

Although we may not like it, we have become somewhat conditioned to the reality that prices increase due to inflation. While inflation is often defined as the slow rise in prices over time, the increase in product prices is more sophisticated than that, and more study in economics and finance is required to truly appreciate the phenomenon. Basically, we examine inflation from two perspectives: as the cost-of-living adjustment (that is, the increase in consumer prices) and as an indication of loss of purchasing power (that is, as prices go up, the real purchasing power of your savings decreases). Let's examine inflation as "price creep" here. Chapter 3 examines how it affects buying power.

Inflation as "Price Creep"

You are a chocolate chip cookie connoisseur, studying them, buying them, and eating them for most of your life. You recall that in 1990 a box of your favorite brand of chocolate chip cookies sold for $3.89. And you have watched as, year in and year out, the price has crept up. One news service has indicated that the rate of inflation for the 1990s has averaged 1.6 percent per year. If this is the case, what will be the price of your box of cookies at the end of this decade? The following equations will determine the new price of the cookies assuming the 1.6 percent growth rate, followed by the keystrokes with the time value of money keys. Note that the price of the cookies in 1990 is the present value.

New price $(t) = 3.89(1.016)^t$

New price $(10) = 3.89\ (1.016)^{10}$

New price $(10) = 3.89\ (1.172)$

New price $(10) = \$4.56$

CALC TIP

Entering Decimal Rates

Normally you need not use a decimal point in entering rates in the time value of money keys because the rate assumes two positions—that is, 8 percent, which is 0.08, is entered as 8. When entering a rate like 1.6%, that is, 0.016, you must include the decimal point because two positions takes you to 6 tenths. You should arrive at the same answer, $4.56.

 Estimating Costs of Goods Sold

Your total cost of goods sold at Cyber Vineyards this year was $200,000. If the costs from your suppliers are expected to increase by a factor of 2 percent each year, what will be your projected costs for each of the next 4 years?

As a dedicated follower of the wine and liquor markets, you know that the costs of producing wine have slowly increased each year a little above the annual inflation rate. Anticipating that this trend will continue for the next few years, you make the assumption that your suppliers' prices will increase 2 percent (an estimate above the annual inflation rate). In Figure 1.7, note that the curve is an increasing function, as opposed to a zero price increase, which is represented by the constant line of $200,000.

MATHEMATICALLY SPEAKING

Compounding on the Existing Rate

The future value of the costs of goods sold is a compounding function of the inflation rate—that is, costs for equipment will increase by a factor of 2 percent each

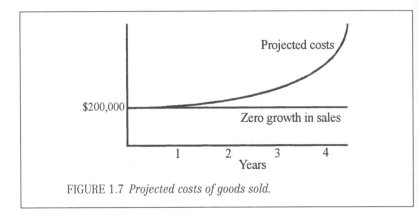

FIGURE 1.7 *Projected costs of goods sold.*

year. This translates to the following function, where *t* represents the number of years in the projection:

Costs $(t) = 200,000 (1 + 0.02)^t = 200,000 (1.02)^t$

Cost $(1) = 200,000 (1.02)^1 = 200,000(1.02) = 204,000$

Cost $(2) = 200,000 (1.02)^2 = 200,000(1.0404) = 208,080$

When using the calculator, the following settings will calculate the future value (cost) for the third year of the projection.

N	I%YR	PV	PMT	Press FV	OTHER
3	1.6	−200,000		to solve for FV.	

Verify that the total sales for years 3 and 4 of the projection are $212,241.60 and $216,486.43, respectively.

KEY CONCEPT Planning for Retirement Now

Let's talk retirement. For many of you this is a very remote topic, but as the following observation will demonstrate, saving early will have a major effect on how you would like to live later in life. We'll assume you will retire at age 60. Consider the effect of time on your annual $2,000 IRA retirement deposit (PV) during your prime earning years when you are 30, 40, and 50 years of age. For those of you still too young to understand this, an Individual Retirement Account (IRA) allows you to deposit a set tax-deferred amount each year for your retirement. For the sake of the demonstration, suppose you make a $2,000 deposit and get, on average, a conservative rate of 5 percent (I% YR) compounded annually over the period of the investment. Use your calculator to determine the future value of each deposit when you are ready to retire and start withdrawing from the account at age 60.

Time Period	Future Value
At age 30, your $2,000 deposit will accrue interest for 30 years.	8,643.88
At age 40, your $2,000 deposit will accrue interest for 20 years.	5,306.60
At age 50, your $2,000 deposit will accrue interest for 10 years.	3,257.79

It is pretty clear from the results of this example what time can do for your savings. After comprehending this example, the use of the time value of money concepts should be more than just interesting! So saving early isn't just a crock, it's for real.

CALC TIP

Finding Future Value the Fast Way

When doing this problem, take advantage of keeping the PV and I% YR entries the same and just changing the n setting for each of the three calculations. At this point in your learning, n and t mean the same thing, number of years. The beauty of the calculator is that it maintains settings until such time as you change them.

KEY CONCEPT — Financing Higher Education

The cost of higher education for our children, if not a current concern of yours, will be shortly. So this application shows how we can start today to pay for some of these college costs that will come due in the future. We analyze many strategies in this book to help you plan the financing. Initially we propose a little forced saving in order to prepare for the inevitable. To focus on an identifiable number to aim for, we assume the following:

- You need to finance one child.
- Your child will graduate from high school in 10 years.
- He or she will attend a four-year college.
- Average annual tuition will be $15,000 per year.

As you can see from the setup of assumptions, you can change those relative to either the costs of the school, the number of kids or years to graduation, and so on. We now determine how much your savings will be worth in the future, given a variety of interest rates.

The following table presents a number of scenarios to help you plan, using different interest rates, as well as a range of present values (deposits). Assume that each alternative will compound your deposit annually for 10 years. The future value will represent the amount that will be available to pay college tuition bills beginning in 10 years. We should also note that whatever is not spent from the first payment stays in the account gathering interest awaiting the next tuition payment. Solve the following future values according to the assumptions stated.

Present Value	Interest Rate	Future Value
$20,000	8%	$43,178.50
20,000	10	
25,000	8	
25,000	10	64,843.56
30,000	8	
30,000	10	77,812.27

Don't hyperventilate. The object of this book is to help you. As you understand more about the time value of money, you will also learn ways to reduce these numbers so that you can make your future desires affordable, as long as you act now.

Related to college education is the very real inflationary behavior of college tuition. Suppose the school your daughter would like to attend currently advertises an annual tuition amount of $18,000. She is currently finishing her freshman year of high school. If we assume that college tuition will continue to rise at 5 percent per year, then how much will her freshman year of college cost you in 3 years?

Answer: $20,837.25. Don't forget that there are a lot of scholarships out there, as well.

END POINT

Our objective in this first part is to define and develop the fundamental relationship between the worth of money today (*present value*) and in the future (*future value*). We show that both time and rate will affect both adversely and positively the amount of interest accrued. And, maybe most important, we introduce the important keys on the calculator that will do the work for us. Whew!

We also illustrate some important applications of the time value of money, ranging from business to personal. They can be used to describe the growth of things other than money; for example, the increase in the number of units of output from your factory could be exponential, as could the increase in the number of applications for a job opening at the factory.

The Dynamics of Compounding

As demonstrated in the previous chapter, the annual compounding technique of generating interest yields a better future value than that determined by simple interest. But, can we do *better?* This chapter investigates ways in which the compounding may produce an even larger yield. What is the effect on your total interest if you increase the number of interest conversion periods within a year—does monthly or daily compounding increase your yield? And if so, what is the best yield you can get—is there a maximum return given a specified rate per annum? This will lead to the development and use of continuous compounding, featuring *e* itself. And, because this chapter focuses on rates, we will need to understand the concept of an effective annual yield, in order to compare the returns on multiple financial opportunities, and use that tool to tell us which is "better."

COMPOUNDING IN A NUTSHELL

What happens when a bank or other lending institution increases the number of conversion periods within a year? Does interest grow even faster by using shorter interest periods within the year? Employing shorter interest conversion periods presents an intriguing question, and one that is important for us to understand because it is truly a double-edged sword.

The process of compounding gets more involved because money grows even faster by increasing the frequency of conversion periods. What does this mean? To attract investors, some institutions will compound in time periods of less than a year—for example, semiannually, quarterly, or monthly. This means at the end of the period—a month, a quarter, and so on—they calculate the interest and add it onto the present value for that period. By increasing the total number of conversion periods per year, the number of times interest gets applied to the principal or present value also increases. As we shall see, this will result in an increase in the total amount of interest accrued.

In this way, you, as an investor, will make more interest on your investment than if your funds were compounded only once a year. But it goes both ways. On the credit card side, banks charge us daily for cash advances and credit card purchases not paid within a certain time limit, thereby increasing the amount of interest they apply to our monthly bills. So, as the saying goes, "What's good for the goose is good for the gander."

How Compounding Works

To see how this compounding works, let's compare two investment opportunities over a one-year period: the Boring Bank of Boston, which features annual compounding, and the Better Bank of Boston, offering quarterly compounding (Figure 2.1). If two banks offer the same interest rate, are their investment returns the same? As you walk into the first bank with your $100, you recall that annual compounding means that the full 8 percent is applied to the $100 once.

Where should you put your money? Is the Better Bank of Boston really better? And, is Boring bad? From Chapter 1 we know that the future value for the Boring Bank of Boston is $108. Consider the effect on $100 invested for 1 year in the Better Bank of Boston at 8 percent, but compounded quarterly. This means that the year is broken down into four equal interest periods and interest is calculated at the end of each of those periods at one-fourth the annual rate. The interest is then added to the principal at the end of each interest period, hence increasing the principal by a small amount for each of

Boring Bank of Boston	Better Bank of Boston
8% Interest Rate	8% Interest Rate
We take very good care of your money and compound once a year. We give a full 8% and a free toaster.	Don't be satisfied with interest periods of one year. We're better! We compound quarterly for your best interest.

FIGURE 2.1 *A tale of two banks.*

the following periods. So when interest is calculated, it is calculated on a principal that is slightly more than the principal of the preceding period. But note that you will not get the full 8 percent each period. Instead, you get 8 percent divided by 4 (the total number of conversion periods per year.) See Figure 2.2 to see how it differs from the Boring Bank of Boston.

So, by increasing the frequency of compounding, the amount of interest will grow slightly. As Figure 2.2 shows, in the *second period,* interest is calculated on $102, not $100. So, by increasing the number of conversion periods per year, we have increased the worth of the entire yearly investment by 24 cents.

MATHEMATICALLY SPEAKING

How to Calculate Future Value with Quarterly Compounding

The key to understanding this process is to take a close look at what happens in the second period. How does the math work for the second period? First, note that the principal or present value at the beginning of the second period is $102, which is the same as the future value for the first period. So the future value for the second period is calculated as follows:

Divide by 4 because quarterly.

$$FV_2 = FV_1 \left(1 + \frac{0.08}{4} \right) = FV_1 \, (1 + 0.02)$$

First period's ending value is 102.

$$FV_2 = 102 \, (1 + 0.02) = 102 \, (1.02)$$

$$FV_2 = 104.04$$

Or, alternatively, since we know that the rate is divided by 4, and we are examining the future value at the end of the second period, the following equation can define what we need:

$FV_2 = 100(1.02)^2$ Power is 2 because two terms.

$FV_2 = 100(1.0404)$ Squaring 1.02.

$FV_2 = 104.04$

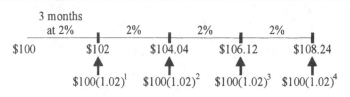

FIGURE 2.2 *Quarterly compounding of 8 percent.*

You try: → ### Quarterly Future Value

Verify that $100 invested for 1 year at the Better Bank of Boston given a rate of 8 percent compounded quarterly results in a future value of $108.24.

You try: → ### Semiannual Future Value

You just determined the future value given quarterly compounding. Suppose you deposited $100 in another bank at 8 percent for 1 year that compounds semiannually? Do you expect the result to be greater or less than $108.24? Yes, it should be less than $108.24 because of less frequent compounding, but more than $108.

Answer: $108.16.

The Big Effect of Compounding Interest

Now that we have seen how increasing the number of conversion periods benefits us, let's get to the general principle of compounding. Recall the original compound interest formula:

$$FV = PV\,(1 + r)^t$$

Here's what happens: Although the number of conversion periods will be increased, the rate will be correspondingly decreased by the same factor. The annual rate is now termed *nominal,* because it is divided by the number of compounding periods per year n. As a result, the number of years t is multiplied by n, so that exponent still reflects the total number of compounding periods.

$$FV = PV\left(1 + \frac{r}{n}\right)^{nt}$$

Recall that earlier we posed the question of which bank is the best investment, the Boring Bank or the Better Bank. Both banks advertised an annual rate of 8 percent. In analyzing the two banks' rates of 8 percent, compounding annually and quarterly, solve the following two equations to determine the best return on the investment (that is, the greatest future value). In the following equations the subscripts refer to the number of years of the investment.

Annually	*Quarterly*
$FV_1 = 100(1.08)$	$FV_1 = 100\left(1 + \dfrac{0.08}{4}\right)^4$
$FV_1 = 108$	$FV_1 = 100(1.02)^4$
	$FV_1 = 108.24$

How Compounding Works on the Lending Side

Suppose you need to borrow $1,000 from either the Boring or Better Bank of Boston, each of which you know offers a 12 percent interest rate on lending. We'll assume the loan must be paid in full at the end of the year. With whom should you take the loan? As you will see, what is good for you on the investing side may not be good for you on the borrowing side. The following calculations show how much you will owe at the end of the year assuming the 12 percent rate.

Boring Bank	Better Bank
$FV_1 = 1{,}000(1.12)$	$FV_1 = 1{,}000\left(1 + \dfrac{0.12}{4}\right)^4$
$FV_1 = 1{,}120$	$FV_1 = 1{,}000(1.03)^4$
	$FV_1 = 1{,}125.51$

So, by going to the Better Bank of Boston for a loan, the quarterly compounding actually means that you will owe the bank an additional $5.51. But if, in fact, different future values are being determined in this process, then the question of exactly what the rate is becomes a very important issue. How can both banks say they offer a rate of 8 percent or 12 percent? The next topic (after a practice example) addresses this.

You try:

Compounding Quarterly for Three Years

How much will $100 grow in 3 years if the Better Bank of Boston gives a rate of 8 percent compounded quarterly? Use the basic formula that we used before, and adjust it for 3 years. You'll need your Power key or the y^x key to get success here.
Answer: $126.82.

CALC TIP

The Beauty of Updating Calculator Registers

This is meant to be an easy calculator exercise to show a number of interesting observations about the compounding process. Let's use the calculator to get to the point. First, verify the annual case without compounding to obtain the $108 future value (i.e., PV = $100, N = 1 year, and the rate is 8 percent). Then make adjustments to the rate by dividing by the number of conversion periods per year and, correspondingly, multiplying the number of conversion periods per year times the number of years—in this case, 1—then press FV. The calculator keystrokes for quarterly compounding follow here:

N	I%YR	PV	PMT	FV	OTHER
4	2	−100			

┌ 4 × 1   ┌ 8/4   ┌ No change

The calculator should show 108.24 for the future value of 1 year. Keep the same settings. What if you wanted to calculate the three-year case as we just did, what would change? The rate and present value would not change. But the total number of periods would be 12 (4 × 3 years), not 4. Try it; you should get the same answer as before, 126.82.

KEY CONCEPT — UNDERSTANDING NOMINAL AND EFFECTIVE RATES

What is the real annual rate in these problems? As you can see from the preceding examples, the actual rate of growth for the money in the Better Bank of Boston is more than the nominal 8 percent. When the rate for the Boring Bank was 8 percent, you had a return of $108. So if the Better Bank yields $108.24, then its real annual rate must be better than 8 percent. The following definitions qualify the use of the term *rate* and set the standard for its use in business.

The Nominal Rate

The *nominal annual interest rate* is the indicated annual percentage when it is divided by the number of interest conversion periods occurring in one year. For example, if the interest rate is stated as 10 percent, compounded semiannually, then the 10 percent is termed a *nominal* rate. The actual interest rate applied to each compounding period is 5 percent (that is, 10 percent divided by 2). In other words, the nominal annual rate is the rate quoted before it is divided by the number of conversion periods.

Indicated Annual Rate	Nominal Annual Rate	Periodic Rate
12% compounded monthly	12%	1%
8% compounded semiannually	8%	4%
6% compounded annually	6%	6%

The Effective Rate

The *effective annual interest rate* or *effective annual yield* (EAY) is the equivalent rate of growth of the investment over one entire year with one compounding period. It represents the percentage change of the investment over 1 year—that is, the rate of growth of $1 with a compounding period of 1 year. The effective annual rate translates the nominal rate to the equivalent rate for an interest period of one year. In this way you can compare the "real" rates of two investment or borrowing opportunities. Examine the following examples. Don't be concerned about where the effective rates were derived; that topic is next.

Indicated Annual Rate	Effective Annual Rate
12% compounded monthly	Slightly more than 12% (12.68%)
8% compounded semiannually	Slightly more than 8% (8.16%)
6% compounded annually	Exactly 6%

Why the Effective Rate Is Greater than the Nominal Rate

When interest is compounded more than once a year, the effective interest rate is always slightly higher than the nominal rate. Why is this so? Since interest is earned in all the compounding periods and added in as principal for the remaining periods, it accrues more interest, thereby yielding a greater future value. You basically get interest on your interest, which results in an increased rate.

Not long ago, because of the complexity in the consumer lending marketplace, it became a law that rates had to be quoted in terms of one compounding period per year in advertisements or loan and mortgage applications so that consumers could tell the real rates when comparing two potential investment opportunities. Look for the terms *effective annual rate* or *effective annual yield* for the true comparative rate.

MATHEMATICALLY SPEAKING

How Future Value Increases

Let's investigate what happens to a $100 investment getting an 8 percent interest rate over a 1 year period as we increase the number of interest conversion periods per year. Table 2.1 will help with this exercise. Recall that you do not have to reenter all the values with your calculator. First calculate the future value using the annual rate of 8 percent. Record the answer in the first line of the table. The calculator is smart enough to remember your entries. Now enter the new adjusted rate for semiannual interest periods and total periods to calculate the new future value. The rate is nominal—that is, you use the stated annual rate divided by the number of compounding periods per year as your I%YR entry. You need not make an entry for the EAY column just yet; there will be an easy way to do it shortly. Be sure to record the appropriate entries in Table 2.1, because the pattern that emerges provides support for understanding the concept of continuous compounding.

How the EAY Grows

Let's examine Table 2.1, because something mathematically intriguing is before us. It would appear as though the future values are increasing as we increase the number of periods per year. For example, your semiannual calculation should yield $108.16, and the daily compounding case should yield an even greater future value, $108.33. So the true rate must be getting larger to return more interest on the initial $100.

Let's make an observation to help us find this true rate, which is the effective annual rate or yield (EAY). Follow along with a trick and then we will demonstrate the proper techniques for calculating the EAY. Note that the EAY for the annual case is 8 percent. Note that if we subtract the $100 from the future value of $108, we have left the percentage yield. This works because we began with a present value of $100. To see the effective annual rate for the appropriate period, subtract $100 from the future value amount. The dollar and cents components become the EAY. See the following example for the quarterly case:

$$108.24 - 100 = 8.24$$

Hence, the EAY is 8.24 percent.

TABLE 2.1 THE INCREDIBLE INCREASING FUTURE VALUE

Periods/ Year	Equation for FV	Nom Rate Periods	Total Periods	Future Value	EAY
Annually	$100(1 + 0.08)^1$	8%	1	$108	8%
Semiannually	$100\left(1 + \dfrac{0.08}{2}\right)^{1(2)}$				
Quarterly		$\dfrac{8\%}{4}$			
Monthly			12		
Daily, 360 days			360		
Hourly	$100\left(1 + \dfrac{0.08}{24 \times 360}\right)^{1(360)(24)}$	$\dfrac{8\%}{24 \times 360}$			

In order to understand the second important observation regarding the behavior of the EAY, carry the effective rate out to four positions after the decimal. There are many ways to determine the effective annual rate. The easiest method is to use the interest conversion menu on the calculator. The other is to find the effect on $1 as it completes its compounding for 1 year. Our first approach is with the use of the calculator, then we demonstrate how to use the second technique.

CALC TIP
Calculating the EAY

Now that you know the correct rates from our exercise in Table 2.1, let's show how the calculator can really help here. Many calculators have an interest conversion menu to help you find the EAY given a nominal rate. Look for "Interest conversion" in the index of your calculator manual to follow along with these keystrokes.

If the rate conversion keys are part of a menu, they should identify three variables: (1) nominal rate, (2) periods (number of conversion periods per year), and (3) effective rate. Procedurally, the steps are very simple (see Figure 2.3).

For example, to find the EAY for 8 percent quarterly, enter the nominal rate, 8 percent, in the Nominal Rate register and the number of interest periods, 4, in the Periods register. Given two factors you can solve for the third, so press the Effective Rate key to derive the equivalent EAY. In Figure 2.3, the EAY for 8 percent compounded quarterly should be 8.24 percent. This works in reverse, as well; to find the corresponding nominal rate, enter the given effective rate, the number of conversion periods per year, and then press the Nominal Rate key. However, the usual use of this menu is to find the effective rate given the nominal rate.

To solve for:	Enter:
Effective rate	The nominal rate and number of periods
Nominal rate	The effective rate and number of periods

Nom	Per	Eff
8	4	

FIGURE 2.3 *Calculating the EAY.*

You try: → ## Finding the EAY

If an investment pays 12 percent compounded quarterly, then show that the effective rate is approximately 12.55 percent.

MATHEMATICALLY SPEAKING

Finding the EAY without the Calculator

When calculators are not available (or the calculator you have does not have an interest conversion menu), then how would you find this elusive rate? Think, what did people do back before the Beatles and calculators? To determine the effective annual rate when given the nominal rate, calculate the future value of $1 over 1 year and then subtract the dollar out of the amount. (This is similar to what we did in the Table 2.1 exercise.) For example, an 8 percent nominal annual rate compounded semiannually results in a 4 percent nominal rate for each 6-month period, which is equivalent to an effective annual rate of 8.16 percent.

In the development of the following formula below, which determines the EAY, n refers to the number of interest conversion periods per year and r_{nom} refers to the nominal rate. We start with the equality, the nominal rate r_{nom} is equal to some effective rate r_{eff}:

Set the equations equal.

$$PV\left(1 + \frac{r_{nom}}{n}\right)^n = PV(1 + r_{eff})$$

Divide out the PV.

$$\left(1 + \frac{r_{nom}}{n}\right)^n = (1 + r_{eff})$$

Solve for r_{eff}.

$$r_{eff} = EAY = 1\left(1 + \frac{r_{nom}}{n}\right)^n - 1$$

So, if you want to calculate the EAY for an 8 percent annual rate that is compounded semiannually, follow these steps:

Divide by the 2 periods/year, and raise to the second power.

$$EAY = 1\left(1 + \frac{0.08}{2}\right)^2 - 1 = 1\,(1 + 0.04)^2 - 1$$

$$= 1\,(1.0816) - 1$$

When done remember to subtract the 1.

$$EAY = 1.0816 - 1 = 0.0816$$

$$EAY = 8.16 \text{ percent}$$

You try:

Doing the EAY without a Calculator

Show that 12 percent compounded quarterly is equivalent to an effective rate of 12.55 percent. Worst part of this problem is all that multiplying!

You try:

Doing the EAY with a Calculator

If an investment pays 24 percent compounded monthly, then show that the effective rate is approximately 26.82 percent. In doing this problem, you will definitely need your Power key if you do not have an interest conversion menu on your calculator.

Is There Convergence?

Let's examine a revised version of your table, found in Table 2.2, because something else mathematically intriguing is before us. Table 2.2 shows the relationship between the number of compounding periods per year and the resulting future value and effective annual yield. Although the future values are increasing as we increase the number of periods per year, the amount of the increase is getting smaller and smaller, indicating that there is a limit to this progression. To help show the significance of this sequence, we have expanded the number of positions after the decimal to four. To get the same numbers as the table, look up "Displaying number of positions" in your manual's table of contents or index. Our last value for the EAY, 8.3287 percent, represents the nominal rate, 8 percent, compounded hourly.

Isn't it strange that as the power of the expression, and hence the number of compounding periods, gets very large, the increase in the amount of the future value slows down? Now that you're get-

TABLE 2.2 THE GROWING EAY AS COMPOUNDING PERIODS INCREASE

Compounding Period	Periods/ Year	EAY	Change in Rate
Annually	1	8.0000%	
Semiannually	2	8.1600	0.1600%
Quarterly	4	8.2432	0.0832
Monthly	12	8.3000	0.0568
Daily	360	8.3277	0.0277
Hourly	360 × 24	8.3287	0.0010

ting the idea of how money grows, you've probably already noticed that the amount of the future value slows down due to dividing the rate by larger and larger numbers. As the numbers in Table 2.2 show, this progression definitely shows a convergence, which gives rise to the following question: Is there a best rate?

THE BEST COMPOUNDING RELATIONSHIP

Certainly the bank that compounds more frequently on the same nominal rate—that is, daily, hourly, or by the minute—will return the better yield. What if a bank offered *continuous* compounding—that is, instead of 360 conversion periods, it compounded over a steadily increasing number of periods, such as by the minute or second? In each of these cases, the period itself gets smaller and smaller, thus allowing more periods throughout the year on which to calculate interest. With a computer we could even take the period down to a nanosecond! As a result of making the period so small, the number of compounding periods per year gets very large—so large, in fact, that we say there are an infinite number of them.

This continuous compounding is a pretty hefty concept. Although increasing the number of periods has a slight effect on the future value, you do nearly as well as the bank that offers daily compounding—360 conversion periods per year.

Continuous Compounding and the Magic of e

The convergence we see from the example in Table 2.2 yields one of the most important constants in mathematics, *e*. The best compounding occurs not just daily, or by the hour, but more frequently—instantaneously, if you will. The last formula in Figure 2.4 is used to derive the future value of a principal PV for *t* years of continuously compounding at an annual rate of *r* percent. In this adjusted formula, *e* (2.71828 . . .) represents the base for continuous compounding where there are an infinite number of interest periods per year. How *e* evolved into this equation is explained in Chapter 13.

The Two Most Famous Numbers in Mathematics: π and e

You have just discovered *e,* a magical number like π. Now *e* requires a little patience on your part; after all, some of you have never seen *e* before, yet you have been

$$FV = PV\left(1 + \frac{r}{n}\right)^n \quad \text{Assumes } n \text{ compounding periods for 1 year.}$$

$$FV = PV\left(1 + \frac{r}{n}\right)^{nt} \quad \text{Assumes } n \text{ compounding periods for } t \text{ years.}$$

$$FV = PVe^{rt} \quad \text{Assumes continuous compounding for } t \text{ years.}$$

FIGURE 2.4 Deriving the best future value.

using π since the fifth grade. It may help you to think of the following analogy: π is to geometry as e is to finance.

Just as π is the limit of the ratio of the circumference to the diameter of a circle, so e is the limit of the compounding formula to the number of compounding interest periods. And just as in those early years you approximated π by 3.14, so e is approximated by 2.71828. But we take advantage of the calculator's exponential function to handle this for us.

This very famous number appears all through mathematics, much like its more famous relative, π. But e's reputation is more like that of an unwelcome in-law, in that it has often been explained through logarithms, which everybody naturally dislikes. So let's set the record straight: e is extremely useful to those of us studying finance in that it is the instrument by which we calculate continuous compounding.

e in Action

This is surely strange to some of you, so let's take a moment to try to increase the quantitative comfort quotient. First, e is a base, just like 2, 5, or 10, which is raised to various powers just like any other exponential function.

So how does this work? We can use the calculator to actually derive the value of e in our calculations. Generally, e will be found in the exponential menu of your calculator. For example, to derive e^2, type 2 and press the e^x or EXP key, depending on your calculator. Figure 2.5 shows the corresponding values of e^x (make sure you are able to get these values) and the graph of the function, so you can understand its exponential behavior.

The points we are trying to make with the graph and table in Figure 2.5 are that e^x is a very well defined function, you are getting valid numbers, and e is a perfectly valid base that can be employed in a wide variety of applications. For those of you who have a curiosity about e, Eli Maor wrote a wonderful book called *e, the Story of a Number* (Princeton University Press, 1994), which will entertain your imagination. But for us, the

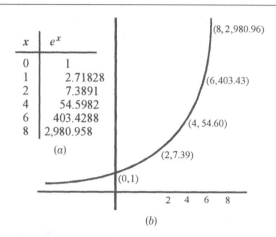

FIGURE 2.5 *Graph of the function y = e^x: (a) table of values, and (b) curve.*

major concern is continuous compounding. Now that you have the idea on how to work with *e*, let's return to our problem.

Suppose some adventurous bank was going to offer us 8 percent compounded continuously for 1 year; how would we calculate the future value? In the formula in Figure 2.4, *e* is raised to the annual rate and there is no *n* to account for compounding periods because they have been replaced with the base value *e*. This is explained in the Chapter 13.

Thank goodness for the calculator to help us find the value of e^x in our calculations. To see the effect of the continuous compounding we compare it to our first example. Let's determine the future value of $100 compounded continuously at 8 percent. We know from earlier calculations that it should be greater than $108, but is it greater than 108.24 or 108.32? To derive *e* raised to the 0.08 power on the calculator (0.08 nominal rate multiplied times 1 year), type 0.08 and press the Exp key. This will produce the continuous compounding multiplier. Once 1.0833 is displayed in the register, multiply it by 100. Figure 2.6 compares the keystrokes for the two calculations.

You try:

Finding FV with Continuous Compounding

A particular investment advertises a 12 percent annual rate compounded continuously. If you invested $5,000, what would the future value be in 5 years?

Answer: $9,110.59.

Hint: Here's the first step.

$$FV_t = PV\ e^{r(t)} = 5{,}000\ e^{0.12(5)}$$

Quarterly compounding	Continuous	Explanation
$FV_t = PV\left(1 + \dfrac{r}{n}\right)^{nt}$	$FV_t = 100\,e^{r(t)}$	General equation
$FV_1 = 100\left(1 + \dfrac{0.08}{4}\right)^4$	$FV_1 = 100\,e^{.08(1)}$	Substitution
$FV_1 = 100\,(1.02)^4$	$FV_1 = 100(1.0833)$	Raising to the power
$FV_1 = 100\,(1.0824)$	$FV_1 = 108.33$	Simplifying
$FV_1 = 108.24$		

FIGURE 2.6 *Calculating FV at 8 percent for 1 year, periodically versus continuously.*

MATHEMATICALLY SPEAKING

What about the EAY for Continuous Compounding?

To answer this insightful question, let's return to our discussion on effective and nominal annual rates. Recall that we must assume all rates are nominal unless they specifically indicate that they are effective. In the periodic case, we divided a nominal rate by the number of compound periods and calculated the return on $1 to determine the effective rate. So how do we determine effective rates for the continuous case? Basically, the same way. The calculations in Figure 2.7 show both methods for determining the EAY of 8 percent: One case is periodic, compounded semiannually, and the other is the continuous case.

You try: **Finding the EAY**

If an investment pays 12 percent compounded continuously, then show that the effective rate is approximately 12.75 percent.

 CALC TIP

EAY for Continuous Compounding

Many calculators have a continuous compounding interest conversion menu to help you find the EAY given a nominal rate. In this case there are only two options since the periods are assumed to be infinite in the case of continuous compounding. To find the EAY, just enter the nominal rate, then press the Effective Rate key (EFF% on the HP 19) to derive the equivalent EAY.

8% compounded semiannually	**8% compounded continuously**
$EAY = 1\left(1 + \dfrac{0.08}{2}\right)^2 - 1$	$EAY = 1\,e^{0.08} - 1$
$EAY = 1(1.04)^2 - 1$	$EAY = 1(1.08329) - 1$
$EAY = 1(1.0816) - 1$	$EAY = 1.08329 - 1$
$EAY = 0.0816 = 8.16\%$	$EAY = 0.08329 = 8.33\%$

FIGURE 2.7 *Calculating EAY: (a) periodically versus (b) continuously.*

The Continuous Interest Conversion menu on the HP 19 series, displayed in Figure 2.8, has only two variables, nominal rate and effective rate, for solving these rate conversion problems. In this case we would like to verify the EAY of 8 percent compounded continuously. We have entered 8 in the Nominal Rate register. To determine the EAY, just press the EFF% key.

You try:

Comparing Two Investment Opportunities

You have just won $100,000 in The Publishers Clearinghouse Sweepstakes. Now, what should you do with the money? You are presented with two potential investment opportunities: The Bank of Strong Times is advertising a rate of 6.1 percent compounded quarterly, but the E Bank of Continuous Good Feelings is offering 6 percent compounded continuously. Determine the effective rate for each fund to decide the best growth opportunity for 10 years.

Answer: These are Strong Times (6.241 percent versus 6.1837 percent).

To solve for:	Enter:
Effective rate	The nominal rate
Nominal rate	The effective rate

Nom	Eff
8	

FIGURE 2.8 *Calculating the EAY for continuous compounding.*

APPLICATIONS OF PERIODIC COMPOUNDING

This section demonstrates how the material in this chapter can be applied to determining the cost of credit, the annual inflation and effective rates, and the best investment among alternatives.

 Determining the Cost of Credit

Cyber Vineyards has received a notice from one of its suppliers, Colonel Mustards, that as of the beginning of next month it will be charged 15 percent interest on any balances that are not paid within 30 days of notice. This is understandable because Honey Brown, a Colonel Mustards mustard sold in your tasting room, is a big product for you, selling hundreds of bottles every month. It should not be Colonel Mustards' responsibility to finance its customers' inventories. This policy is one of the reasons you applied for the credit line described in Chapter 1. In order to compare this rate to that offered by other institutions, you need to express it as an effective annual rate.

Determine the equivalent effective annual rate to a 15 percent rate that compounds daily, assuming 365 days per year.

Answer: 16.18 percent.

Upon closer reading of the notice, it indicates that interest will be charged as of the day of purchase for any items not paid in full within the 30 days. Their method of applying the interest calculation is to take 1/365 of the effective annual rate and multiply it times the number of days. Determine the amount of interest you owe if Cyber Vineyards purchased 200 cases of Honey Brown for $1,200 on June 1 and paid the bill on July 15.

Answer: Determine the daily rate and apply as follows:

$$\text{Interest} = \frac{1}{365} \times 0.1618 \times 45 \times \$1,200 = ?$$

 Determining the Annual Inflation Rate

It was reported today in the Wine Investment Analyzer *(WIA) that inflation jumped up a little more than expected last month, 0.32 percent for products in the wine and liquor industry.*

While preparing the four-year projection of costs, as indicated in Chapter 1, you read in the *WIA* that the

Bureau of Labor Statistics has stated that last month's CPI grew a surprising 0.32 percent. Inflation is often reported on a monthly basis, and then, magically, we are supposed to understand the significance of that statistic. Is 0.32 percent surprising if you have been assuming that prices would rise 1.6 percent annually?

CALC TIP
Determining the Effective Annual Rate

We'll assume that the supplied rate is the rate that the CPI grew just during that month. The trick in this problem is to determine the associated nominal rate and convert it to the equivalent effective rate. It requires that we go in the opposite direction than we did earlier. That is, since we know the month's rate, then by multiplying it by 12 we will have the corresponding nominal rate for the year. Once we know this rate, we can use the Interest Conversion menu on the calculator (Nom = 3.84, Per = 12) to translate from the nominal annual rate to the effective annual rate. The equation, expressed in percentages, can be used with your calculator's interest conversion keys:

$$\text{Nominal annual rate} = r_{monthly} \times 12$$

$$\text{Nominal annual rate} = 0.32 \times 12$$

$$\text{Nominal annual rate} = 3.84$$

Yielding an effective annual rate of 3.908 percent.

Mathematically, the equivalent rate on an annual basis is found by expressing the monthly rate raised to the twelfth power (12 months):

$$EAY = 1(1 + 0.0032)^{12} - 1 = 1(1.0032)^{12} - 1$$

$$EAY = 1(1.03908) - 1$$

$$EAY = 1.03908 - 1$$

$$EAY = 0.03908 = 3.908 \text{ percent}$$

You try:

Determining the Best Investment Opportunity

What should you do? You've just received a small (yet significant to you at this age) inheritance from Aunt Rosie for $10,000. You decide it is important to invest it so you don't spend it all right away. You do a little research on the Web and find two investment options: One offers 12 percent annually with continuous compounding; the other, 12.2 percent compounded semiannually. Which is better?

Answer: Using EAY, 12.7497 percent (continuous) is better than 12.5721 percent (semiannual).

END POINT

This chapter shows the significance of the number of compounding periods per year and the rate of return on an investment. Increasing the number of compounding periods per year increases the future value, thereby changing the actual annual rate of growth of the investment. For this reason we need a standard way to compare returns between these competing investment rates. Knowing how to calculate the true effective annual rate from the nominal rate is extremely important in business. The applications show how compounding applies to cost analysis, inflation, and investing.

Finally, this chapter introduces *e*, a very important number in the mathematics of finance and continuous compounding. The following chapter uses the varieties of compounding to determine *present value*, one of the most important topics in all of finance.

The Significance of Present Value

Present value is the most important tool employed in financial decision making, and as such, deserves its own chapter for exploration. It is rich in capability and application, and is the building block upon which many important concepts such as cash flow analysis and bond valuation are based. Consider the following situations:

- How should you decide between two projects that require capital funding of $100,000?

- What is the effect on the purchasing power of $25,000 10 years from now, assuming a 2 percent rate of inflation?

- If a union agrees to a certain amount for pension benefits, then how does management adjust its funding to support benefit payments in the future?

- How much do you invest today to fund a year of retirement in 30 years?

The seed to understanding the criteria for making these decisions is present value.

KEY CONCEPT

DEFINING PRESENT VALUE

Present value is the value or worth today of a cash amount that will be received in the future. It is the means of measuring the worth of a dollar in the future in terms of today's dollar. Another way to look at it is how much you need today to have a certain amount at some future point in time. Hence, the present value of a future dollar amount. It is often used as a means of measuring the value of two or more alternative cash flows by relating them back to their value in present-day dollars.

What financial objectives come to mind that require this type of analysis? The cost of a year's worth of education in 10 years, the down payment on a house in 5 years, the purchase of a sailboat or luxury car in 3 years, or the worth today of a retirement annuity. Determining the best decision in meeting all of these financial objectives requires that you know the worth today of a dollar that will be received in the future. For example, you can either write a check for $18,000 in 10 years for your child's freshman year of college or fund it now for considerably less. This is the real beauty of the time value of money.

Your Parents and Present Value

Consider the following situation as an example to help you understand the behavior of present value. It might even have happened to you. Your father and mother have rewarded your hard work in high school by giving you money as a graduation present to buy a car, but not until you have completed two years of college. You both agree that you can get a good used car for $5,000. The problem is they only gave you $4,535.15. You feel cheated. Have they tricked you?

To help understand this concept, let's analyze what your parents did. The idea is that you will need the $5,000 in 2 years based upon doing well in college. So, being smart folks, they put the money near you, actually in your bank account, so you will remember to continue to study. But it was not enough for the car, presently. In tricking you, they also needed to know the interest rate in your local bank, which they found to be 5 percent.

GRAPHICALLY SPEAKING

How Present Value Grows

Before continuing with this concept, verify for yourself that the future value of $4,535.15 in 2 years invested at 5 percent is $5,000.

Since $4,535.15 grows to become $5,000 in 2 years, it's called the present value of $5,000 in 2 years at 5 percent. From Figure 3.1 we can make an important observation: The value of a dollar today is less than the value of a dollar in the future—the essence of the time value of money.

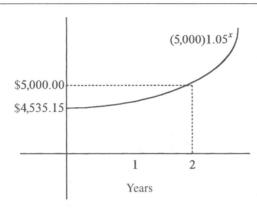

FIGURE 3.1 *In 2 years, $4,535.15 grows to become $5,000 at 5 percent.*

How Present Value Is Calculated

Present value is simply the opposite of future value. In determining the future value you are trying to find the value of an amount (money in your hand) at some time in the future, given a certain rate at which interest is calculated. Present value is the worth today of some future value.

Mathematically, how is present value related to future value? A little simple algebra in the following derivation answers this burning question. Remember the equation for the future value of a principle, given a rate r and time $t?$

Start here to solve for PV:

$$FV = PV(1 + r)^t$$

Divide both sides by $(1 + r)^t$:

$$\frac{FV}{(1 + r)^t} = PV\,\frac{(1 + r)^t}{(1 + r)^t}$$

Cancel the $(1 + r)^t$ on the right side:

$$\frac{FV}{(1 + r)^t} = PV$$

Employ a negative exponent:

$$FV(1 + r)^{-t} = PV$$

What is the significance of the negative exponent in this last equation? This is important to understand, because a negative exponent creates a reciprocal relationship—that is, it makes a number greater than 1 become less than 1, and vice versa. And, note carefully, the negative exponent does not make the result of these calculations negative. Consider some examples:

Algebra	*Finance*

$$2^{-1} = \frac{1}{2^1} = 0.5 \qquad 1.08^{-1} = \frac{1}{1.08^1} = 0.9256$$

$$2^{-2} = \frac{1}{2^2} = 0.25 \qquad 1.08^{-2} = \frac{1}{1.08^2} = 0.8573$$

In particular, we are most interested in the second set of examples (1.08), because that base represents the 8 percent relationship that we have seen with future value—that is, the interest rate that we used to calculate the growth of an investment. It was clear that the powers of 1.08, like $1.08^2 = 1.1664$ or $1.08^5 = 1.469$, were used to calculate the future value of an investment for 2 or 5 years, respectively. But now we change perspectives: In present value the calculation must yield a smaller value; that is, there must be a way to show that from $5,000 you can determine $4,535.15. That, algebra fans, is the significance of the negative exponent. The table in Figure 3.2 shows the corresponding values of the function $y = 1.08^{-x}$ as x takes on positive values. As time x increases from 0 years to 5, notice that the result (the present value multiplier) gets smaller. This is exactly parallel to the derivation of the multipliers for future value in Chapter 1. In that situation we had a positive exponent and the amount grew because it produced multipliers greater than 1. We have just the opposite here.

Now let's apply it to money. Suppose you want to know how much money you should deposit today in order to have $100 in 1 year, if interest compounds at a rate of 8 percent annually.

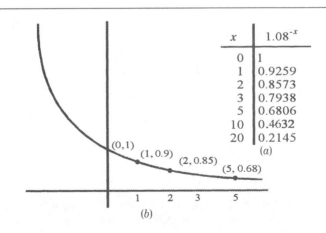

x	1.08^{-x}
0	1
1	0.9259
2	0.8573
3	0.7938
5	0.6806
10	0.4632
20	0.2145

(a)

(0,1)
(1, 0.9)
(2, 0.85)
(5, 0.68)

(b)

FIGURE 3.2 *Present Value and graph of the function* $y = 1.08^x$: *(a) table of values, and (b) curve.*

$$PV_{t \text{ years}} = FV(1 + r)^{-t}$$

$$PV_{1 \text{ year}} = FV(1 + r)^{-1}$$

$$PV_{1 \text{ year}} = 100(1.08)^{-1} = 100 \ (0.9259) = 92.59$$

What this basically means is that to have $100 in the bank at the end of 1 year, you must invest $92.59 today. But in finance they really don't talk that way. Instead, they will say that the present value of $100 to be received in 1 year at 8 percent interest is $92.59. Another convention employed in finance is to say that $100 discounted at 8 percent for 1 year is $92.59. The use of the word *discounted* makes sense, since we are looking for a smaller value. So now, how do we actually get these multipliers that will yield the discounted present value?

CALC TIP
Negative Exponents and the Power Key

The only difference between present and future value keystrokes is that you need to activate the negative sign. To do so, you usually need only hit the CHG or ± key (these keys will change the sign of the number in the register from plus to minus or vice versa). Here is how you do it for these problems:

1. Type in the base, which is 1.08.
2. Press the Power key, ^.
3. Type in the power, which is 1.
4. Press either the CHG or ± key.
5. Press = to calculate the multiplier.
6. Multiply by the amount, 100.

What is the effect of increasing the conversion periods? Compounding with conversion periods of less than one year—for example, quarterly or daily—is handled the same as in the future value calculations. In the following equation, n represents the number of conversion periods in a year.

$$PV_{t \text{ years @ } 8\%} = 100 \left(1 + \frac{0.08}{n}\right)^{-nt}$$

$$PV_{t \text{ years @ } r\%} = 100 \left(1 + \frac{r}{n}\right)^{-nt}$$

MATHEMATICALLY SPEAKING

Determining Present Value

Does increasing the number of conversion periods result in a smaller or larger present value? To answer this question, we determine the present value of $100 discounted at 8 percent for 2 years with two different conversion periods.

Compounded annually	*Compounded quarterly*
$PV_{t \text{ years}} = FV(1 + r)^{-t}$	$PV_{t \text{ years}} = FV\left(1 + \dfrac{r}{n}\right)^{-nt}$
$PV = 100(1.08)^{-2}$	$PV = 100(1.02)^{-8}$
$PV = 100(0.85734)$	$PV = 100(0.85349)$
$PV = 85.73$	$PV = 85.35$

So, in the annual case, we would have to deposit $85.73 into the account so that in 2 years the future value of the account would grow to $100, but only $85.35 for quarterly compounding case. Note that we have the same behavior as our findings in the future value case; we benefit from increasing the number of compounding periods. Or, put another way, with more frequent compounding we can deposit even less!

You try:

Solving for Present Value

What is the worth today of $1,000 that you will receive in 3 years discounted at 6 percent compounded semiannually?
Answer: $837.48.

GRAPHICALLY SPEAKING

Introducing the Cash Flow Diagram

Now that you have some experience with these types of problems, we introduce a convention used in working with time value of money. Problems are often displayed in a cash flow timeline diagram like the one in Figure 3.3. The present value amount is facing down indicating a negative amount (cash out), and up arrows indicate a positive amount.

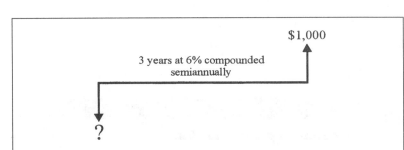

$1,000

3 years at 6% compounded semiannually

?

FIGURE 3.3 *Basic cash flow diagram.*

CALC TIP
Solving for Present Value with the Time Value of Money Keys

Ah, the excitement of your first car and present value. Your parents asked the following question: "How much should we place in the bank or investment account so that you will have the sum of $5,000 when you want to buy the car in 2 years?" Again, this is an example of present value because you need to know how much the $5,000 is worth in today's dollars. Or, what is the value of $5,000 discounted at 5 percent for 2 years? In solving this mathematically you would set up the following equations and solve. But let's do this using the calculator's time value of money keys.

$$PV_{t \text{ years}} = FV(1 + r)^{-t}$$
$$PV = 5{,}000(1.05)^{-2}$$

		Press		This time enter a value for FV.	
N	I%YR	PV	PMT	FV	OTHER
2	5	to solve for PV.		5,000	

Since you are solving for the PV, you will press that option last. So enter the required settings as shown, and then press PV. You should get the same answer as stated earlier, $4,535.15.

You try:
Present Value of $40,000, Please

What is the value today of $40,000 that the company will receive in 10 years discounted at 12 percent compounded daily? Use 365 days.
    Answer: $12,050.14.

KEY CONCEPT **Present Value and Continuous Compounding**

The last calculation you must be able to perform is solving for the present value with continuous compounding. Recall that in the future value case, continuous compounding introduced the financial constant e. So how do you calculate the present value if you were to get continuous compounding on your $5,000 at a rate of 5 percent? The parallel between periodic and continuous compounding is very simple:

Periodic	*Continuous*
$PV = FV(1 + r)^{-t}$	$PV = FV\, e^{-rt}$
$PV = 5{,}000(1 + 0.05)^{-2}$	$PV = 5{,}000\, e^{-(0.05)2}$
$PV = 5{,}000(0.9070)$	$PV = 5{,}000\, e^{-(0.1)}$
$PV = \$4{,}535.15$	$PV = 5{,}000\, (0.90484)$
	$PV = \$4{,}524.19$

CALC TIP
Competence Check

Complete Table 3.1 to check your understanding of how to calculate present value, and then we will do a few real-world problems. Analyze the present value of $5,000 for 1 year at 5 percent with increasing conversion periods. What should be the nature of the progression of the present values?

KEY CONCEPT — DETERMINING RATE OF RETURN

Being able to determine the annual rate of return on an investment is necessary in order to make the right choices in the use of funds, whether it is a company investing in a project or you personally, investing in a business opportunity. Consider the following example.

Your company has been asked to fund a project that is expected to return $200,000 in 5 years. The project is requesting $100,000, and you have been asked to determine if the company should invest in the project. The company has a history of investing only in projects that return at least 25 percent on their use of capital, on an annual compounding basis.

You should realize that this problem requires that you solve for the rate when given the remaining three variables, future and present values and time. Because the calculator does it so easily, we will use the calcula-

TABLE 3.1 THE INCREDIBLE SHRINKING PRESENT VALUE

Periods/Year	Total Periods	Present Value
Annually	1	$4,535.15
Semiannually		
Quarterly		
Monthly		$4,525.13
Daily, 360 days		

tor to solve these types of problems, then we will go through the mathematics of solving for the rate. Figure 3.4 shows the structure of the problem, and the relationship between the variables to determine the rate.

CALC TIP
FINDING THE ANNUAL RATE OF RETURN

When using the calculator it is critical that the present value be entered as a negative—that is, cash out is different from cash in. With most calculators, you will get an error message if the entries do not have opposite signs. It makes sense from the business perspective as well, because you are spending money and looking for a positive amount back on the investment. As we now understand the problem, the actual keystrokes should be like the following:

	Press				
N	I%YR	PV	PMT	FV	OTHER
5	to find 1%YR.	−100,000		200,000	

If, as previously stated, your company requires at least a 25 percent return on its capital investments, then this project would fall short, because this investment returns an annual compounded rate of 14.87 percent. If you had difficulty with these entries, and you got an error message or a beep it is most likely because you did not enter the present value as a negative.

You try:
Shorter Time Period, Better Rate

Show that if the investment period were reduced to 3 years then the investment would return a satisfactory return, 25.99 percent. Please do this problem the easy way, just enter a new value for

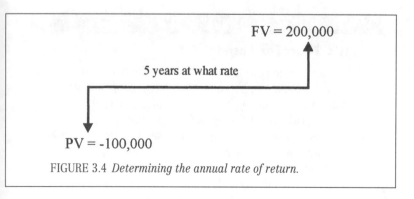

FIGURE 3.4 *Determining the annual rate of return.*

n and press I%YR. Remember, the registers retain their entries until you either clear them or replace one with a new entry.

DETERMINING TIME TO ACHIEVE A SPECIFIED RETURN

The remaining factor for which you should be able to solve is *time*. That is, given an initial investment and an estimated rate of return, can you determine the number of years and/or months it will take to achieve the expected future value? This could be a bit tricky inasmuch as some calculators will not calculate this number exactly, often rounding to the next whole number. To demonstrate this option, consider a variation of our last problem.

The project team is requesting $100,000 for a $200,000 return on the investment, and you have been asked to determine if the company should invest in the project. The company has a history of investing only in projects that return at least 25 percent, on an annual compounding basis. If 25% return is required, then what should be the length of the investment period?

Assuming annual compounding, and the same values as the preceding example, then the calculator keystrokes will be as follows:

Press

N	I%YR	PV	PMT	FV	OTHER
to solve for N.	25	–100,000		200,000	

The HP 19 or 17 series will return the correct answer of 3.1063, which should be interpreted as a little more than 3 years to achieve the desired return. You must be careful when using some calculators, because they will automatically use the next whole number. For example, the HP 12C series will return 4 for this answer.

MATHEMATICALLY SPEAKING

It's Time for Logs!

Because some calculators will ignore the decimal value in this calculation, it can be a source of confusion. We will take the time to show how to solve this problem algebraically through the use of logarithms. For a more detailed explanation of logarithms see Chapter 13. This problem displays one of the few opportunities in business mathematics where logarithms are not only appreciated, but needed, because some calculators can't solve for time accurately. When working with logarithms please note that in business we only work with the natural logarithm system (ln and your friend e). Recall the original formula for annual compounding:

The original compounding formula.

$$FV_{t \text{ years @ } r\%} = PV \left(1 + \frac{r}{n} \right)^{nt}$$

Substitute our values into the formula.

$$200,000 = 100,000 \, (1.25)^t$$

$$2 = 1 \, (1.25)^t$$

Employ the power rule of logarithms.

$$\ln 2 = t \, (\ln 1.25)$$

Find the natural logs (lns) of 2 and 1.25.

$$0.6931 = t \, (0.2231)$$

$$3.106 = t$$

Now, substituting the values into the equation and simplifying, you will come to the important step, which requires that you take the logarithms of both sides of the equation. Applying logarithms to both sides makes the problem solvable by reducing it to a first-degree equation in a single variable.

The reason this problem so beautifully displays the need for logarithms is that there is no way to solve the exponential equation without logs. Thus far in our financial equations we have solved simple equations that have the variable to the first power. In this case the variable is the exponent, which requires a very special technique for solving the equation. Thank you, Napier, the father of logarithms. The applications section explores how to solve this with the calculator.

APPLICATIONS OF PRESENT VALUE

This section demonstrates how the material in this chapter can be applied to determining the cost of borrowing and inflation, and to planning for selected financial goals.

KEY CONCEPT   **The Cost of Borrowing**

To get Cyber Vineyards positioned into the next century, you want to launch a website so people from all over the world can log on, review your wine, and make purchases by credit card. A technical consulting company is interested in giving you guidance and supplying the necessary hardware as well as the initial software development to get the website on line.

They have proposed the following investment scenario: They will supply the hardware and software at a cost of $100,000. In 5 years, they want a cash return of $240,000. Alternatively, the bank has evaluated your business plan and extended Cyber Vineyards a credit line of $100,000 at 18 percent. Which alternative should you select?

This problem can be solved many ways, but let's make sure we understand what we are analyzing. We are comparing two alternatives for the funds of $100,000—the bank, with a rate of 18 percent compounded annually, and the technology consulting group, which wants a return of $240,000 on its investment. Essentially, the answer will be found by determining which investment gives you the best rate. You already know that the bank is charging 18 percent; now determine the rate that is assumed in the offer from the consulting firm.

CALC TIP
Finding the Comparative Rate

Use the time value of money keys to solve for the rate, I%YR. But be careful—remember, the present value amount must be entered as a negative; otherwise, it will result in an error.

Answer: The bank has the lowest rate, 18 percent versus 19.14 percent.

KEY CONCEPT — How Inflation Weakens Buying Power

Earlier we described inflation as *price creep*—that is, the slow rise in the price of consumer goods and services over a given economic period. As prices slowly rise, the result is that current dollars buy less in the future. Here is an example of how this might affect you.

Suppose you got a 4% raise on your job. You would naturally expect to be able to spend that extra money on a new washing machine or HDTV, or save it for the kids' education. If you were currently earning $40,000 a year, then your raise would constitute $1,600 additional income. But suppose inflation grew 5 percent over that year, which would mean that the prices of goods you purchase would have increased by 5 percent. Figure 3.5 shows how your 4 percent raise would fail to cover the 5 percent inflationary increase, which would result in a loss of buying power for you. Essentially, it would cost you more than your raise to maintain the same standard of living.

Let's take a specific example of how this works. If food for the family was 25 percent of your salary—$10,000—then that same amount of food 1 year later

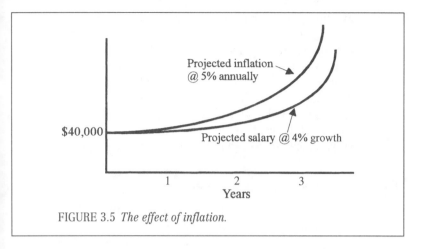

FIGURE 3.5 *The effect of inflation.*

would cost you $10,500 simply because of inflation. So almost a third of your raise would be gobbled up by inflationary increases in maintaining the exact same level of food intake. Inflation causes an erosion of your buying power. This is why unions and employee bargaining groups have a cost-of-living adjustment in their labor contracts, in addition to their negotiated raises, so that their memberships can receive the full benefit of the additional compensation.

Anticipating price increases is a function of determining future value. Anticipating the loss of purchasing power is a discounting relationship—that is, a dollar saved today will be worth less than a dollar in the future, thanks to inflation. Sounds like a present value situation. If you put $1 away today for your savings, what is its buying power in the future? Figure 3.6 shows how this happens, assuming an average 3 percent per year inflation over some investment period. The following equation calculates the inflation factors and represents the curve in Figure 3.6.

$$\text{Today's \$ value}_{t \text{ years @ 3\%}} = \$1\,(1 + 0.03)^{-t}$$

Because prices go up, today's dollar buys less in the future. This is made very clear when you consult

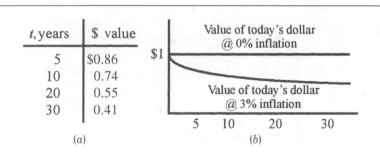

t, years	$ value
5	$0.86
10	0.74
20	0.55
30	0.41

(a)

(b)

FIGURE 3.6 *How inflation weakens your dollar: (a) table of values, and (b) curve.*

investment counselors, because their objective is to carefully select investments that will generate returns that will exceed inflation—generate a "real" return on your investment, if you will. The *real interest rate* is defined as the difference between the interest rate and the annual rate of inflation. For example, in the preceding example, if the interest rate for an investment is quoted at 8 percent per year, and inflation is 3 percent per year, then the real interest rate is 5 percent.

The Cost of Inflation

Currently inflation is out of control in many of the countries in South America. If inflation is running at 48 percent per year in Brazil, what effect will it have on the purchasing power of $1 in that economy in 1, 2, or 5 years?

Answer: $0.68, $0.46, and $0.14.

If your company put aside $2 million for construction of a new office in San Paulo, Brazil, and it was delayed 2 years because of government negotiations, what would the purchasing power of the $2 million be, 2 years later?

Answer: $913,075.24.

The Role of Inflation in Financing College Tuition

In no area do we see the ugly face of inflation more than in the spiraling costs of college tuition. A recent *New York Times* article by Ethan Bronner, "College Tuition Up 4%, Outpacing Inflation" (October 8, 1998), indicates that college tuition costs are rising much faster annually (4 percent) than inflation (1.6 percent). Bronner states that the average tuition at a four-year private college is $14,508, which is actually up 5 percent over the preceding year.

If we assume that the specified rate for tuition increases in private colleges (5 percent) will be maintained for the time period your children are preparing for and attending college, then what can you expect to pay for your oldest child's first-year tuition when he or she will start in 6 years? Do you have the idea that you are shooting at a moving target? You can either use the time value of money keys or work it out mathematically as follows:

$$FV_{t \text{ years}} = 14,508 \, (1.05)^t$$

$$FV_{6 \text{ years}} = 14,508 \, (1.05)^6$$

$$FV_{6 \text{ years}} = 14,508 \, (1.3401)$$

$$FV_{6 \text{ years}} = \$19,442.11$$

But here is the point: If you assumed that tuition would be $14,508 in 6 years, you'd be in for a surprise—you wouldn't have saved enough! Determine the true amount that you must put away today at 9 percent to meet the inflationary tuition fee in 6 years—that is, what is the present value of $19,442.11?

$$PV_{6 \text{ years}} = 19,442.11 \ (1.09)^{-6} = \$11,592.69$$

Financing Your Second Honeymoon

Paris is without a doubt the most romantic city in the world, and there is probably no better place to spend a honeymoon. But, alas, you went to Miami. Later you surprise your spouse with the idea of spending your tenth anniversary in Paris. Let's assume you have 10 years to save. How much would you need to put away today so that in 10 years you will have accumulated the necessary amount for your trip? Let's assume that expenses—airfare, food, wine, hotel, local transportation, more food and wine, and so on—will require $10,000. So you will need $10,000 in 10 years.

Ah, the excitement of Paris and present value, two wonderful thoughts. *Mais oui,* how much should you place in the bank or investment account so that you will have the sum of $10,000 if you receive a rate of 8 percent? That is, what is the value of $10,000 discounted at 8 percent for 10 years?

Mathematically
Now you determine the present value of $10,000 to be received in 10 years at a rate of 8 percent compounded annually ($n = 1$).

$$PV_{t \text{ years @ } r\%} = FV \left(1 + \frac{r}{n} \right)^{-nt}$$

$$PV = 10,000(1.08)^{-10}$$

$$PV = \$4,631.93$$

Calculator Tip 1
To verify your work, calculate the present value of $10,000 to be received in 10 years at a rate of 8 percent. Which keys are affected?

N	I%YR	PV	PMT	FV	OTHER

Calculator Tip 2

Using the calculator, determine the cost today of
this trip if you were fortunate enough to find a fund
that compounded the 8 percent on a daily (360-day)
basis.

Answer: $4,493.69.

 Financing Retirement: The "Buy a Year" Model

How much do you need to be comfortable in your
retirement, and when do you want to retire? These are
important questions that require some tough decisions.
The following questions, along with others in the
remaining chapters on the time value of money, will
help you come to some important realizations about the
growth of money.

One way to plan for your retirement is to try to determine the lump sum that you will need at retirement to
finance it, and then hope you win the lottery. Another
way is to "buy a year" each year. To consider the latter
strategy, you first need to estimate how much money
you will need each year to live comfortably: $40,000,
$60,000, or more? For the sake of the example, we'll
assume that you need $40,000 a year. The second step
is to determine how much you need to put away now to
have $40,000 available at age 55, which is dependent
on the number of years left before you retire (that is, the
number of years that the money will be invested). Here's
how the "buy a year" strategy works. Once you know
what one year will cost by solving the present value,
invest that amount. This pays for the first year. Next
year, put away the same amount to buy the second year
of retirement—that is, your fifty-sixth year. Keep doing
this until you retire, and you'll be in pretty good shape.

Use Table 3.2 to determine how much money must
be put away today in an account yielding 8 percent
interest to have $40,000 in 30 years. These present val-
ues are rather dramatic, are they not?

TABLE 3.2 THE "BUY A YEAR" RETIREMENT PLAN

Compounding Period	Present Value
Annually	$3,975.09
Quarterly	
Monthly	$3,657.73
Daily, 360 days	
Continuously	$3,628.72

Real Estate, Rates, and Time

How long does it take for an investment to double? Let's take a situation that most likely occurred for your parents or grandparents. In the late 1950s and 1960s in the United States, housing developments were constructed for returning veterans, who were then able to buy an inexpensive home in the suburbs. One such town is Levittown, New York, named for the men who created a number of these developments, William and Alfred Levitt. Suppose your parents bought their first house for $6,000 in 1952. And let's assume that real estate, on the average, appreciated 6 percent per year. How long did it take for their investment to double in value?

Answer: 11.9 years.

The trick in doing these types of problems is how you enter the PV and FV values. Hint: The PV must be a negative entry (see Figure 3.7). Although this is a straightforward problem with the calculator, if you get a whole number, it is not correct. If you get 11 or 12 as the answer, then to get the true rate you will have to resort to logarithms.

You might have heard of the Bankers' Rule of 72, which gives an approximate time for money to double. The rule states that the product of the rate and the time it takes for funds to double at that rate must equal 72. So, for example, if the rate is 8 percent, then money will double in approximately 9 years; 12 percent, then 6 years, and so on. The actual derivation is from ln 2, which can be seen by using logarithms to solve the following relationship using 8 percent. Reduce from the basic FV equation, take the natural log of both sides, and solve for t.

$$12,000 = 6,000\ e^{0.08t}$$

$$2 = 1\ e^{0.08t}$$

$$\ln 2 = 0.08t(\ln e) = 0.08t$$

$$0.6931 = 0.08t$$

$$t = 8.66$$

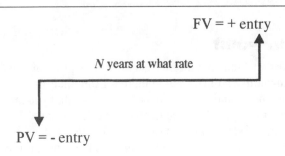

FIGURE 3.7 *How long it takes for money to double.*

You can see that the approximation is really associated with the natural log of 2. Although 69 is more valid, you can see that 72 is more divisor-friendly.

Examples from Today's Headlines

Here are some present value problems from current events.

Yo, Taxi

Sixty years ago a New York City taxi medallion cost $10. This medallion is placed on the automobile, thus making it an authorized vehicle to transport passengers for hire. This year it was announced that the New York City Taxi and Limousine Commission would issue 200 new medallions at a fee of $160,000 each. If your grandfather had bought a medallion 60 years ago and sold it at the city's current price, what would be the annual rate of return on his investment? What if he received monthly compounding?

Answer: 17.51 percent and 16.24 percent. Did you expect a lower rate? Think about it: Because of the increased frequency of periods, the rate adjusted down.

If inflation averaged 3 percent annually over this time period, then determine the real rate of interest for the period.

Answer: Approximation is 14.51 percent; actual is 14.08 percent.

Sad Stats for 16-Year-Olds

In the September 28 edition of *Newsday*, Marta Genovese of the Automobile Club of New York stated that, "although overall highway fatalities (nationwide) have declined over the past 10 years, fatality rates for 16-year-olds have nearly doubled." When statistics like this are presented, we may be alarmed or unfazed depending on the subject matter. It may be more striking to know the actual annual rate of increase. What is the annual rate of increase of highway fatalities of 16-year-olds over the 10-year period cited?

Answer: 7.18 percent.

END POINT

Present value of a future cash amount is probably the most important concept in finance. And analysis of cash flows and decision making requires that you know how to employ it and understand its significance. By using present value you can evaluate the relative worth of competing proposals or determine the rate of return on an investment, again for potential comparisons. Knowing what a project will cost today—its present value and its associated future return—you can calculate the rate that will return that yield.

By understanding how to calculate either the present value or the rate of return on a single payment, we can build to multiple payments and more complicated cash flows. But in this study, we walk before we run. Make sure you know the material from this chapter before moving on to the more robust financial topics in the next chapter.

The Fundamentals of Cash Flows

There are many situations in business, as well as in life, when you are asked to make a choice between two or more options, such as leasing or purchasing. The options usually involve either paying a single one-time payment or making a series of equal payments over some time period in the future. Typically, in business you encounter this when making lease or purchase decisions for computer equipment or an automobile, and in your personal life, you encounter similar decisions when you must decide to lease or buy your next set of hot wheels or a minivan, depending on your age. The essence of the decision is finding a standard or tool that allows you to compare the options.

Currently, there is a very interesting example of just this situation in New York State. The state lottery, called New York Lotto, now requires that you specify on your lottery ticket that you will accept either a single lottery payment (for example, $2 million) or a series of annual payments for life (for example, $125,000) if you should win. So, which should you do?

The process by which we can decide what to do requires that we find a tool that compares all the options with a standard measure. That measure will be found by using either present value or future value calculations to determine the worth of the series of payments, either in the future when payments are completed, or now at the beginning, as in the present value. Although we present both calculations at this point, later we concentrate on the present value calculation, since it is the more widely used tool in business analysis. Let's consider an example as a way to illustrate cash flows and decision making.

As Cyber Vineyards expands, so does its need for additional technology to support the increase in usage. With more people trying to access the network, the increased volume has caused busy signals and customer frustration. A new network server will solve the volume problems. The salesman from the local LANs-R-Us computer store has indicated that you can either lease the computer you need for $1,249 per month for 4 years, or you can purchase it outright for $52,000. The choice is yours. Which should you do?

KEY CONCEPT — DEFINING A CASH FLOW

Up to now we have focused on the present value and future value of a single cash amount, which is different from the situations just described. In these financial situations there are multiple payments over a period of years. Figure 4.1 displays the difference in examining the future value in the two situations. Although both cash flows begin with a $100 payment, over the following 2 years you will make two additional $100 payments. So, obviously, the multiple payments will result in greater future and present values. The question now becomes how we determine the present or future value of this cash flow.

KEY CONCEPT — DEFINING ANNUITIES

The series of $100 payments in Figure 4.1 demonstrates an annuity. An *annuity* is a series of equal cash amounts paid regularly over a period of time. The period of time is the same between each payment—for example, annually, semiannually, or monthly. There are

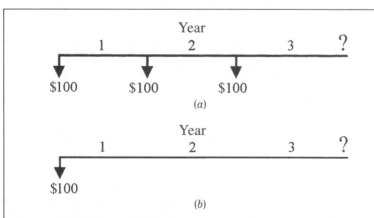

FIGURE 4.1 *Comparison of a single payment to a series of payments: (a) single payment, and (b) series.*

many examples, including those previously mentioned—every year, as in an IRA payment; twice a year, as in coupon bonds; or monthly, as in a car payment or rent. So an annuity is when the same cash amount is received or paid out on a defined periodic basis.

Many factors influence the amount of the future or present value of an annuity:

- *The time period.*   The longer the length of time in which the payments are made, the more interest the future value accrues or the present value discounts.

- *The rate.*   The greater the rate, the larger the future value, or the smaller the present value. An important note about rate: In doing an annuity, we assume that the specified rate is held constant over the life of the annuity.

- *Timing of the payments.*   Payments can be made either at the beginning of the period (termed *up-front* or *in advance*), or at the end of the period (termed *ordinary* or *in arrears.*) These are specified during the negotiation of the annuity.

One question that often comes up is, payments to whom? This is a good question because at times you make the payment to a company (bank, realtor, or insurance company) or an organization (credit union). Or, the payment could be made to you, as as in a retirement or pension benefit. Some individuals will buy an annuity today for a guaranteed cash flow in the future to enhance their retirement income. Later sections present more on these possibilities.

GRAPHICALLY SPEAKING

How a Beginning-of-Term Annuity Works

Let's take a closer look at the example. Suppose we needed to determine the future value of an annuity featuring payments of $100 made at the beginning of the year, for 3 years, at an annual rate of 8 percent. Somebody will surely ask, "What is this whole thing worth at the end of three years?" This is a perceptive question, because it alludes to a comparison: That is, there are other opportunities for investment; which one is best? One way to answer the question is to determine the future values of the investments and compare. Before calculating and summing the future values, it is helpful in your understanding of the solution to have a picture of the payment structure (called a *cash flow;* see Figure 4.2).

So, how does a 3-year annuity of $100 work? Since Figure 4.2 is an example of an up-front or in-advance annuity (beginning of period payment), the first pay-

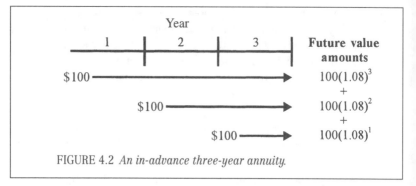

FIGURE 4.2 *An in-advance three-year annuity.*

ment of $100 is made at the beginning of the first year, and, as a result, it has 3 years in which it can accrue interest at the specified rate. Each successive year's payment in the annuity will have one less year's interest accrual. So the third payment, at the beginning of the third year, will accrue interest for only one year.

MATHEMATICALLY SPEAKING

Calculating the Future Value of This Annuity

So, how do we solve this mathematically? To help define the cash flow in the mathematical sense, we make use of summation notation—specifically, the summation symbol Σ (capital sigma)—to express sequential sums. (You can find more on sigma notation in Chapter 13). This notation means that you should sum the following terms substituting the appropriate values for the variables. Each term in the sequence is generated by the product of the payment amount ($100) and the financial multiplier $(1 + r)$ raised to the appropriate power as t takes on values from 1 to 3 years. Here is how the whole solution plays out:

$$FV = \sum_{t=1}^{3} PMT(1 + r)^t$$

Now make the substitutions.

$$FV = \sum_{t=1}^{3} 100(1 + 0.08)^t$$

This notation generates these sums:

$$FV = 100(1 + 0.08)^1 + 100(1 + 0.08)^2 + 100(1 + 0.08)^3$$

$$FV = 100(1.08)^1 + 100(1.08)^2 + 100(1.08)^3$$

$$FV = 108 + 116.64 + 125.97 = 350.61$$

So, mathematically, the sum of the future values of these 3 beginning-of-term payments of $100 at 8 percent interest is $350.61. Each payment has 1, 2, or 3 years in which to accrue interest, the sum of which is $350.61. Now, how did you do this? Did you calculate each term as a power problem (using the y^x key), or did you use the time value of money keys, and just change the N key from 3 to 2 and then to 1? If you did it the latter way, you are really getting the idea. If you did not, take a moment to try it as a review; you know the answer has to be $350.61.

KEY CONCEPT — The End-of-Term Annuity

How does the end-of-term annuity change the analysis if the annuity payments occur at the end of the period, that is, an ordinary (or arrears) annuity? Should its future value be less or more than $350.61 (or even the same)? Since you are putting the money in later at the end of the payment period, it stands to reason that your future value should be less because each payment has one less term in which to accrue interest. Think about it. Maybe a diagram will help; see Figure 4.3.

As you examine the two flows, note that the major difference between the beginning- and end-of-term cash flows is that each of the end-of-term payments accrues interest for one less term. In fact, it may seem silly, but the last payment in the ordinary and arrears case actually gathers no interest, because it is made at the end of the third year. This may seem strange, but as you will learn later, most cash flows are made at the end of the period, not the beginning. Note how the summation changes from the earlier derivation—there are still three periods, but the powers shift from 1 to 3 to 0 to 2. In terms of the amounts of the future values, this is a big difference.

$$FV = \sum_{t=0}^{2} PMT(1 + r)^t$$

Now make the substitutions.

$$FV = \sum_{t=0}^{2} 100(1 + 0.08)^t$$

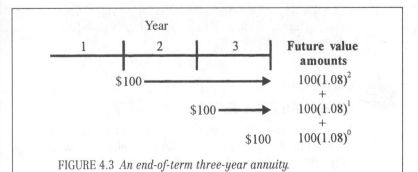

FIGURE 4.3 *An end-of-term three-year annuity.*

69

This notation generates these sums:

$$FV = 100(1 + 0.08)^0 + 100(1 + 0.08)^1 + 100(1 + 0.08)^2$$

$$FV = 100(1.08)^0 + 100(1.08)^1 + 100(1.08)^2$$

$$FV = 100 + 108 + 116.64 = 324.64$$

Alternatively, you could factor the payment amount out from the summation since it is a constant belonging to each term. Then the summation process will yield a pure multiplier very much like what we saw in analyzing single amount calculations. In the old days you would look up present and future value annuity multipliers to find the 3.2464 to calculate the respective present or future value. If you examine Table A.3 in the appendix you will see the multipliers for an in-arrears annuity. Look down the 8.00 percent column to the third row, indicating the multiplier for a three-year annuity. But now, as long as you are careful, the calculator will do this for you. Here is the math:

$$FV = \sum_{t=0}^{2} 100(1 + 0.08)^t$$

Factor the constant.

$$FV = 100 \sum_{t=0}^{2} (1 + 0.08)^t$$

Now expand 1.08 to each power.

$$FV = 100[(1.08)^0 + (1.08)^1 + (1.08)^2]$$

$$FV = 100(1 + 1.08 + 1.1664)$$

$$FV = 100(3.2464) = 324.64$$

It should be clear now that the future value of a cash flow that makes payments at the beginning of the term will allow you to accrue more interest than an annuity plan having end-of-period payments.

You can appreciate that these annuity calculations could become tedious and time-consuming as they are projected out for 20 years, as in, for example, retirement planning. So when analyzing these large cash flows, you should be thankful that the calculator was invented. First, make sure you have the right idea by using the calculator to determine the future value of 3 $100 payments of an in-advance annuity, assuming an interest rate of 8 percent.

CALC TIP
Calculating the FV of an Annuity

You already know the structure of these cash flows from the initial annuity presentation, as well as the two different answers. So, use the calculator to verify your answers. There are a couple of tricks in doing an annuity on the calculator, but as before, start at the Time Value of Money menu. Table 4.1 lists the keys required in the calculation of an annuity.

CALC TIP
The Effect of Begin and End Modes on Future Value

On the HP 19 and 17 series there is the Other key on the time value of money keys, which presents a menu to change settings for the calculations. After pressing Other, select BEG from the menu. Begin mode automatically sets the calculator to perform the future or present value calculation for the annuity, assuming the in-advance case. Be advised that this setting affects only PMT entries. It does not have any numerical effect on the future or present value of a single cash amount, as discussed in the previous chapters. On other calculators, such as the HP 12C, you may see two keys actually named BEG and END. If this is the case, pressing them before executing FV or PV will calculate the answer in the selected mode.

The HP annuity keys should take values like those shown here:

TABLE 4.1 THE ANNUITY KEYS

Key Name	Purpose
N	The number of years you will be making annuity payments. This entry is adjusted as was done with present and future value when payment frequency (semiannual, for example) changes.
I%YR	The interest rate over the years of the investment period.
PMT	The amount of a single annuity payment is entered into the PMT register. If it is cash out, then it is a negative number.
FV or PV	What are you solving for, the worth of the cash flow today or the value in the future? Know the type of calculation you need, either future value or present value. (In this case you want the FV.)
BEG or END	You should assume an annuity is ordinary (payments at end of term) unless specified otherwise. There is usually a setting related to the time value of money keys that states BEG or END mode, which refers to the payment occurring at the end (ordinary) or at the beginning of the term (up-front). In the example, select the Begin option.

			Enter the coupon value (PMT).	Press	
N	**I%YR**	PV	**PMT**	**FV**	OTHER
3	8		−100	to solve for FV.	

Once you have entered the number of years, rate, and payment amount into the appropriate registers, you need only know what you are solving for. Pressing the FV key will calculate the future value of the 3 payments and their interest accrual at 8 percent for 3 years—namely, $350.61. If you had pressed PV you would have solved for the present value of the cash flow—that is, what the worth of those 3 payments is today, discounted at 8 percent.

You try: ➤ **Future Value of the Annuity— End Mode**

Using the preceding technique, show that the $1000 you put in the bank at the end of each year for your 6 percent rainy day fund will grow to $13,180.79 after 10 years. It's a sunny day, thanks to the calculator.

You try: ➤ **Future Value of the Annuity— Begin Mode**

Now suppose you put the payment in at the beginning of the term. Make the simple change to the annuity by switching to Begin mode and press FV again. Ah, the beauty of paying early— $13,971.64, nearly an $800 increase.

 You Can't Do PV and FV at the Same Time

This probably seems crazy, but on most calculators you can solve for only one of these functions at a time— that is, you can't press PV after calculating the FV. The reason is that the calculator now holds the future value calculation in its register. To calculate the present value, you must first *zero it out*—enter a zero in the future value register—so you can get the true value for the PV. Otherwise, it calculates the PV assuming 3 flows of $100 and a final payment of $350.61. Although you may wish for that $0.00 amount, it is not correct.

With all these settings still in place, suppose you needed to determine the future value of 10 yearly payments of $100. All you need to do is enter 10 for the number of payments; that is, replace the *N* value of 3 and again press FV. Answer: $1,564.65.

N	I%YR	PV	PMT	FV	OTHER
10	8		−100		

ANNUITY STRUCTURE OF AN IRA PLAN

An Individual Retirement Account (IRA) is a self-initiated retirement account. You can make tax-deferred contributions to the IRA while you are working and withdraw from it after you reach the age of 65, when your tax rate will presumably be lower. The U.S. Congress sets a limit on the maximum amount you can deposit in the account. The good news is that these payments can add up significantly. Let's take an example. What is the future value of 20 $2,000 end-of-term IRA payments? Assume a conservative rate of 6 percent.

Now, math fans, you can really appreciate the use of the calculator—otherwise, this would be at least a 10-minute exercise to calculate each of the flows individually and add them. Answer: $73,571.18.

It should now be clear that the consequence of making payments at the end of a term, as opposed to the beginning of the term, to a fund such as a retirement account or an IRA account is that you earn less interest on each individual payment. Therefore, your savings will accrue even more interest if payments are made sooner in the period. In this way, you get more interest on your principal as opposed to waiting until April 15, which is when most people make their IRA payments. If the value of the ordinary annuity is $73,571.18, then what is the future value if you make the payments at the beginning of the period? Now that's retirement planning. *Vive la différence:* $4,414.27. Yes, you've earned an additional $4,414 just by making your deposits early.

 THE PRESENT VALUE OF AN ANNUITY

Earlier we examined the future value of a series of $100 cash payments. How might we consider the present value of this cash flow? Suppose you wanted to assure yourself that you will be able to receive a series of payments in the future—in this case, three $100 payments, each at the end of the next 3 years.

An insurance company might sell you an annuity program similar to this (only at a greater amount) as a retirement vehicle. The question is how much you must pay them *now* in order to receive these payments in the future. The answer is the present value of the cash flow at their given rate.

GRAPHICALLY SPEAKING

The Present Value Picture

Calculating the present value of a cash flow is a necessary skill for finance. The beauty of the annuity is that it is easy to understand how it works and to calculate the solution. Let's start with a diagram.

How does the payment structure in Figure 4.4 differ from the future value scenario we just analyzed? First of all, you are being asked to pay for this entire cash flow before receiving any payments. For that one-time amount, you will receive 3 payments of $100. That's the way this annuity works. Now, since this is an ordinary annuity, the first payment of $100 is received at the end of the first year, and has only 1 year in which it can be discounted at the specified rate. The second payment, at the end of the second year, will be discounted for 2 years at 8 percent. The last payment actually gets discounted for all three years. So, to determine the worth of the cash flow today, you take the present value of each payment and add them. How do we solve this mathematically?

MATHEMATICALLY SPEAKING

Calculating the Present Value of the Annuity

$$PV = \sum_{t=1}^{3} PMT\ (1 + r)^{-t}$$

Now make the substitutions.

$$PV = \sum_{t=1}^{3} 100(1 + 0.08)^{-t}$$

This notation generates these sums:

$PV = 100(1 + 0.08)^{-1} + 100(1 + 0.08)^{-2} + 100(1 + 0.08)^{-3}$

$PV = 100(1.08)^{-1} + 100(1.08)^{-2} + 100(1.08)^{-3}$

$PV = 100(0.9259) + 100(0.8573) + 100(0.7938)$

$PV = 92.59 + 85.73 + 79.38 = 257.70$

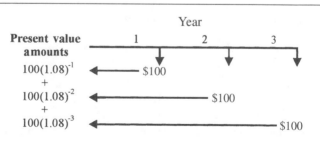

FIGURE 4.4 *Present value of a three-year annuity.*

So, if you want to guarantee those payments for yourself it will cost you $257.70 to lock in that cash flow. Now you can see how an annuity might be set up to establish a certain lifestyle for retirement, or even a child's college education, but you would need a little more than $100!

In the old days prior to calculators, you would use a table for the present value of an annuity, as shown in appendix Table A.4. You would look down the 8.00 percent column for the 3-year row to find the desired multiplier. You would then multiply 2.57710 times the $100 payment to obtain the present value. Incidentally, the penny difference in the result when using Table A.4 or the calculator ($257.71) is due to rounding.

An Interpretation of Indifference

There is an alternative interpretation to the significance of the present value calculation yielding $257.70 in the preceding annuity. Suppose you are investing with the following goal: You need to attain the amount of $324.63 at the end of 3 years. As shown earlier, you could make 3 annual end-of-term payments of $100 to satisfy the goal. This present value calculation indicates that you could also invest $257.70 today for 3 years at 8 percent to arrive at the same amount. Check it out with the calculator—determine the future value of $257.70 invested for 3 years at 8 percent. As they like to say in economics, you are *indifferent* to the method; either strategy will achieve the $324.63.

CALC TIP
Calculating the PV of an Annuity

The only difference from what we were employing earlier is that you are solving for the present value and not the future value. Recall the note mentioned earlier: You can't do both at the same time, so do not press FV. If you make an FV entry by mistake, enter 0 in the FV setting and continue doing the PV keystrokes. To do the previous problem, the annuity keys should take values like those shown here:

		Press	Enter the coupon value (PMT).		
N	**I%YR**	**PV**	**PMT**	**FV**	**OTHER**
3	8	to solve for PV.	–100		

Once you have entered the number of years, rate, and payment amount into the appropriate registers, you need only know that you are solving for present value. Pressing the PV key will calculate the present value of the 3 payments discounted at 8 percent for the

3 years—namely, $257.71. If you do not obtain this amount, check that you are in End mode and make sure there is no value in the FV register. Otherwise, clear it all and try again.

 Determining the Effect of
CONCEPT **Monthly or Quarterly Payments**

You are probably familiar with monthly payments for things like cars and rent. How does this change the future or present value? For example, recall the $100 ordinary 3-year annuity, whose future value was $324.63, that was studied earlier. Comparatively speaking, which has the better future value—3 ordinary annual payments of $100, 6 semiannual payments of $50, or 12 quarterly payments of $25? Recall that *ordinary* refers to end-of-period payments. Essentially, the question is whether making smaller payments more frequently will increase the future value of the investment.

Using the calculator, modify the keystrokes in exactly the same manner as you did in the single cash flow case. Divide the rate by the number of periods per year, and multiply the number of periods times the number of years. Don't forget to modify the amount of the payment to reflect each situation. The HP annuity keys should be adjusted to reflect values like those shown here for the semiannual case:

N	I%YR	PV	PMT	FV	OTHER
3 × 2	8/2		−50		

 CALC TIP

On the HP 19 and 17 series you can use the Other key and adjust the P/YR register, which will automatically adjust the rate to the frequency of the payments entered. However, as mentioned earlier, you must remember to reenter the number of years by pressing the Shift key prior to pressing the N register. While you are in the Other menu you should also make sure you are in the appropriate mode: Begin or End.

Table 4.2 is an exercise to make sure you have the concept and keystrokes down.

 DETERMINING THE PAYMENT
CONCEPT **AMOUNT**

This topic is a variation on the effect of making more frequent payments. How are those car payments determined? In this variation of our analysis we want to

TABLE 4.2 INCREASING THE FREQUENCY OF PAYMENTS

Payments/ Year	Periodic Payment	Nom Rate	Total Periods	Future Value, Ordinary Mode	Future Value, Begin Mode
Annually	$100	8%	3	$324.64	$350.61
Semiannually (2)	$50	8%/2	2 × 3	$331.65	
Quarterly (4)	$25	8%/4	4 × 3	$335.30	
Monthly (12)	$100/12	8%/12	12 × 3		$340.05

determine the payment amount when given the future or present value, the time period, the periods per year, and the rate. Let's rethink an earlier problem: planning the second honeymoon. In that problem you wanted to have $10,000 at the end of 10 years for your trip to Paris. In that analysis you determined that you needed to put away $4,493.68 now to pay for that trip in 10 years. But now suppose you ask, "How much should I put away each year so that at the end of the 10 years, we have enough to pay for the second honeymoon?" This is the soul of financing. You have a target value either presently (buying the car in the showroom) or in the future (the second honeymoon), and you need a palatable way to pay for it, as they say, *over time.* In solving this problem, the missing variable is the payment amount. To solve for the payment, in addition to the future or present value, you also need to know frequency (monthly or annually) and the interest rate. In this problem we will assume a monthly payment. To solve for the monthly payment you must set the P/YR register to 12, enter the nominal annual rate, and enter the number of years. If you do not have a P/YR register, multiply the years by 12 and divide the nominal rate by 12, as pictured here. We'll assume the same rate of 8 percent, and the FV value will be $10,000.

N	I%YR	PV	PMT	FV	OTHER
10 × 12	8/12			10,000	

The answer, assuming Begin mode so you can start saving right away is, $54.30. If you do not get this answer, the source of confusion could be in the use of the P/YR register. If you have this register you must

enter the nominal annual rate because the P/YR register will divide the rate automatically. And when entering the N setting, type the number of years, then press
Shift and N. The shift automatically multiplies the years
times the P/YR register. This is the beauty of an annuity
or any forced savings program: Smaller amounts more
frequently paid grow to become very sizeable indeed.
Good enough for a trip for two to Paris with style!

Why did we enter $10,000 for FV? We did not enter
the $10,000 in PV because we want the money to be
available in 10 years. But beware—suppose you
were financing an automobile, and wanted the money
available now, to pay the dealer. Since it is money today
you are financing (not an amount to have in 10 years),
then the cash flow requires a present value setting.
This is an important observation, and it is addressed in
the applications section.

APPLICATIONS OF CASH FLOW ANALYSIS

This section demonstrates how the material in this
chapter can be applied to determining the cost of buying versus leasing, and to planning for selected financial goals.

Buying versus Leasing

The salesman from the technology center has
indicated that you can either lease the server at $1,249
per month for 4 years, or you can purchase it outright
for $52,000. Which should you do?

There are many other factors that may enter into
your decision on this problem—most notably, do you
have the cash to pay the full amount, or could the capital be used in another more attractive financial opportunity? Our criterion will be simple: Is the present value
of the payments reasonably close to the purchase
price?

To solve the problem you need to know what the
rate of return would be on your money if you left it
either in the bank or in its current investment. Assume
that the bank is offering 6 percent. Also, assume that
the dealer will want the first payment at the lease signing; therefore, you should look at the annuity as an in-
advance cash flow with monthly payments. The trick in
doing this problem is that the annuity must be set up in
Begin mode and the rate and time must be adjusted for
monthly payments. If done properly, you find that the
present value of 48 payments of $1,249 discounted at 6
percent is $53,448.73, indicating that at the 6 percent
rate the dealership could charge you less per payment.

If you got a negative amount in the PV register, it is because the payment was not entered as a negative.

To determine the annual nominal rate used by the dealer for financing this deal, enter $52,000 in the PV register, 48 payments in the N register, a negative payment amount of $1,249, and press the I% YR key. Answer: 7.48 percent.

Finding the Equitable Payment Amount

You could find the appropriate payment amount by solving for the payment. This is done by entering the same rate and time values as before, but entering $52,000 as the PV value. When solving for PMT you should get $1,215.15, which is much less than the amount suggested by the dealer—if you're going to pay $1,249 a month, then get more computer for the value.

Retirement Planning Made Easy

In earlier chapters we investigated the cost of financing a retirement nest egg at various saving periods. This time we'll tackle the problem from a different perspective. You know the amount you want to retire with—for example $200,000. The question is how much you must sock away on a regular basis to get there.

Retirement planning requires careful selection of a fund, and attention to its expected annual rate of return and the payment schedule. To be safe, assume an average rate of return over the period of 7 percent (it may be high when you are young and not afraid of risk, and low when you get older and want to protect your investment). Assuming you will retire in 30 years, how much money must you invest in the fund at the end of each year to be assured of achieving your $200,000 goal? Figure 4.5 should help define the problem.

Figure 4.5 represents an annuity problem because you are solving for the equal amount (payment) that you must deposit each year. You know the future value because that is the amount you're investing toward in 30 years. On an annual basis you would have to deposit $2,117.28 into the fund at the end of each year. If you considered making the payment at the beginning of the year you would save some money, $1,978.77.

An interesting note: Suppose you made monthly payments toward your objective. Simply adjust your calculator to 12 periods per year and recalculate, and you'll find the monthly payment is only $163.94, assuming End mode, which is very doable. But start now. This number is probably half your current car payment. Think about it.

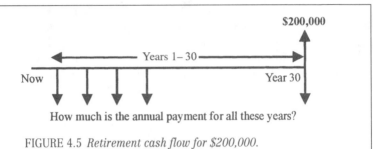

How much is the annual payment for all these years?

FIGURE 4.5 *Retirement cash flow for $200,000.*

KEY CONCEPT — A Key to Financing Higher Education

Your oldest child is graduating from high school in 10 years. It's time to plan for the cost now. Assuming the cost of each year of his or her four-year college program is $15,000, how much should you save annually to guarantee his or her successful higher educational experience?

It is time to become a little more analytical. To set you up to do this type of problem, we'll ask a more basic question, then take it to the next level. Suppose your child was to begin college tomorrow—how much would you need to put aside today to fund four years of education? No graduate school, please! As you set up a diagram, remember that you pay in advance for a year's worth of education, so this is an in-advance annuity. Assume that you will be conservative with the type of investment that you will use to hold these funds; therefore, assume an annual rate of 7.5 percent on your educational nest egg. Figure 4.6 displays the cash flow.

The important point of Figure 4.6 is to show that the amount you need is actually not $60,000, but, in fact, some amount less than that because your money will be accruing interest over the time period. Yes, time value of money is here to help you. The solution is the present value of an in-advance annuity of 4 payments discounted at 7.5 percent, which is $54,007.89. Now you know what it will cost to finance your objective.

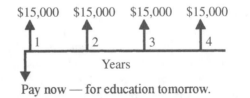

Pay now — for education tomorrow.

FIGURE 4.6 *The present value of education.*

This is an important point to note. $54,007.89 is what 4 years of education is going to cost at $15,000 per year, whether your child starts school tomorrow or in 10 years (assuming the same tuition amount). And here is where it gets interesting—the more time you have to save to get to that number, the easier it will be to finance—or, at least, the more palatable the numbers.

This last point is a very important principle. It is important to understand that there will be many situations where you will need to save today for a cash flow to be received in the future. In this case, what does it really cost for a 4-year cash flow that you will receive in 10 years? This wonderful model will help you with education, retirement, expensive toys, you name it.

Now, the final step is to determine how much must be put aside today to attain the $54,007.89 in 10 years. In other words, what is the cost today of 4 years of education that will begin in 10 years? The adjusted diagram in Figure 4.7 helps show the task required.

This is a simple present value problem, asking us to find the worth today of an amount of money ($54,007.89) to be received in the future. At this point in the problem it is not an annuity problem, but a simple future and present value problem. Assuming the same rate of 7.5 percent, compounded annually for 10 years, we get $26,204.30. That's right, my friends, you have reduced the problem down to $26,204 to finance the 4 years of education. That's the good news. The bad news is, what if you do not get the 7.5 percent interest rate, or you have more than one child!

Alternatives in Financing Higher Education

Actually, although we reduced a $60,000 problem to a $26,204 solution, this might still be a rather difficult number to attain. So instead of thinking about abstinence or birth control, might we try to bring this number into a better perspective, and by that I don't mean a less expensive school (always an option) or suggesting a career in the armed forces. Here are a few options to consider.

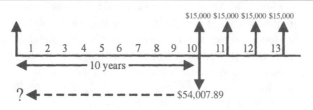

FIGURE 4.7 *Present value of the annuity.*

Better Rate

It may be a risky strategy, but would it be possible to get a better rate? For example, suppose you invested in an equity mutual fund that advertised an average growth rate of 12 percent compounded annually. Considering the same 10-year time period (you will keep the money in the 7.5 percent fund during the 4 years of college), how much is the present value? Answer: $17,389.09. This represents an approximate $9,000 savings in obtaining the more aggressive rate.

And if you got more frequent compounding—for example, monthly—then how does the present value change? Answer: It's even better, now it's $16,364.11.

More Frequent Payments

How about a strategy using monthly payments? It may mean treating your objective as if it were another mortgage. Again, consider the same 10-year time period with a slightly more aggressive rate—namely 8 percent, compounded monthly. What is the payment that must be made on a monthly basis that will achieve a future value of $54,007.89 in 10 years? Assume an ordinary annuity for the 10-year period; there will be no appreciable difference between an in-advance or ordinary annuity. Answer: $295.21 per month, which represents a very realistic way to achieve your financial objective. It works, folks—all you have to do is stick to the program, be attentive, and don't skip payments. The in-advance annuity is $293.26.

Other Options

Some may wonder why we have limited the discussion to only the same amounts for the entire 10-year period. This is because we have an easier tool for handling different cash flow amounts, which is explained in the next chapter.

KEY CONCEPT   Automobile Financing

It's sticker shock time. You just went into the local dealer's showroom to check out a four-wheel-drive SUV to get you and the family up to ski country safely this winter. The dealer is offering a special 2 percent financing on a brand new SUV with all the options that costs $28,000. Your spouse insists that the most you can afford is $600 per month. If you finance the auto over four years, what will be the monthly payment?

As in the preceding problem you must be in monthly periods; assume monthly compounding for both the financing and the payments. There are two ways to do this problem. One way is to determine the future value—that is, the amount actually to be financed—then determine the monthly payment that will satisfy that amount. The other way, which will yield the same answer, is to solve this for the payment that yields the present value of $28,000.

The first way finds the payment by referencing the future value. Today, the car is valued at $28,000 (this is your present value), and there is a 2 percent rate, compounded monthly over 48 months, which yields a future value of $30,330.02. Now the payment that will meet this amount is $606.45. Since the first payment must be paid at the signing, consider this an in-advance annuity. If this did not work, make sure you have entered 0 in the present value setting. Once you zero out the PV register, solve for PMT. As well, remember that this is a monthly payment and compounding problem.

The second way to find the monthly payment is quicker, but possibly not as easily understood—that is, you can finance on the present value just as well as the future value. In fact, that is exactly how a mortgage is financed. The best way to think about it is that the amount you need to finance is the present value of the car, house, or whatever. With this in mind, the following keystrokes will determine the $606.45 payment, assuming Begin mode:

N	I%YR	PV	PMT	FV	OTHER
4 × 12	2/12	28,000			

If you did not get this answer and you used the P/YR register, check that you are in Begin mode. Otherwise, see the earlier calculator tip on using the P/YR register.

CALC TIP
Finding the Price to Negotiate To

You're so close. By entering the payment amount of $600 and solving for the present value, you can find the amount you will need to negotiate the dealer down to in order to satisfy your spouse's requirement ($27,702.08), assuming Begin mode and monthly compounding.

Various Ways of Financing a Mortgage

$150,000, that's the final price on your dream house. Of course, money will be tight and you'll borrow from Aunt Tillie and the in-laws for some of the down payment, but it's yours. Now what about the mortgage? Mortgage rates are truly reasonable; they are down to 9 percent. The problem is, should you go for the 30-year or 15-year mortgage? What, you never knew they had 15-year mortgages?

Your parents probably had at least three important pieces of financial advice as you grew up: (1) Save your pennies, (2) go to college, and (3) buy a house. In my house, none of these was negotiable. This last item was particularly important to my parents because it meant a great deal to them to own their own home. Owning a home was part of America's great opportunity. Do you remember the happiness Mr. Martini expressed to Jimmy Stewart, our hero, upon buying a house in *It's a Wonderful Life*? It is interesting that such a financially fulfilling concept is defined by a word that in French means something like death, maybe "Till death do us part."

What makes owning a house possible for most people, is that they can qualify for a mortgage. A *mortgage* is a financial contract whereby you get a large sum of money from a lender, most likely your local bank, to pay the owner or contractor of the house. You then make monthly payments to the lender over an extended period of time until the loan is paid off—a very long time, usually 30 years. Most home mortgages are *fixed rate,* that is, they have a fixed interest rate over the life of the mortgage, and require a fixed monthly payment to the lender.

How does a fixed-rate mortgage work? A fixed-rate mortgage is the most familiar example of an annuity in our society; most people make an outlandish payment, on a uniform basis, for most of their working careers (Figure 4.8). I know people who have had parties when their mortgages were paid off. Since payments are made monthly, interest is compounded monthly on the amount borrowed. And as will be seen later, the total amount of interest paid to the bank on a mortgage is incredible. Hence, look carefully at what we show you about 15-year mortgages.

Suppose you are required to put a 20 percent down payment on the house, thus reducing the amount of the mortgage to 120,000. The advertised rate is 9 percent, compounded monthly, and we will look at a 30-year

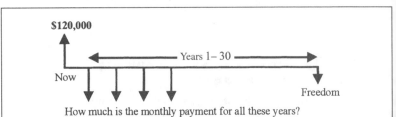

$120,000

Now

Years 1– 30

Freedom

How much is the monthly payment for all these years?

FIGURE 4.8 *The mortgage cash flow.*

time period. The trick in looking at the setup of the mortgage is that the amount you are borrowing is actually the present value. Why? Because this is the amount you want now, at signing, so you can pay the owner. And this is why a mortgage is so expensive, because you pay interest on this amount all the way through the period of the loan. Yikes!

CALC TIP

Finding the Annuity Payment

When doing the keystrokes, remember that you are paying on a monthly basis; therefore, you must adjust for monthly valuation by either using the P/YR register or adjusting the N register for 360 periods, and dividing the rate by 12. Also, mortgage calculations assume end-of-period payment. If you do not get the correct answer, clear and try again. You should get $965.55.

N	I%YR	PV	PMT	FV	OTHER
30 × 12	9/12	−120,000			

The Benefit of Shorter Time Frames and Lower Rates

This $965.55 is an interesting number, and it deserves a little perspective. To be clear, my friends who are seeking home ownership, you will be paying this amount every month for 30 years. This number is just south of $1,000. Hence, if you were asked how much you will pay the bank in total, you would estimate $350,000, or in that vicinity. Well, the actual number is $347,598, as displayed in Table 4.3, and the amount of interest is $227,598. That's right, interest accounts for almost twice your mortgage principle. As the table shows, there is a lot of interest going into the bank's pockets. Incidentally, there was a time in the early 1980s when mortgage rates were in the mid- to upper teens. So, when reality bites, we would like to know what we can do about it.

TABLE 4.3 THE BEAUTY OF A 15-YEAR MORTGAGE

Years	8% PMT	Total	Interest	9% PMT	Total	Interest
30	$ 880.52	$316,987.50	$196,987.20	$ 965.55	$347,598.00	$227,598.00
20	1,003.73	240,875.20	120,875.20	1,079.67	259,120.80	139,120.80
15	1,146.78	206,420.40	86,420.44	1,217.12	219,081.60	99,081.60

Let's consider your mortgage amount of $120,000 with a range of rates so you can see the significance of lower rates, as well as the significance of a shorter mortgage period. Suppose you do a little shopping around (you should, because you will be surprised at the range of rates available), and find institutions ranging from 8.5 to 9.5 percent in their annual mortgage rates. How will a small rate change affect your payment? Dramatically.

Use the calculator to verify the payment calculations in Table 4.4. A few cells have been left blank for you to show your proficiency. This table clearly shows the significance of a small difference in the rate and, therefore, the importance of shopping around at banks, credit unions, savings and loans, and so on. For example, if you can get half a percent reduction on the mortgage, this will yield approximately $40 in saving each month, or $15,000 over the life of the mortgage, which is approximately the amount of one year's college tuition. One full percent reduction will yield an additional $80 a month for your use.

Now, how does the length of the term affect payments? Clearly, the payments will be more, due to the shorter period, but this presents a very interesting opportunity. If you can afford only a little bit more, you can get out of long-range debt significantly sooner, thereby leaving yourself free to make payments toward the next big-ticket item—your children's education!

Table 4.3 shows very clearly the opportunity afforded by a drop in the mortgage rate. Not only do you lower the amount of your monthly payment over the 30-year period, but you also open the opportunity to pay off the loan in less time. Examine the table closely. By paying approximately $180 more a month, the 8 percent mortgage is paid off in half the time of the 9 percent mortgage. And it gets even more advantageous as the rates get lower. So, when rates get low and you consider refinancing your mortgage, look closely at the 15-year mortgage opportunity.

TABLE 4.4 HOW DECREASING RATES HELP YOU

Rate	PMT	Total	Interest
8.50%	$922.70		$212,172.00
8.75		$339,854.40	
9.00	965.55	347,598.00	227,598.00
9.25	987.21	355,395.60	235,395.60
9.50		363,250.80	243,249.00

How Much Can You Mortgage?

Finally, let's examine this topic from the perspective of what you can afford as a monthly payment. Suppose you and your spouse sit down for a heart-to-heart talk to determine exactly how much your family can afford for a monthly mortgage, and you arrive at $1,200 per month. How much of a mortgage can you get with that monthly amount? Assume you have sufficient savings or resources for the down payment. In this problem you know the payment, the time period, and the rate; simply solve for the present value and you'll have the answer. And don't forget the lessons learned in this section—vary the percent, and vary the time period. Good luck!

END POINT

This chapter's objective is to define and develop the fundamental concept of an annuity, examining both its present value and future value. An annuity is simply a series of equal payments received or paid out over uniform time periods. The real value in understanding an annuity is that it provides a wonderful opportunity to understand the fundamentals of cash flow analysis. And solving the present or future value of an annuity is relatively easy thanks to the important keystrokes used on the calculator.

There is a wide range of applications for annuities, from more refined retirement planning to lease purchase analysis. The hard work on annuities gets you ready for the next chapter on bonds.

CHAPTER 5

The Beauty of Bonds

Before defining a bond, let's try to explain why bonds evolved. Consider some of the following examples:

- A company wants to make a new product and must build a new manufacturing plant.
- A government requires funding to facilitate interstate commerce by building a new interstate highway.
- A municipality requires funds to build a new school.

In each of these situations an entity needs to borrow substantial sums of money. Whether it is a corporation needing funds to expand or modernize its manufacturing operation, or a city needing funds for a technology initiative to bring its classrooms into the twenty-first century, each requires sums beyond its normal annual budget. They fund these efforts by borrowing money from investors, to be paid back over a long period of time. For the use of these funds, the issuer (the organization doing the borrowing) pays the lender (you, or an organization buying the bond) interest, through either annual payments (coupon bonds) or a discounted purchase price (zero-coupon bonds). At maturity, the lender is paid the face value (a very close relative of future value) of the bond. Because of this "borrow–pay back" obligation, bonds are known as *debt instruments*.

THE NATURE OF BONDS

Let's take a specific example to see how this works. When you were young, somebody surely gave you a U.S. Savings Bond as a gift for some special occasion. First thing you noticed was that you couldn't do anything with it, except give it to Mom and Dad. Talk about frustrating—I mean, it wasn't like a toy, a book, or a bike. Now, suppose somebody had given you tickets to a baseball game as a gift. The tickets would allow you entrance into a game at some point in the future. They would secure your seats for a game in the future, if you will. That wouldn't have been so bad, particularly if they were World Series tickets.

A bond is like a baseball ticket in that somebody pays money today for a seat you will use in the future. In the case of your U.S. Savings Bond, an aunt or uncle spent, for example, $50, so that you would be able to collect $100 in 10 years. So, why bonds? Issuing bonds is a way in which the government or a corporation can get money to support its capital-raising efforts. Because most bonds are issued in units of $1,000, they appeal to both individuals and large investors who look for a safe investment. They are considered *safe* because the likelihood that either a municipality or a large corporation will default on the payments is very unlikely.

KEY CONCEPT — DEFINING BONDS

A *bond* is a form of corporate or government borrowing. The government or private corporation issues bonds for a purpose—for example, General Motors may want to build a new factory to assemble a new automobile, as it did with Saturn, or the State of New York may want to issue bonds to build new university housing at its Albany campus. In selling the bond, the issuer (GM or the State of New York) gets the money and the purchaser gets a guaranteed cash amount or series of cash amounts in the future. The time period often ranges from 10 to 20 years or more. It is a long-term contractual agreement between the issuer and the bondholders. There are two types of bonds, coupon and zero-coupon bonds.

HOW COUPON BONDS WORK

Most corporate bonds are termed *coupon bonds* because they yield a periodic payment (the coupon), usually every six months, over the life of the bond. The coupon is determined by the *coupon rate,* which is the guaranteed rate on the bond agreed to by the issuer. This rate is in effect for the life of the bond, which produces the coupon payments, and hence the guaranteed cash flow. At issuance, the purchaser buys the bond at or near its face value, usually $1,000, and then receives the face value of the bond upon maturity. Depending on market conditions, the price of the bond may deviate above or below the face value. The conditions of the coupon bond are much like a contract; they automatically lock in a defined cash flow over the life of the bond. This type of financial instrument is very attractive for personal retirement plans because it guarantees an income flow in the future, which can compensate an individual's social security or pension plan.

They Are Bonds—James Bonds

The James Corporation announced today that it will build a new distillery to support the sudden worldwide interest in gin martinis, a powerful drink once consumed by the equally powerful businessmen of the 1960s and a famous special agent known for preferring them "shaken, not stirred." To finance the effort, James has indicated that it will sell corporate bonds at an attractive 8% coupon rate.

Let's take an example from this fictional newspaper article and apply the key definitions employed in bonds. Table 5.1 defines the key terms used with bonds and relates them back to the specifications set in the James bonds.

GRAPHICALLY SPEAKING

James' Coupon Bond and the Cash Flow

Suppose the James Corporation issues a 10-year bond at a coupon rate of 8 percent, with a face value of $1,000. What is the corresponding cash flow for the investor? To clearly see how the cash flow is created, examine Figure 5.1. Assume that the coupon payments are annual, and the price to the buyer is $1,000. Amounts on up arrows represent returns to the investor; amounts on the down arrows represent costs to the investor. Note that the final payment includes the face value of $1,000, as well.

How Risk Affects Coupon Rates

KEY CONCEPT   The discount rate and market interest rate, although close in value, are not the same. The *discount rate* is the rate the Federal Reserve Bank uses to lend to commercial banks. Commercial banks, in turn, lend money to a wide range of customers, from their very best customers (safe companies), to those needing funds to refinance (riskier), and to individuals for mortgages or short-term loans. In each of these situations the bank establishes a rate above the discount rate that will assure its profitability, yet be competitive with the other banks for the same level of lending service. The term *interest rate* can apply to any of these market

TABLE 5.1 BOND DEFINITIONS FOR THE JAMES BOND

Issuer James Corp.	The company or government agency that is borrowing the money.
Face value $1,000	The value of the bond at maturity, also referred to as *par value*. This could be the price of the bond at issuance. At maturity, this is the amount paid to the lender.
Coupon rate 8%	The rate employed in the contract at issuance of the bond to determine the coupon. The coupon rate is usually very close to the discount rate but may be higher for an issue due to perceived risk on the borrowing company.
Coupon $80	The interest payment to the lender—face value times the coupon rate (0.08 × $1,000). If these are annual coupons, the lender receives the full amount once a year; if semiannual, the lender receives half the coupon amount every six months. Most corporate bonds are semiannual coupons.
Term 10 years	The number of years of the investment. Bonds can go from short term, 6 months, out to long term, 30 years.
Discount Rate	The rate currently employed by the Federal Reserve Bank in short-term lending. To attract buyers to the bond, the coupon rate has to be higher than the short-term rate.

rates. The key point is that interest rates, and, specifically, coupon rates for generating interest payments on bonds, will fluctuate up or down in relation to the behavior of the discount rate at the time of issue. But once the bonds come to market, the coupon rate is locked so that investors can assess the relative quality of the investment.

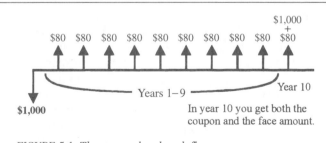

FIGURE 5.1 *The coupon bond cash flow.*

Why do coupon rates vary? As stated, the behavior of the discount rate will influence the bond market, and, particularly, it will affect those companies planning an issue. But another factor that influences the choice of the coupon rate is the financial health of the issuer. A company with a good credit rating will be able to obtain a lower rate for borrowing than a company in fear of bankruptcy, which, as a consequence, will be forced to offer a higher rate due to risk and the absence of banks willing to take that risk. As a result, when these riskier companies issue bonds, they must set their coupon rates higher than the current market rates for safe companies. Purchasers of the bonds require a premium for investing in such companies. The riskier the company, the greater the amount of the premium. The decision as to what the rate should be is usually made by the underwriters of the issue, who work on behalf of the borrowing company to market and sell the bonds. The better, more established companies will offer a lower rate (but with little risk to the lender), and struggling companies must offer a higher rate to attract lenders to buy their bonds.

Once a coupon rate is established for a bond's issue, it is in effect for that bond until maturity, when the last coupon and face value are paid back to the lender. The discount rate may change, thereby affecting new issues; that is, new bonds will be coming to market with smaller or larger coupon payments depending on the discount rate. This after-purchase market behavior does not affect your payments—they are guaranteed—but it does affect the worth of your bond if you decide to sell it. The sections on premium and discount bonds present more on this.

Setting Up the Bond's Cash Flow

Check out the cash flow for the James Corporation 10-year $1,000 coupon bond at the rate of 8 percent. Do you recall the annual coupon amount, and how much you paid for the bond? Suppose you bought that bond on February 1, and on February 2 the groundhog saw its shadow and the Fed raised the discount rate to 9 percent. If other bonds were being issued February 2 with coupon rates of 9 percent, what would the cash flow look like (see Figure 5.2)? Note that both bonds were purchased for the same amount, $1,000.

CASH FLOW FOR A ZERO-COUPON BOND

Let's take a quick moment to describe the cash flow for zero-coupon bonds. These are bonds that are issued without any interim payments—that is, no coupons. So, instead of coupons you get a discounted price. To see

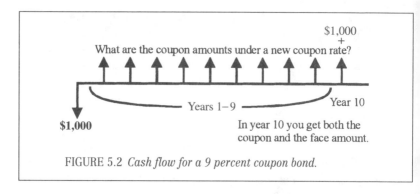

FIGURE 5.2 *Cash flow for a 9 percent coupon bond.*

how it works we'll again return to when you were young and received that $100 U.S. Savings Bond. Why do you think your Aunt Sheila and Uncle Bill gave it to you? No, not to keep Mom and Dad's hands off the money. It was probably done to help pay for your future college education. It cost them some amount less than the $100, say in this case $50. Then, by the time you needed the money, it had grown to a much greater amount, namely, $100, the face value. Many government agencies issue these types of bonds with a 30-year maturity.

Defining a Zero-Coupon Bond

Unlike corporate bonds, *zero-coupon bonds* are financial instruments that sell at a discount, have no coupons, and upon maturity pay the face value of the bond (see Figure 5.3). The price of the bond is usually the present value of the face amount discounted at the issue rate (the published rate on the bond, similar to the coupon rate), which is used to calculate the price, that is, the discounted value.

Let's put this all together in an example. Suppose New York State Dormitory Authority issues a 10-year 8 percent zero-coupon bond to help construct new dormitories for the Albany campus. What is the corresponding cash flow for the investor? Note that the face value of the bond is $1,000, and there are no coupon payments.

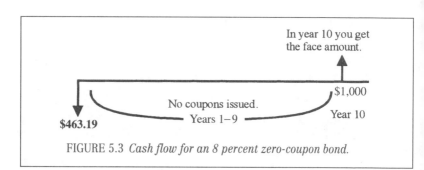

FIGURE 5.3 *Cash flow for an 8 percent zero-coupon bond.*

MATHEMATICALLY SPEAKING

Calculating the Price of the Zero-Coupon Bond

Zero-coupon bonds are pure present value instruments; that is, the key to determining their price is to simply calculate the present value of the $1,000 discounted at 8 percent for 10 years. So the issuer receives the present value of the face value (same as future value) of the bond discounted at the current interest rate.

$$PV_{t \text{ years @ } 8\%} = FV (1 + 0.08)^{-t}$$

$$\text{Price (PV)} = 1,000(1.08)^{-10} = \$463.19$$

CALC TIP

Use your calculator with the following entries to determine the present value, $463.19. There are no coupons, so do not enter any value in the PMT register.

		Press PV	PMT	FV	OTHER
N	**I%YR**	**PV**	PMT	**FV**	OTHER
10	8	to solve for PV.		1,000	

You try:

Finding the Price of a 20-Year Zero

Bonds that are issued by municipalities (for example, New York State) usually employ longer periods to maturity (for example, 20 years). Determine the price of the $1,000 bond with an 8 percent coupon rate, if it matures in 20 years.
Answer: $214.55.

KEY CONCEPT — How Time Affects Price

There is a very important relationship between the length of time that a zero-coupon bond is held and the worth of the bond—namely, the closer the bond gets to maturity, the closer the price approaches the face value. We will consider the worth of a bond to be its price should you wish to sell it. To help work our way through the mathematics, consider a case where the Massachusetts Turnpike Authority is issuing 20-year zero-coupon bonds in order to fund highway improvements. Suppose you buy the $10,000 face value bond as a retirement strategy at issue with a coupon rate of 7.5 percent for $2,354.13. Use the calculator to find the present value to verify the worth (price) of the bond at a rate of 7.5 percent.

As you hold on to the bond, how does its worth change? Specifically, what is the price as you get closer to the maturity date? That is, if you needed to sell the bond prior to maturity for a family emergency, how much would it be worth? To determine the price (assuming an interest rate of 7.5 percent during the period), simply calculate the present values with varying entries for the number of years remaining to maturity. What you should find is that as you get closer to maturity, the price gets closer to the $10,000 face value. See the following equations as an illustration.

$$PV_{t \text{ years @ 7.5\%}} = FV (1 + 0.075)^{-(20-t)}$$

$$Price_{0 \text{ years}} = 10,000(1.075)^{-20} = \$2,354.13$$

$$Price_{5 \text{ years}} = 10,000(1.075)^{-15} = \$3,379.66$$

$$Price_{10 \text{ years}} = 10,000(1.075)^{-10} = \$4,851.94$$

$$Price_{15 \text{ years}} = 10,000(1.075)^{-5} = \$6,965.59$$

$$Price_{18 \text{ years}} = 10,000(1.075)^{-2} = \$8,653.33$$

These calculations show that the longer you keep the bond, the more the value approaches the face value. The graph and data in Figure 5.4 show that as the bond approaches maturity, the closer the price approaches $10,000. Although this trend will be the case, the specific present values may change if prevailing interest rates move above or below the issue rate. Next we explore this relationship.

How Changing Discount Rates Affect Price

This last point is extremely important—the discount rate and the worth of a bond are inversely related. That is, when the discount rate goes up, the bond's worth will fall, and vice versa: If the discount rate goes down, the bond's worth increases. So, why? Let's demonstrate this inverse principle between the discount rate and the price of the bond using the $10,000 zero-coupon bond. We'll consider two calculations, one in which the discount rate rises to 8 percent at a time 10 years into the bond period, and a situation where the discount rate falls to 7 percent. To determine the price, simply calculate the present value of the face amount discounted at the new discount rate for the number of years remaining to maturity. The price of the bond (that is, its worth) will be determined with respect to each of these rates as follows:

$$PV_{10 \text{ years @ 8\%}} = FV(1 + 0.08)^{-(20-10)}$$

$$Price_{10 \text{ years}} = 10,000(1.08)^{-10} = \$4,631.93$$

$$PV_{10 \text{ years @ 7.5\%}} = FV(1 + 0.075)^{-(20-10)}$$

$$\text{Price}_{10 \text{ years}} = 10,000(1.075)^{-10} = \$4,851.94$$

$$\text{PV}_{10 \text{ years} @ 7\%} = \text{FV}(1 + 0.07)^{-(20 - 10)}$$

$$\text{Price}_{10 \text{ years}} = 10,000(1.07)^{-10} = \$5,083.49$$

Table 5.2 and Figure 5.5 show that as the discount rate increases from 7 to 8 percent, the worth of the bond decreases. Yet as you approach maturity the prices converge to the face value of the bond. The section on coupon bonds explores this inverse relationship in greater depth.

WHAT MAKES BONDS ATTRACTIVE INVESTMENTS

Private investors (probably like yourself) purchase bonds because of the guaranteed cash flow that they secure for the future, such as for retirement, college education, or a special gift. Large investors (for exam-

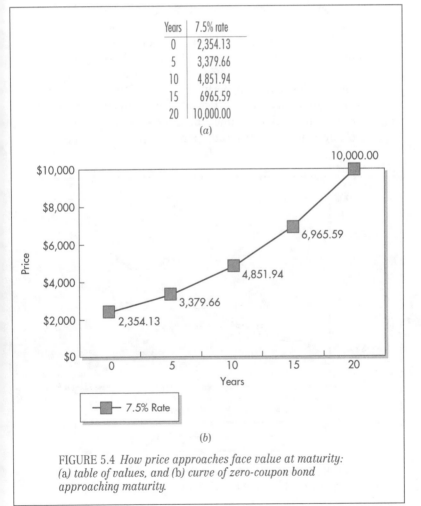

Years	7.5% rate
0	2,354.13
5	3,379.66
10	4,851.94
15	6965.59
20	10,000.00

(a)

(b)

FIGURE 5.4 *How price approaches face value at maturity: (a) table of values, and (b) curve of zero-coupon bond approaching maturity.*

TABLE 5.2 PRICE IN RELATION TO INCREASING DISCOUNT RATE

Years	Discount Rate		
	7%	7.5%	8%
0	$ 2,584.19	$ 2,354.13	$ 2,145.48
5	3,624.46	3,379.66	3,152.42
10	5,083.49	4,851.94	4,631.93
15	7,129.86	6,965.59	6,805.83
20	10,000.00	10,000.00	10,000.00

ple, pension funds and insurance companies) purchase large amounts of these bonds (in units of 1,000 bonds) to lock in a cash flow that will assure that they are able to make payments to their constituencies, for whom they hold retirement plans. The *locked-in* nature of the cash flow is why bonds are often called *fixed-income* instruments, because the cash flow is fixed—that is, predictable—unlike equities (stocks) that fluctuate based upon market and/or business conditions.

The beauty of the bond is that you have the payments locked in. But is there risk involved? Do some investors actually use bonds as investment vehicles to be sold off when the opportunity arises? To answer these questions, we have to study the cash flow of the coupon bond and see how it behaves with respect to changes in the interest rate. Here's where it gets inter-

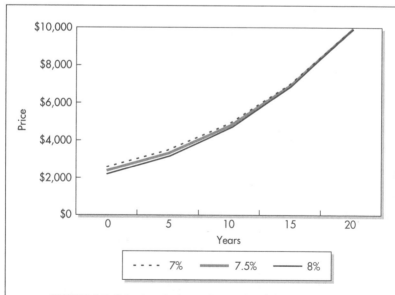

FIGURE 5.5 *Price in relation to increasing discount rate—comparison at 7, 7.5, and 8 percent.*

esting, if not downright intriguing. Suppose you had the following opportunity presented to you: How would you benefit from the behavior of the interest rate?

Your broker has called indicating that you should buy a 10 year James Corporation coupon bond that is being issued with an 8 percent coupon rate. The face value of the bond is $1000. "Get in now," he says. "When interest rates go down, you'll be looking pretty. Right now it is selling at par." Now exactly what does *looking pretty* mean, or, for that matter, *selling at par?*

Defining Selling at Par

The expression *selling at par* refers to the fact that the bond will sell at its face value, in this case, $1000. *Par value* and *face value* refer to the amount received at maturity. Shortly, you will see that bonds can be purchased or sold *above par* or *below par.*

Before you can understand the significance of "looking pretty," which suggests some kind of positive investment position, you need to find a way to determine the value of the bond at any point in time. In particular, let's try to answer the main question currently before us: What is the value or worth at issuance?

GRAPHICALLY SPEAKING

Cash Flow for a Coupon Bond

Consider the cash flow in Figure 5.6. Then you should examine the tools that you have learned thus far to see if you can determine the present value of the cash flow at issuance. The trick (as the diagram suggests) is to see the problem as two separate present value calculations, an annuity and a single payment.

Shortly you will learn how to do this calculation as

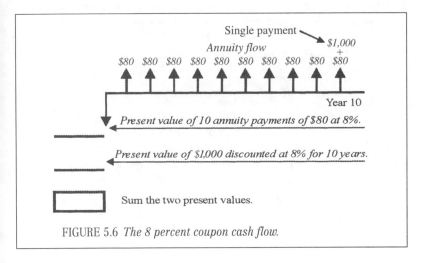

FIGURE 5.6 *The 8 percent coupon cash flow.*

one cash flow with unequal payments. In this method we'll observe that the answer can be found by summing these two present values, because as of this point in your learning the two tools available to you are annuities and single cash amount. That is, you could solve your problem in three steps:

- First, determine the present value of the annuity of $80 per year for 10 years.

- Second, determine the present value of the $1,000 received at maturity, discounted for 10 years at 8 percent.

- Once you determine each of these calculations, you can add them to determine the worth of the bond at issuance.

MATHEMATICALLY SPEAKING

Finding Price Using the Present Value

When solving these present values, we are discounting them back for the full period, that is, 10 years. In this way we can display a fundamental relationship between the price of the bond and the discount rate. The objective is to sum the results of the following two equations:

$$PV_{10 \text{ years @ 8\%}} = \sum_{t=1}^{10} PMT(1+r)^{-t} + FV(1+r)^{-10}$$

$$PV_{10 \text{ years @ 8\%}} = \sum_{n=t}^{10} 80(1+0.08)^{-t} + 1,000(1+0.08)^{-10}$$

First, the present value of the annuity:

$$PV_{10 \text{ years @ 8\%}} = \sum_{n=1}^{10} 80(1+0.08)^{-n} = \$536.81$$

Press

N	I%YR	PV	PMT	FV	OTHER
10	8	to solve for PV.	80		

Second, the present value of the face:

$$PV_{10 \text{ years @ 8\%}} = 1,000(1+0.08)^{-10} = \$463.19$$

Press

N	I%YR	PV	PMT	FV	OTHER
1	8	to solve for PV.		1,000	

Third, the sum of the present value of the annuity and the present value of the face value yields $1,000. Both calculations will yield negative present values because they represent the worth or price of the bond (i.e., what someone would pay for it).

Wait a minute! Is that right? Can the sum be the face value of the bond? Well, the answer is *yes*. The reason the worth is exactly equal to the face value is because the bond's coupon rate is equal to the prevailing discount rate. At issuance, the coupon rate must be close to the discount rate, or investors will go elsewhere for a better return with an equivalent level of risk. And if the discount rate were never to change, then, in a strange way, you would have broken even in the sense that, had you gone to another investment at the 8 percent discount rate, you would have done no better. So you can see that the present value of the cash flow when discounted at the discount rate (same as coupon rate here) is exactly equal to the price of the bond. But, here is where the fun begins with bonds. A bond is a gamble on the future behavior of the discount rate, which is subject to the whims of many factors beyond the monetary policymakers, including political unrest, economic conditions in other areas of the world, and so on. How, pray tell, is it a gamble? This book is about the math that is behind numbers that help us make decisions, not about economics. But as economists will tell you, when there is instability, there is risk, and when there is risk, discount rates become volatile.

Determining the Price for the James Bond

Suppose you buy that bond for $1,000 as recommended by your broker/brother-in-law. You now own a cash flow like the one in Figure 5.7, and no matter what happens (excluding default and bankruptcy by the James Corporation) you will be receiving the $80 each year, at the specified date in the bond's agreement, and the face value upon maturity.

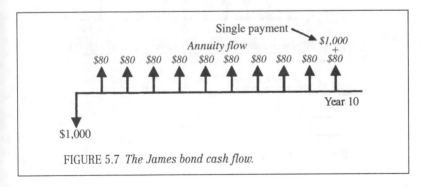

FIGURE 5.7 *The James bond cash flow.*

How Bonds Become Premium

To understand how investors employ bonds in their investment strategies, consider the worth of your bond if the discount rate changes. Recall that the worth of your bond was exactly the face value when the discount rate remained at 8 percent. Consider change. Suppose that, unbeknownst to you, after you buy the bond the chairman of the Federal Reserve Bank makes an announcement indicating that he or she would like to get capital spending moving, and so has decided to lower the discount rate. Suppose that moments after you buy your 8 percent bond, the discount rate magically changes to a lower rate, for example, 7 percent. What will that do to your bond?

It is important in this discussion that you remember that your 8 percent coupon rate bond is locked in; you know you will be receiving the cash flow previously shown. Next, think about what the 7 percent bond would look like. What are the coupons and resultant cash flow going to look like? Will it be as good as the cash flow you locked in with your 8 percent bond? Of course not. Because if another buyer took $1,000 and bought a 7 percent coupon bond, he or she would be getting only $70 coupons. So your investment of $1,000 is a better investment compared to the purchase of the 7 percent bond. That astute awareness should be worth something in the market.

Then, what is the worth of the 8 percent bond that you purchased earlier if the discount rate falls to 7 percent? Here is the key to the problem. Take the cash flow of the 8 percent bond and discount it at the new interest rate—that is, find the sum of the present values of the cash flow determined by the 8 percent bond but at the rate of 7 percent. Figure 5.8 shows the cash flow

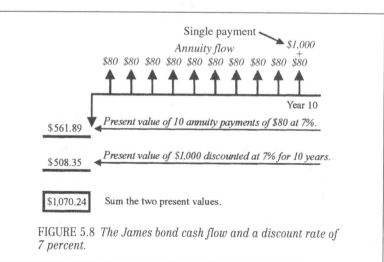

FIGURE 5.8 *The James bond cash flow and a discount rate of 7 percent.*

diagram required for solving the problem. Again, note that you are working with the James bond because you want to know its worth.

Solving for the Price of a Premium Bond

Mathematically, you are calculating the two present value calculations at the revised rate of 7 percent, as follows:

$$PV_{10 \text{ years @ } 7\%} = \sum_{t=1}^{10} 80(1 + 0.07)^{-t} + 1,000(1 + 0.07)^{-10}$$

First, the present value of the annuity:

$$PV_{10 \text{ years @ } 7\%} = \sum_{t=1}^{10} 80(1 + 0.07)^{-t} = \$561.89$$

Press

N	I%YR	PV	PMT	FV	OTHER
10	7	to solve for PV.	80		

Second, the present value of the face:

$$PV_{10 \text{ years @ } 7\%} = 1,000(1 + 0.07)^{-10} = \$508.35$$

Press

N	I%YR	PV	PMT	FV	OTHER
10	7	to solve for PV.	80		

Third, the sum of the present value of the annuity and the present value of the face value at a market rate of 7 percent yields $1070.24.

Examine this closely. Does it make sense? It is worth more, as it should be, because you have a better flow than the folks out there who are buying those 7 percent bonds. Therefore, you are entitled to a premium ($70.24), because you bought the bond when the discount rate was higher and returning better coupons.

Defining a Premium Bond

A bond is termed *premium* when it is trading at a price above par (the face value) due to changes in the interest rate or concerns about the economic health of the issuer. Compared to bonds that are trading at par or below, a premium bond will receive a higher price in the market. Premium refers to the actual amount above par.

But before you get too excited, if your objective is retirement or your children's education, you're not interested in selling the bond. The bond market doesn't fluctuate as dramatically as the equity market, where the individual investor can truly take advantage of such changes in the discount rate. But understand that there is a bond market where institutional investors who have sizeable positions in a particular issue (number of shares in the thousands resulting in positions in the millions) can trade on a small increment either way and make a sizeable profit.

Market Behavior: How Bonds Seek Parity

An important point is that the bond market strives in its own way to achieve parity between previously issued bonds and current issues. That is, as bonds with more or less attractive interest rates come onto the market, how do they affect the value of previously issued bonds? Well, as noted earlier, the cash flows of your purchased bonds can't change; they're locked in. But what *can* change is the price or worth of the previously issued bonds. In our example, the market fell to a rate of 7 percent. If you insist on buying that 8 percent James Corporation bond, and it is trading above par, then you will have to pay more for it. How much, you ask? Get ready to pay $1,070.24, not $1,000. Now here's the significant point: The James bond, now selling at $1,070.24, is equivalent in rate of return to the 7 percent issue selling at par. This is one of the more mathematically fascinating aspects of the bond market. The later section on yield to maturity discusses this.

How Bonds Become Discounted

Suppose that due to world tension, discount rates go up to 9 percent, reflecting market uncertainty. Recall what your initial 8 percent bond looked like with its $80 coupons. As before, think about what the 9 percent bond would look like. Suppose someone took $1,000 and bought a 9 percent bond—what will the coupon and resultant cash flow look like? Does it look as good as your 8 percent bond? Remember, these buyers also went to the market with $1,000, but now they are getting a cash flow based on $90 coupons. So, what do you expect will be the affect on the value (price) of the 8 percent James bond? Compared to these 9 percent bonds, your 8 percent bond is not as attractive (a nonquantitative word indicating the bond should be worth less). If you are not sure, just take the pencil and draw the cash flow from the coupons and you'll see why.

How does this change in the discount rate affect the value of your 8 percent bond? Specifically, what is the worth of the 8 percent bond that you purchased earlier if the discount rate grows to 9 percent? Once again, the key is to take the cash flow of the 8 percent bond and discount it at the new interest rate—that is, find the sum of the present values at 9 percent. Figure 5.9 shows the James bond cash flow and the appropriate discount rate for the analysis.

MATHEMATICALLY SPEAKING

Solving for the Discount Price

Mathematically, you are calculating the two present value calculations at the revised rate of 9 percent as follows:

$$PV_{10\ years\ @\ 9\%} = \sum_{t=1}^{10} 80(1 + 0.09)^{-t} + 1,000(1 + 0.09)^{-10}$$

First, the present value of the annuity:

$$PV_{10\ years\ @\ 9\%} = \sum_{t=1}^{10} 80(1 + 0.09)^{-t} = \$513.41$$

N	I%YR	PV	PMT	FV	OTHER
10	9			1,000	

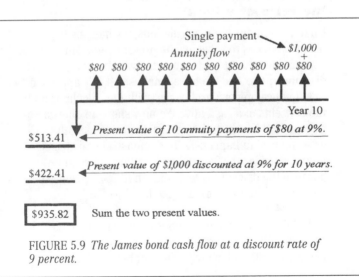

FIGURE 5.9 *The James bond cash flow at a discount rate of 9 percent.*

Second, the present value of the face:

$$PV_{10 \text{ years @ } 9\%} = 1,000(1 + 0.09)^{-10} = \$422.41$$

N	I%YR	PV	PMT	FV	OTHER
10	9		80		

Third, the sum of the present value of the annuity and the present value of the face value yields $935.82.

Examine this result very closely. The James bond is worth less, as it should be, because you do not have as good a cash flow as the folks out there who are buying those 9 percent bonds. Therefore, you will not command as high a price because you bought the bond when the discount rate was lower. The discount amount is $64.18.

Defining a Discount Bond

A bond is termed *discount* when it is trading at a price below par due to changes in the interest rate or concerns about the financial health of the company or organization issuing the bond. Compared to bonds that are trading at par or above, a discount bond will receive a lower price in the market. The amount of the discount is equal to the actual amount below par (1,000 – 935.82).

 CALC TIP

The Fast Way to Determine the Price of a Bond

Up to now in our bond calculations, we have been using two steps to solve for the present value, and then adding the values to determine the worth under various discount rates. And we have emphasized this approach to help develop your proficiency with the calculator and the concepts of a cash flow. We now show an alternative method in which the calculator performs both operations simultaneously. To demonstrate this technique, consider the James bond trading at premium because the discount rate has fallen to 7%. Earlier we determined that the price of the bond would be $1070.24.

In joining the two operations in one calculation, enter both the payment ($80) and the face value (future value is $1,000) along with the number of years (10) and the rate, in this case 7 percent. And note that since you get both the face amount and the coupon payments, they are both the same sign, positive. When you press the present value key you should get $1,070.24.

N	I%YR	PV	PMT	FV	OTHER
10	7		80	1,000	

You try:

The Consequences of the Interest Rate

Your company needs to raise capital for expanding the plant to support a new product line. You are going to issue bonds with a face value of $1,000 that will mature in 20 years. Currently the discount rate is 8.2 percent. You have been advised by the investment firm managing the issue that although your company has a good credit rating, market conditions suggest that you should issue the bonds with an attractive coupon rate of 8.6 percent, issuing the coupon on March 17.

If the discount rate went down and other companies with the same credit rating as yours were issuing bonds at 7.5 percent, what would be the worth of your bond in that market? Assume the full 20 years to maturity. Would your bond be trading above par or below par?

Answer: Above par and worth $1,112.14.

If the discount rate went up and other companies with the same credit rating as you were issuing bonds at 9.5 percent, what would be the worth of your bond in that market? Again, assume the full 20 years to maturity. Would your bond be trading above par or below par?

Answer: Below par and worth $920.69.

◆K◆E◆Y◆ Determining Rate of Return
CONCEPT

Suppose you are offered the opportunity to buy a 9 percent corporate IBM bond with a par value of $1,000 that is selling below par for $951.70. It matures in 20 years, about the same time as a fine burgundy from France.

Often bonds are quoted in terms of their price, much like VCRs from the back of someone's truck. What does this mean about the prevailing interest rate in the bond market? First, if the bond was selling at par, then you would conclude that the market rate was in the neighborhood of 9 percent. And, if the bond was selling above par, then the price of the bond would be greater than $1,000 because your bond is more attractive than other bonds in the market—that is, it is a premium bond. If your bond is premium, then that means other bonds are not offering coupon rates as good as your bond. Now analyze the situation—suppose you are offered a 9 percent bond for $951.70; it is selling below par. Once again, make the coupons annual to make it simple, and construct a diagram, as shown in Figure 5.10, to show what you know.

The only difference between this problem and determining the price is that you are now solving for the rate. As you look at Figure 5.10, you are trying to find the rate that makes the sum of these two present values equal to the price of the bond. This rate will put the up arrows in equilibrium with the cash out down arrow.

Here are the key entries for the calculator as shown in the following diagram. You know the price, which is entered as a cash out for present value (PV). This means it must be entered as a negative value. The PMT value will be the product of the coupon rate (9 percent) and the face value amount. The face amount is $1,000 for the future value (FV). Once you set N equal to 20 years, solve for interest (I% YR). Answer: 9.55 percent.

Press

N	I%YR	PV	PMT	FV	OTHER
20	to find I%YR.	–951.70	90	1,000	

APPLICATIONS OF BOND CASH FLOWS

This section demonstrates how the material in this chapter can be applied to determine bond cash flows, prices, and yield to maturity.

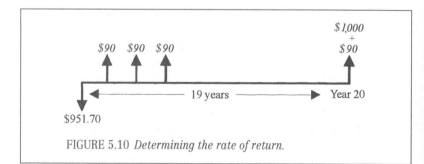

FIGURE 5.10 *Determining the rate of return.*

**How to Handle Semiannual
Coupon Cash Flows**

CONCEPT

Soho Industries is issuing $10,000 face-value bonds at par, which feature a 12 percent coupon rate with semi-annual coupons. The bonds mature in 10 years and the coupon payments will be made on March 5 and September 5. Given the following cash flow, verify that the worth of the bond is the face amount when the interest rate is 12 percent.

Up to now we have used only annual coupons so we could concentrate on the concept of a cash flow, the mathematics employed in it, and the use of the calculator as a tool to facilitate these calculations. Specifically, two factors actually determine the coupon amount, the coupon rate, and the period of the coupon. Because the coupon rate is 12 percent and the coupon is distributed semiannually, then the coupon amount will be determined by the following equation. To see how this affects the cash flow, see Figure 5.11.

$$\text{Coupon} = \frac{\text{coupon rate} \times \text{face value}}{\text{number of coupons/year}}$$

$$= \frac{12\% \times 10,000}{2} = \$600$$

CALC TIP

**Determining the Price
with Semiannual Coupons**

There are a number of ways to solve for the present value for this problem. Conceptually you should recognize that the cash flow calculation changes slightly to reflect the fact that two coupons are paid per year. This means, simply, that the cash flow is twice as long as the annual case but with half the coupon amount and half the rate. The equation for the mathematical calculation should help define what we are about to do with the calculator.

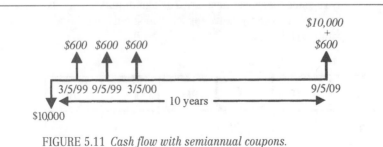

FIGURE 5.11 *Cash flow with semiannual coupons.*

First, consider the annual coupon case:

$$PV_{10 \text{ years} @ 12\%} = \sum_{t=1}^{10} 1{,}200(1 + 0.12)^{-t} + 10{,}000(1 + 0.12)^{-10}$$

Now, the changes for the semiannual coupon case:

$$PV_{20 \text{ periods} @ 6\%} = \sum_{n=1}^{20} 600(1 + 0.06)^{-n} + 10{,}000(1 + 0.06)^{-20}$$

In the second equation, we have changed from the annual indicator t to n to convey the total number of payments over the 10 years. When using the calculator, first enter the annuity payment (PMT = 600), and the face value of the bond (FV = 10,000). Remember, your annuity setting should be in End mode.

Now, what to enter for the rate and payment number? This depends on how your calculator manages the frequency of compounding when periods are less than a year. Recall that Chapter 2 explained this in discussing semiannual and quarterly compounding, and Chapter 4 discussed increased frequency of annuity payments. In these situations you have to adjust the rate as well as the number of periods. There are two ways to handle this.

If Your Calculator Has a P/YR Register

Set P/YR to 2 in order to ensure that the calculator adjusts the cash flow to semiannual. Once this adjustment is made, enter the rate of 12 percent in the Rate register and 10 in the N register. Remember, using the P/YR register automatically adjusts the rate, so you must enter the annual rate—12 percent. On some calculators you have to press the Shift key before pressing N in order to multiply the number of years and the number of payments per year. Solve for PV. You should get the value $10,000. If you do not get $10,000, look up the periods per year option in your manual to determine how to compensate for the adjusted rate and number of periods.

If Your Calculator Has No P/YR Register

Enter half the rate of 12 percent in the Rate register (because this is a semiannual cash flow) and 20 in the N register (because there are 20 semiannual payments over the 10 years). Solve for PV. You should get the value $10,000.

Press

N	I%YR	PV	PMT	FV	OTHER
20	6	to solve for PV.	600	10,000	

Selling Below Par

Luck wasn't with Soho Industries. Just as the company announced its new issue, other companies with the same credit rating came onto the market with a more favorable coupon rate of 14 percent, anticipating a rise in the interest rate. Assuming these other bonds possess the same time and face characteristics, then the Soho bond will sell below par. The cash flow remains the same, but the rate at which it is being valued will be higher. Your task is to determine the worth (price) of the Soho bond at the interest rate of 14 percent. The new cash flow is seen in Figure 5.12.

In determining the new market price you should use the exact same keystrokes as you did in verifying the par value in the previous problem, but employ the new rate of 14 percent (or 7 percent, depending on your calculator).

Answer: $8,940.60.
Discount amount: $1,059.40.

Selling Above Par

Let's change Soho's luck. Just as the company announced its new issue, the Federal Reserve Bank lowered interest rates. As a result, other companies with the same credit rating came onto the market with a lower coupon rate of 10 percent. Assuming these other bonds possess the same time and face characteristics, then the Soho bond will sell above par. The cash flow remains the same, but the rate at which it is being valued will be set at the lower interest rate. Determine the worth (price) of the Soho bond in its premium position.

Answer: $11,246.22.
Premium amount: $1,246.22.

 DETERMINING YIELD TO MATURITY

What should you do? You have just received an inheritance and would like to invest it in a bond that will

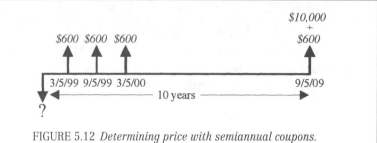

FIGURE 5.12 *Determining price with semiannual coupons.*

mature in 20 years and provide an income stream during the interim. Two interesting bonds have been presented to you from a financial consultant, with the following comments.

MBI is a good, solid, reliable company, issuing 20-year semiannual 9.4 percent coupon bonds, face value of $10,000 for $10,737.55. Computer products sector looks good; MBI has done particularly well in completing a very successful turnaround led by two gurus from Peach Computer.

TTA is a good telecommunications company, issuing 20-year semiannual 8.2 percent coupon bonds, face value of $10,000 for $9,092.90. Regional Bells are becoming competitive, but market looks good. TTA has recently merged with 1-800-FLOWERS, going through merger turmoil, but should come out smelling like a rose.

This example illustrates that at any point in time there will be a variety of bonds available to the purchaser, whose coupon amounts and prices reflect the companys' risks, various economic forecasts of interest rates, and perceived market profitability within the business sectors to which the companies belong. These factors all play together to create a decision problem for buyers.

Each seems to have attractive qualities, a low price for TTA and high interest payments with MBI. So you need a way to assess each with a common metric in order to make the best decision. You need a tool that will determine the rates of return for each of the cash flows and allow you to select the one with the greatest return. The *yield to maturity* of the bond is defined as the rate at which the cash flow, when discounted, is equal to the price of the bond in the market. Figure 5.13 attempts to show a balance between the cost of the bond and the sum of the present value of the cash flows.

The concept that there exists a rate that equates the present value of the cash flow to the price of the bond deserves some thought. First, focus on the cash flow for the MBI bond in Figure 5.13. Next, consider various rates at which the entire cash flow gets discounted (but not too long—time is money!). Now, there is one unique rate such that when it is used as the discount percentage the result is equal to the price of the bond. That rate is defined as the yield to maturity for the bond. That rate, if you will, puts the cash flow in balance.

A sketch of the two flows that require comparison is presented in Figure 5.14. Given these two cash flows, you should be able to solve for the rates. To solve for the yield to maturity, enter the price PV (remember that

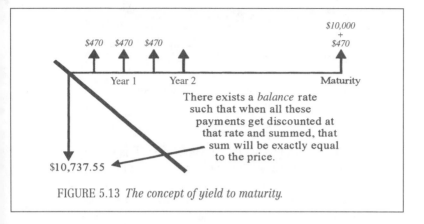

FIGURE 5.13 *The concept of yield to maturity.*

it must be negative), the coupon amount PMT, and the face value FV. But how should you handle the number of periods? If your calculator supports a P/YR register, use it to specify 2 periods per year and enter 20 for the total number of periods (N register). If you do not use the P/YR register, enter 40 in the N register. Solve for the rate. Answer: 8.62 percent for the MBI bond; 9.2 percent for the TTA bond. If you set up the 40-year entry, then you must double the rate to compensate for doubling the number of periods.

It is important to understand what you have solved for in this problem. You have found the rate at which, if all the coupon payments and face value amount were discounted to today (that is, the present value of the cash flow), this sum would be exactly equal to the price of the bond. Take the MBI bond: If each payment of $470 was discounted for its appropriate length of time, at the rate of 8.62 percent annually, and added to the present value of $10,000 discounted at 8.62 percent, the sum would be exactly what was paid for the bond—namely, $10,737.55. Awesome mathematics!

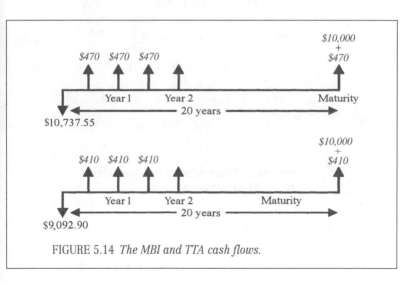

FIGURE 5.14 *The MBI and TTA cash flows.*

MATHEMATICALLY SPEAKING

Mathematically, you are solving for the value of r such that the present value will be equal to \$10,737.55.

$$PV_{40 \text{ periods} \, @ \, r}\% = \sum_{n=1}^{40} 470(1 + r)^{-n} + 10{,}000(1 + r)^{-40}$$

$$= \$10{,}737.55$$

We certainly don't intend you to solve this equation without a calculator. But the concept that a rate exists that solves this equation is very important—as is the fact that with the aid of the calculator this break-even percentage can be solved. The next chapter approaches this subject again under the topic of internal rate of return.

So, back to the problem of choice. What does the yield to maturity tell you about each of these securities? In the decision before you, the BMI bond, with its higher coupon and high premium, is not as good a return as the TTA bond, which has been discounted to \$9,092.90. The next chapter shows how to calculate the infamous internal rate of return, which is essentially what you solved in the yield to maturity analysis. Using the calculator, it is very easy to solve for the yield by using this tool, but, you must wait a few pages for that discussion.

You try:

Doing Yield to Maturity

Chrysler is looking strong. It has just merged with Daimler-Benz and, based upon sales returns, it has once again shown itself to be a strong marketer of minivans. It has announced that it intends to build a new plant to design and build the ultraminivan, the Benz-O-Van. To raise capital, Chrysler is issuing a bond that has a face value of \$1,000 and will pay semiannual interest at a 10 percent annual rate. Investors are buying the bond, and the current price is \$968.30.

In order to compare this investment to those of other fixed-income securities with similar risk, you have been asked to determine the yield to maturity of the Chrysler 10 percents maturing in 10 years.

Answer: 10.52 percent.

 **Pricing Zero-Coupon Bonds— One More Time**

JFK–LGA–NWK to Connect

It was announced today that there is consideration by the Port Authority of New York and New

Jersey to build a rail link connecting all three regional airports. "There is a sizable bond issue proposed to the governors of each state to fund the effort. It should be enacted," said the Mayor.

It's time for a fictional newspaper headline. The Port Authority of New York and New Jersey wants to build a rail link that would connect all three local area airports. Bonds will be sold by the Port Authority to fund this effort. Current discount rate is 7 percent, and there is a slight concern about inflation, so the Board of Directors along with their financial consultants have decided to issue the bonds at a 7.2 percent rate. What will be the price of a 20 year 7.2 percent zero-coupon bond with a face value of $10,000 if purchased at issuance?

Answer: $2,489.46.

END POINT

Bonds can be attractive and safe investment vehicles because, in general, they assure a locked-in cash flow for a price that reflects the company's creditworthiness. The company has use of the funds over the term of the bond, and has a responsibility to make interest payments to the holder of the bond on a regular basis as specified by the coupon rate and period. This cash flow is locked in, and at maturity, the company returns the face value of the bond to the purchaser, along with the last coupon. Zero-coupon bonds do not have coupons, but instead sell at a price, which is discounted up front. At maturity the purchaser receives the full face value of the bond. The key point to remember out of this chapter is that price and the discount rate are inversely related. As the discount rate goes up, the worth of the bond (price, as determined by the present value of the cash flow) will go down, and vice versa. As a result, bonds can be traded based upon the activity of the discount rate.

The Decision-Making Power of Internal Rate of Return and Net Present Value

We have been carefully developing the core topics of time value of money to prepare for the two main tools employed in financial decision making: *internal rate of return* (IRR) and *net present value* (NPV). Both of these calculations yield a measure of return, which can be used to assess the financial merits of an investment opportunity. This chapter not only demonstrates these two important tools but applies them to a number of situations where you will need them.

- Determine the rate of return of a project or use of capital. *Use of capital* is a term meaning the use of funds that the company employs to invest in projects that will improve its operation, support new products, introduce efficiencies, and so on.

- Evaluate competing proposals to determine which yields the best use of the company's funds.

- Determine bond pricing and yield to maturity the easy way.

Up to now we have studied even cash flows—cash flows in which all the payments are the same amount, occurring uniformly over some time period, such as an annuity. The strength of the internal rate of return and net present value is that they are not limited to even cash flows. Not only can the cash flows have different amounts, they can also be positive, where money is coming in, or negative, where money is going out. Amounts can be different, even zero, but they will occur on an annual basis, and unless specified clearly, the payments are at the end of the period. This chapter presents both tools through their decision-making capabilities in a typical capital investment analysis and then revisits bonds to show how these topics can be employed to determine pricing as well as yield. Let's introduce the need for these tools with a typical problem confronting management: Which proposal represents the best use of funds? We'll make the assumption at this initial point that management can fund only one of the projects.

HOW COMPANIES COMPARE RETURNS AMONG COMPETING PROJECTS

"We need computers that talk to each other and can tell us what we have in inventory, what's on order, and, in general, how we are doing," complained your brother. He has come to you with a technology proposal that will achieve tighter control of costs to the organization and expand revenues by installing a new, state-of-the-art local area network (LAN), which will link all of the offices and the warehouse. It will return incremental savings each year by identifying high inventories, advising sales personnel of promotional opportunities, and projecting sales for better purchasing with suppliers. Anticipating your questions, he has even prepared a forecasted cash flow of the savings over the next four years. There is agreement among the technology vendors that the effort will cost approximately $120,000 for the hardware, software, and training. Interestingly, the two guys who manage the distribution center have talked to you about purchasing a forklift. They say the cost is $120,000, but it can be easily made up with reduction in personnel and insurance costs. With the new equipment they can let two people go at an annual savings of $22,500 each in salary alone.

A choice is required. The first step is to map out the proposed cash flows, as shown in Figure 6.1. Note that one flow behaves like an annuity and the other flow has different values for the payments.

 **Introducing Internal Rate**
CONCEPT **of Return (IRR)**

The tools used thus far will no doubt take very good care of your personal finance issues. This situation, however, demonstrates the need for stronger analytical capabilities because of the uneven payments in the cash flow. How can we assess the financial well-being of these projects, and make an informative comparison? Does it make sense for the organization to go forward with either of these efforts? The problem is we need criteria. We need a metric that assesses each proposal's worth with respect to the corporate standard as well as with respect to each other.

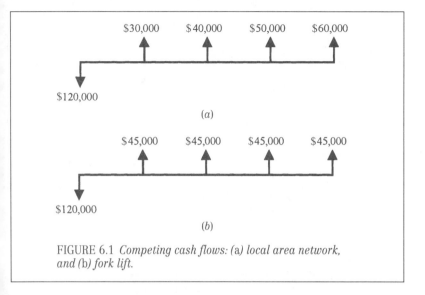

FIGURE 6.1 *Competing cash flows: (a) local area network, and (b) fork lift.*

This last sentence may need a little explanation. As we have done so often previously, let's go back to a simple example. Suppose you had to borrow the money to fund one of these efforts, and assume that there is an interest fee. From what we have seen thus far, the commonsense perspective would be to make sure you get a return better than the rate charged by the bank so you can make all required payments. And it would be nice if there was some money left over as profit. If you could not get sufficient return to pay the bank, then this would not be a wise investment, and it may not be a wise investment if it only breaks even. So our objective is to find a way to determine if an investment breaks even, costs more than it returns, or is profitable with respect to the associated costs.

We'll adopt a strategy similar to analyzing the worth of an annuity or coupon bond. In each of those cases we determined either the rate of return against the cost of the annuity or bond, or we summed the present values of the cash flow discounted at some rate, and compared the sum to the cost of the project. But in these situations we need more generalizable tools. To work our way through this, we'll first consider the LAN proposal. Initially we refer to the proposed savings amount in any year as a *payment,* to be consistent with earlier usage of the term employed with annuities.

GRAPHICALLY SPEAKING

The Objective Is to Find the Rate

As you examine the cash flow in Figure 6.2, note that the payments are at the end of the period. This is a convention in cash flow analysis, and should be

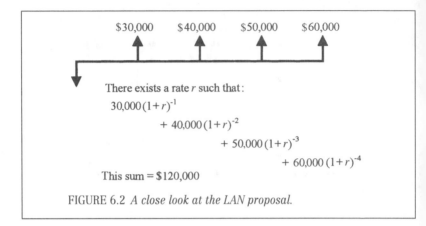

FIGURE 6.2 *A close look at the LAN proposal.*

assumed by you unless clearly indicated otherwise. When you employ the cash flow menu in the calculator, it will assume that payments are annual and received at the end of the period.

As you examine the cash flow, you can't say that $120,000 gets you $180,000 because you know that future cash payments are worth less in the present. You have surely been in meetings where someone has in fact made just such an observation of equating the sum of the cash flows with the cost of $120,000, hence yielding a 50 percent return. Chapter 3 shows that cash in the future is worth less today, and that the exact amount for that present value of that particular payment is determined by the discount rate and the length of time of the discount period. For example, the $40,000 payment in the second year is not worth $40,000 today, but some discounted amount. It makes sense that the criteria for breaking even is intimately tied to the rate employed for discounting. Specifically, you could claim that this project would break even if a discount rate were selected such that when all the payments are discounted to today—that is, the day you borrow the $120,000—their sum is exactly the cost of the investment, namely $120,000. Once you know that rate, each project can be compared to each other, to assess which is best. And, most important, the company can compare the respective rates of each project to its own internal hurdle rate, sometimes referred to as *cost of capital* or *opportunity rate*. Cost of capital is a rate determined by the company as the minimum return it must have on all investments made with its own capital.

Hurdle Rate and Cost of Capital

John Tracy, in *The Fast Forward MBA in Finance* (John Wiley & Sons, 1996), refers to cost of capital as a special type of return on investment (ROI) used with capital investments, where it is defined as the *after-tax weighted cost of capital* of the business. This rate is either used directly in the comparative analysis, or it serves as the benchmark for evaluating the capital investment. It is often referred to as the *hurdle rate* because it is the minimum acceptable rate of earnings on capital investments by the business—the company should do at least as well, and, hopefully, better.

The point is, if you show a rate of return of 12 percent and the cost of renting money is 18 percent, then you are not entering into a profitable investment. In fact, it will be critical that the investment return at least the cost of those funds, hence the nature of the "hurdle." Continuing the analogy, if you can't jump it, you're not going to be in the running.

MATHEMATICALLY SPEAKING

Determining the Rate of Return (Hurdle Rate)

When sketching a cash flow there are a few standards in notation, some of which were defined previously. Up arrows refer to cash that is coming in from the investment, which are entered in the calculator as a positive number. Down arrows, like the cost of the project, refer to cash that is going out, such as the initial funding of the project. Costs are entered in the calculator as negative numbers. When presenting the equation of the cash flow, we let CF_n refer to the cash flow payment for the nth year, and Proj (CF_0 or INIT) refer to the cost of the project. In the following equation, remember that a negative exponent on a base becomes positive when it is inverted.

$$\text{Proj} = \sum_{n=1}^{4} CF_n(1+r)^{-n} \quad \text{is the same as} \quad \sum_{n=1}^{4} \frac{CF_n}{(1+r)^n}$$

$$120{,}000 = \sum_{n=1}^{4} \frac{CF_n}{(1+r)^n}$$

$$120{,}000 = \frac{30{,}000}{(1+r)^1} + \frac{40{,}000}{(1+r)^2} + \frac{50{,}000}{(1+r)^3} + \frac{60{,}000}{(1+r)^4}$$

The objective is to find the value of rate r that will make this equation true. Obviously this is "now" time for the calculator. This type of problem requires special attention, because it cannot be performed on the previously defined calculator keys. We show how to solve this problem generically on the calculator. To prepare for this discussion, you should look up "Internal Rate of Return" in your calculator manual and become familiar with the necessary keys for this calculation. Figure 6.3 demonstrates a cash flow diagram employing the stan-

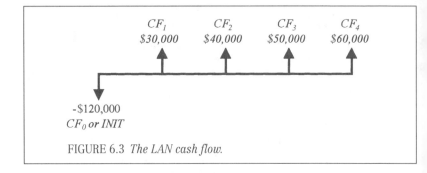

FIGURE 6.3 *The LAN cash flow.*

dard terms and notation used by most calculators for this procedure.

CALC TIP

Now that the cash flow has been described, how will it be translated to the calculator? Before entering a cash flow you should note that on most calculators this is not part of the general keys for the time value of money section. You will not use the PMT or FV keys for a cash flow; it will have its own menu and keystrokes. Table 6.1 defines the keys used in most calculators for entering a cash flow. To help with the definitions, the keys reference the LAN proposal.

CALC TIP

Entering the Cash Flow on the Calculator

A few tips on entering the cash flow, beginning with making sure there is nothing else in the cash flow registers. This usually requires that you clear a list or flow. Usually you begin by entering the cost of the project as a negative in the CF_0 register, followed by entering the sequential payments. Pay attention as to whether the payment is positive or negative. Your entries should follow those in Table 6.2.

After entering the cash flow, follow your manual's instructions on calculating the internal rate of return. Depending on the number of positions on your display, your answer should read 16.28178 percent. We have expanded the number of places so we can use this result to verify our definition of IRR. But now, exactly what does this number mean? May we introduce one of the most respected numbers in all of finance?

WHAT THE INTERNAL RATE OF RETURN TELLS YOU

The internal rate of return (IRR) is probably the first statistic any manager is going to have to provide to jus-

TABLE 6.1 KEY DEFINITIONS FOR CASH FLOW ENTRY AND ANALYSIS

INIT or CF_0	INIT or CF_0 refers to the cost of the project. It is important that this value be entered as a negative if it is a cash outlay. It is highly unusual for this to be a positive entry. After entering this value ($-120,000$), you should begin entering the annual cash flows.
CF_n	CF_n refers to the nth year's cash flow. For example, after entering the cost of the project, you will enter (or be prompted) for the first year's payment, CF_1. The entry for CF_1 will be 30,000. In the example you will enter four cash flows, CF_1 to CF_4. Do not enter any values for CF_5, because doing so will increase the number of years in the analysis to five.
# Times or Nj	After entering the first cash flow amount, most calculators present you with the ability to enter a "Number of Times" value, which will indicate the number of consecutive payments that are exactly the same amount as CF_1. This is a very handy feature when doing a bond or a problem like the fork lift cash flow because there are sequential payments in which the amount is the same. It has a default value of 1. If there are no repeated equal payments for this entry then press Input or Enter to continue the entry process.
CALC or IRR	Once the cash flow has been entered, depending on the type of calculator, you can either calculate the internal rate of return directly (press IRR), or you may have to select CALC to put you into a menu where IRR is an option.

TABLE 6.2 CALCULATOR ENTRIES FOR THE LAN CASH FLOW

Year or CF_n	Amount/Entry	# Times or Nj
INIT or CF_0	$-\$120,000$	
CF_1	30,000	1
CF_2	40,000	1
CF_3	50,000	1
CF_4	60,000	1

tify a request for funds, or ask when assessing the merits of a project. Why is it such an important number? First, it is a rate determined solely by the amount and sequence or position of the cash flows with respect to the cost of the project. It is independent of the existing market discount rate. In a way, this is why it is called *internal*—it is defined by the nature of the cash flow. The IRR is the rate at which each of the cash flows, when discounted and summed, will, in fact, be equal to the cost of the project. In our specific example, the sum of the present values of the cash flow CF_1 to CF_4 will equal $120,000. Figure 6.4 takes the present values of each one of the cash flows at their respective number of years to show this summation.

The mathematical formula defining the IRR is displayed to confirm the nature of our calculations. If you are not sure of these values, you should take a few moments to verify that when each of these cash flows is discounted at the derived rate, and summed, the answer is $120,000.

$$120,000 = \sum_{n=1}^{4} \frac{CF_n}{(1+r)^n} = \sum_{n=1}^{4} \frac{CF_n}{(1+0.1628178)^n}$$

$$120,000 = \frac{30,000}{(1+0.1628178)^1} + \frac{40,000}{(1+0.1628178)^2}$$

$$+ \frac{50,000}{(1+0.1628178)^3} + \frac{60,000}{(1+0.1628178)^4}$$

$$120,000 = 120,000$$

IRR: Some Cautionary Notes

There are two cautionary notes about calculating the internal rate of return. First, that level of return assumes that you can actually reinvest the flows at that rate for the remainder of the time period. For example, when the second flow of $40,000 is received at the end

$ 25,799.39 ← 30,000(1+r)^{-1}

29,582.62 ← + 40,000(1+r)^{-2}

31,800.57 ← + 50,000(1+r)^{-3}

32,817.42 ← + 60,000(1+r)^{-4}

$120,000.00

FIGURE 6.4 *Demonstration of the IRR.*

of year 2, the IRR calculation assumes that it can be reinvested at that 16 percent rate. If, in fact, it cannot yield as good a return—for example, only 10 percent—then the actual return on this investment will be less than the calculated 16.28178 percent. For more information on this you should see a finance textbook.

The second cautionary note involves a rather sophisticated concept (from our initial perspective) found in higher mathematics regarding the solution to the equation previously defined. An unusual possibility occurs when the cash flow itself contains some negative payments (an example of which is found in the applications section), in that there may be multiple solutions to the equation. The problem with the calculator is that only one solution is displayed, and there may be others. Usually, when this occurs the calculator will prompt you to enter an estimated rate from which it can iteratively try to solve for the IRR. This is your alert that two roots exist. You can find the other root by entering a very large starting rate, for example, 200 percent. Be careful—a shortcoming of spreadsheets is that they will not prompt you for an alternative. See Richard Brealy and Stewart Myers, *Principles of Corporate Finance, Fifth Edition* (McGraw-Hill, 1996), for more information on multiple roots.

But relax, 99 percent of the time you will be fine. Despite these cautionary notes, the internal rate of return is the premier tool in quickly assessing the return on a project.

You try: **Performing the IRR**

There is an interesting observation to make here—yes, another opportunity for learning. How is the internal rate of return affected when more money is received up front? For example, suppose the cash flow for the LAN were reversed, as shown in Figure 6.5? Determine the IRR in this case.

Examine the revised LAN proposal in Figure 6.5. Why is the IRR for this cash flow higher than the original cash flow? Well, that was exactly the point of the first cautionary note. Since you are getting the $60,000 at the end of the first year, you can

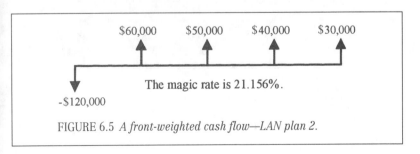

FIGURE 6.5 *A front-weighted cash flow—LAN plan 2.*

get more of a return on that payment from reinvesting at the IRR for the remaining 3 years of the cash flow. By reinvesting $60,000, you will get a better yield than when the $30,000 was reinvested.

Netting Cash In and Out for Payments

Both of the examples we are analyzing have sequential positive cash payments over the life of the investment. And, as mentioned, these cash flows assume one payment per period, occurring at the end of the year. If there is a flow out and in during the same period, you must net the two transactions into one payment; see the applications section for an example. If there is no payment for a particular year in the sequence, it must be entered as a zero cash amount; it cannot be skipped. A skipped payment will slide all the remaining payments down by one year, thereby decreasing the entire life of the analysis by one year and affecting the value of your calculation.

CALC TIP

Entering Repeated Equal Payments

Now, how do you determine the IRR for the forklift proposal? Now that we have put all the theory together, this becomes an easy problem because of the number of times (Nj or # Times) entry in the cash flow. As Figure 6.6 shows, there is only one cash flow value since all the payments are the same.

So, when making the entries (see Table 6.3), you'll continue to enter the cost of the project CF_0 as a negative. But when entering the payments, since they are all the same value they are entered once, and then take advantage of the number of times entry.

Take advantage of the number of times entry to specify that there will be four equal sequential payments. To help, compare Figure 6.6 with the cash flow entries found in Table 6.3. The fact that the payments are sequential is important here. If the second payment were different, but the third and the fourth payments were the same, then the third payment could be employed with a number of times value of 2. The answer for the forklift proposal is 18.45 percent.

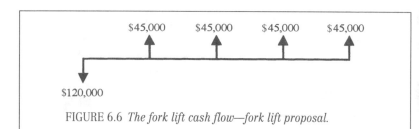

FIGURE 6.6 *The fork lift cash flow—fork lift proposal.*

TABLE 6.3 THE FORK LIFT ENTRIES

Year or CF_n	Amount/Payment	# Times or Nj
INIT or CF_0	−$120,000	
CF_1	45,000	4

So, based on the internal rate of return analysis, the forklift proposal has the greater return; hence, it represents the best use of funds, assuming there are no other factors in our analysis. To prepare for the next section let's tie this all back to the cost of capital or hurdle rate discussion. If the company required a minimum of 25 percent return on any funded project, then neither of these projects would be accepted as they are currently defined. If the company could support multiple projects, in the sense that it felt both projects were worthwhile efforts, and the hurdle rate were 10 percent (highly unlikely), then both projects could be accepted. And finally, if the hurdle rate were 18 percent, as shown in Table 6.4, the forklift proposal would be acceptable, but the LAN implementation would not. So, as Table 6.4 shows, relative to the hurdle rate of 18 percent we could say that the fork lift proposal would yield a positive return, but the LAN project would result in a negative return.

INTRODUCING NET PRESENT VALUE (NPV)

One problem in using the internal rate of return is that it does not account for the prevailing discount rate. That is, when assessing the worth of an investment, you should also consider the current discount rate (or the company's hurdle rate) and how changes in that rate may affect your investment, not to mention your decision. To do this you take advantage of a related tool, net present value (NPV).

TABLE 6.4 PROPOSAL COMPARISON AT 18 PERCENT

Proposal	Less than Hurdle Rate	Hurdle Rate = 18%	Greater than Hurdle Rate
LAN system	IRR = 16.28% Unacceptable		
Fork Lift			IRR = 18.45% Acceptable

The NPV is another important number, but it differs from the IRR in that it requires a rate at which each payment in the cash flow will be discounted—it is dependent on the value employed as the discount rate. By definition, the NPV of an investment is the difference between the discounted cash flow for the project at the selected rate and the cost of the project—that is, your initial cost of the investment. To derive the formula, it is very similar to the IRR formula with the exception that you are providing the rate r and not solving for it.

$$\text{NPV}_{@\,r} = \sum_{n=1} \text{CF}_n(1+r)^{-n} - \text{Proj} = \sum_{n=1} \frac{\text{CF}_n}{(1+r)^n} - \text{Proj}$$

It is important to note that the output of this analysis is a monetary number which is the difference between the sum of the present value dollars discounted at the specified rate and what the proposal requests for funds. It is not a rate. We make the assumption in this calculation that the indicated discount rate used on this cash flow is in effect for the life of the cash flow period. With respect to the initial investment then, one of the following three results will be true with respect to the derived net present value at the selected discount rate.

$\text{NPV} = 0$ For the NPV to equal zero implies that, at the given rate of discount, the sum of the present values of the cash flow is equal to the cost of the project. In this situation it must be true that the rate employed for discounting was, in fact, the internal rate of return. We show this later.

$\text{NPV} > 0$ With respect to the rate employed, the sum of the present values of the cash flow is greater than the initial investment. Or, at the selected rate, the discounted cash flow yields a positive return when compared to the initial investment.

$\text{NPV} < 0$ With respect to the rate employed, the sum of the present values of the cash flow is less than the initial investment. Or, at the selected rate, the discounted cash flow yields a negative return when compared to the initial investment.

You can see from these definitions and relationships that an alternative definition for the internal rate of return is the rate at which the net present value is zero. The advantage of using the NPV instead of the IRR calculation is that the results are in present-day dollars, and can be compared across a variety of rates depending on your belief on probable discount rates or your company's required rate of return.

CALC TIP
Determining the NPV on the Calculator
Now that you know mathematically where the NPV takes its meaning, let's make it work for us. Let's enter the

cash flow for the LAN proposal and determine its NPV. First, keep in mind that the keystrokes are exactly the same as those used for entering the cash flow for the IRR. First, there is probably a cash flow from the last exercises in your calculator, so when prompted, clear it out. The CF_0 (or INIT) entry will be –120,000 as before; then enter the remaining cash flow as you did earlier. See Table 6.2 for all the key entries for this project.

Once the cash flow has been entered, you are ready to do the NPV. Depending on your calculator, you may have to press a CALC key to access the NPV calculations as you did with the IRR. But what is different from calculating the IRR is that the NPV requires a rate at which it will discount the cash flow. Most likely there will be an I% key, which identifies the rate entry (not to be confused with IRR%, which indicates the internal rate of return).

Let's test your intuition. With respect to the LAN project, suppose management indicated that the discount rate (or the minimum return) must be 10 percent—that is, calculate the NPV using 10 percent as the discount rate. As Figure 6.7 demonstrates, the NPV analysis is a wonderful example of a function. The value of the NPV is a function of the value you enter for the rate. So, assuming the rate of 10 percent, which of the three results should we get: NPV < 0, NPV = 0, or NPV > 0? To give you a hint, remember that the internal rate of return for the LAN Project was 16.28 percent.

Here's an example that should make your choice very clear. Suppose you went to the bank to borrow money and they charged a rate of 10 percent. Now, you know that your project will give a return of 16.28 percent from your IRR analysis. Wouldn't it be profitable? Or, stated another way, shouldn't your project yield a positive return? And the answer should be a resounding *yes*. There is even some cash left over.

Figure 6.8 shows the positive return of $18,877.13. What this means is that the sum of the present values for this cash flow discounted at a rate of 10 percent is $138,877.13. Once it is netted out with the project cost of $120,000, you get an NPV of $18,877.13. The important factor to remember in all this is that the discount rate can take on a range of values depending on what you or management decide regarding rate behavior.

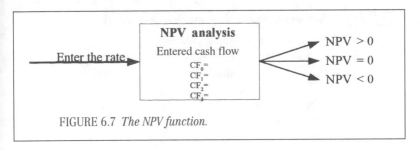

FIGURE 6.7 *The NPV function.*

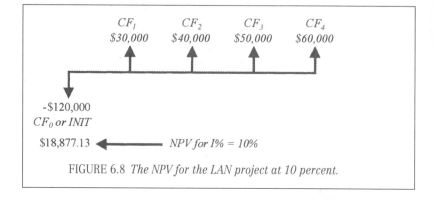

FIGURE 6.8 *The NPV for the LAN project at 10 percent.*

Determining the NPV

In the following equation, each of the cash flows CF_n are discounted to the beginning of the project at the entered rate of 10 percent. If you are still unsure of these calculations, you could solve for each of the discounted flows at 10 percent, for their respective number of years, and then add them to verify this result. Use the equations to help you arrive at the correct values for the NPV. This certainly will confirm your understanding.

$$NPV_{@r} = \sum_{n=1} \frac{CF_n}{(1+r)^n} - Proj$$

$$NPV_{@10\%} = \frac{30{,}000}{(1+0.10)^1} + \frac{40{,}000}{(1+0.10)^2} + \frac{50{,}000}{(1+0.10)^3}$$

$$+ \frac{60{,}000}{(1+0.10)^4} - 120{,}000$$

$$NPV = 138{,}877.13 - 120{,}000$$

$$NPV = \$18{,}877.13$$

It should make sense that the NPV produces a positive number in this situation. Put it in the perspective that the rental of funds is 10 percent, yet the rate of return of the cash flow itself is in excess of 16 percent, and bingo, you're ahead of the game. And "ahead of the game" translates to $18,877.13 in today's dollars.

You try:

Solving for NPV at 20 Percent

Suppose, alternatively, you were to use a discount rate of 20 percent—what would be the value of the net present value? Now, the beauty of this exercise is that it requires no further keystroke entries. All you need to do is to enter the rate of 20 percent in the I% register, and solve for NPV. It's that easy. See the solution in Figure 6.9.

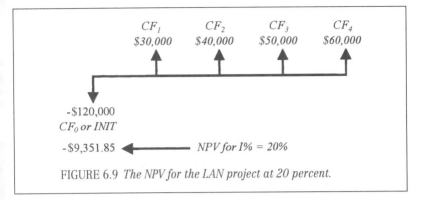

FIGURE 6.9 *The NPV for the LAN project at 20 percent.*

You try:

Solving for NPV at 16.28178 Percent

Now that you have the idea that solving for the NPV of the LAN project is simply entering the proposed rate, verify an important principal discussed earlier. Verify that the NPV is zero (or very close) when the selected rate is the internal rate of return. Enter the rate of 16.28178 percent in the I% register, and solve for NPV. It's that easy.

So, there is a range of values for the discount rate and associated values of the net present value, ranging from positive to negative, based on the entries made for the rate. There is something mathematically beautiful in these last few comments, and that is that this relationship between the NPV and the selected value for the discount rate can be graphed to enhance your understanding of the decision process. We used Excel to demonstrate this functional relationship. Although you may not have the software, you do have enough understanding based upon what you have done in these last few pages to appreciate this financial goodie.

Finally, note the importance of NPV to decision making with respect to management's investment in the LAN project. The graph in Figure 6.10 displays the necessary information to support the significance of the NPV calculation.

Everything done in this chapter to show how these two tools can be invaluable to financial decision making can be explained from the curve in Figure 6.10.

- If the net present value is greater than zero for the required discount rate, then the project is favorable, hence returning a positive return on the investment. As you examine the x axis, the curve takes on positive values for a discount rate less than 16.28 percent. So, if the rate used is the company's cost of capital, or the internal hurdle rate for all projects is less than 16.28 percent, then this

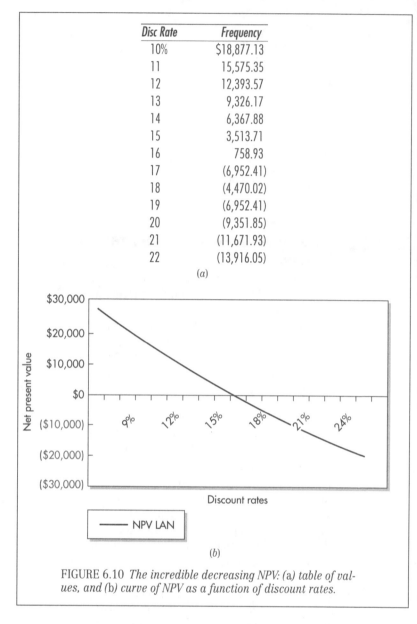

Disc Rate	Frequency
10%	$18,877.13
11	15,575.35
12	12,393.57
13	9,326.17
14	6,367.88
15	3,513.71
16	758.93
17	(6,952.41)
18	(4,470.02)
19	(6,952.41)
20	(9,351.85)
21	(11,671.93)
22	(13,916.05)

(a)

(b)

FIGURE 6.10 *The incredible decreasing NPV: (a) table of values, and (b) curve of NPV as a function of discount rates.*

project would be considered an attractive investment.

- If the net present value is equal to zero, then the project will just break even with respect to the discount rate, which is exactly equal to the internal rate of return. This is the point where the NPV function crosses the axis of the independent variable, 16.28 percent.

- If the net present value is less than zero for the required discount rate, then the project is not favorable, hence returning a negative return on the investment. As the graph shows, values of the NPV function are less than 0 for values of the discount rate greater then 16.28 percent.

Analyzing the Alternative Proposal

Now that you have the tools, analyze both cash flows, calculate their internal rates of return, and determine their net present values for discount rates of 16, 18, and 20 percent. What decisions would you make with respect to funding these projects based upon the projected cost of capital used by your company? Figure 6.11 and Table 6.5 compare the two cash flows.

So, what conclusions can you draw about what the company should do? The IRR tells you that the forklift proposal has the highest return on the investment of $120,000. In addition, if the cost of capital is 16 percent, then either proposal is acceptable since they both return a positive net present value. But if you think that the cost of capital is going to increase to either 18 or 20 percent, then you must be more careful. At the 18 percent rate, the fork lift is acceptable but the LAN is not, and at 20 percent, neither project is acceptable. Figure 6.12 presents an Excel solution that demonstrates both proposals and shows each one's NPV and trend.

APPLICATIONS OF IRR AND NPV

This section demonstrates how the material in this chapter can be applied to analyze cash flows and bond prices.

 Analyzing Projects with Different Time Periods

The expansion of your product lines has certainly had its impact on the revenue of the company. However, with expansion has come the problem of cellaring all that wine (inventory). There are two locations that are appealing in their proximity to customers, both of which will cost you $600,000. The Main Street location is a seven-

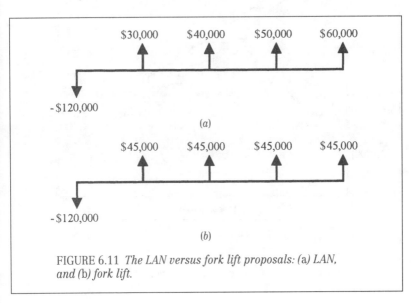

FIGURE 6.11 *The LAN versus fork lift proposals: (a) LAN, and (b) fork lift.*

TABLE 6.5 ANALYSIS TABLE: LAN VERSUS FORK LIFT

Proposal	IRR%	NPV @ 16%	NPV @ 18%	NPV @ 20%
LAN	16.28178	$758.93	−$4,470.02	−$9,351.85
Fork lift	18.45048	5,918.13	1,052.78	−3,506.94

year plan, while the Interstate Center is a nine-year plan. Given the following cash flows, which should you select?

This example demonstrates that cash flows over differing time periods can be compared and, in fact, analyzed to determine the critical cost of capital that makes both of these opportunities equal. There is a second opportunity in this analysis, as well. With many competing proposals, there could be a rate point where you are indifferent to the selection of the project because the net present values for both will be the same. This problem is intriguing and will have more meaning once you analyze the projects and demonstrate relationships on a graph. Figure 6.13 displays the cash flows for the two projects.

Handling Negative or Zero Cash Flows

The Interstate Center proposal demonstrates that cash flows may be negative or zero in some of the

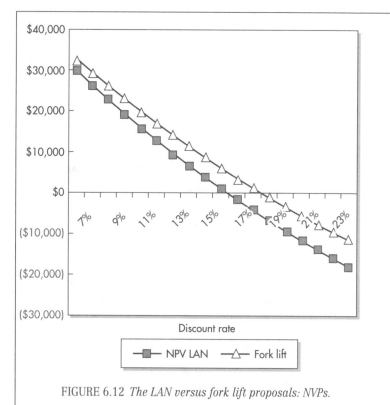

FIGURE 6.12 *The LAN versus fork lift proposals: NVPs.*

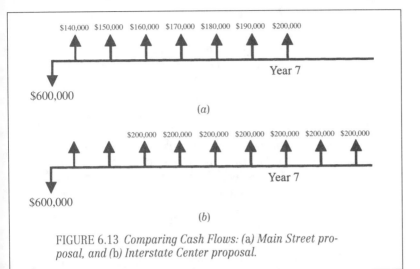

FIGURE 6.13 *Comparing Cash Flows: (a) Main Street proposal, and (b) Interstate Center proposal.*

early periods. In this case it may be due to offsetting flows—for example, additional renovations or technological investments that exactly offset any positive return. This is a very important point; you must do your own adjustments to come up with the final period value. An example might clarify the concern. Suppose as part of the Interstate project you had to automate the facility to meet your distribution requirements (we'll assume that Main Street is truly in condition to move in, thereby requiring no further costs). The cost for this modification and enhancement of the location will be $200,000 for each of the first 2 years. After these two periods there will be no further requirements. As a result, you must consolidate the costs and savings within the appropriate period, as demonstrated in Figure 6.14. The net amount for each of the first 2 years is therefore $0 ($200,000 – $200,000).

If you assume that the company is going to choose only one of the locations, and that investors have advised you that your cost of capital benchmark should be 16 percent, which proposal should be selected?

Enter the cash flow starting with an initial cost of –$600,000, followed by 7 annual payments beginning with $140,000. The fact that there are no cash pay-

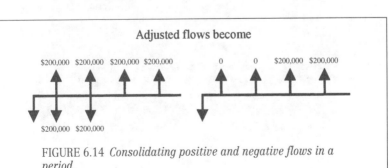

FIGURE 6.14 *Consolidating positive and negative flows in a period.*

ments coming in during years 8 and 9 will have no effect on either the IRR or NPV calculation. The present value of the zero payment amount is zero, and will have no effect on the sum of the present values as long as they are at the end of the flow. Zeros in the beginning of the flow cannot be disregarded because they force future positive payment amounts farther out into the cash flow, thereby affecting their present value.

By examining the results in Table 6.6, at the 16 percent cost of capital criterion, both proposals are acceptable, but the Main Street proposal has the better return and NPV. Hence, it would be the choice based upon the financial data. If the company investors required a higher cost of capital of 20 percent then neither proposal would acceptable, although a little negotiation might bring Main Street in easily.

GRAPHICALLY SPEAKING

Comparing the Two Proposals

If you have a spreadsheet available, you might want to try to reproduce the table of net present value calculations shown in Figure 6.15 because something is very interesting here. Note that at low rates Interstate has the higher NPV, and after approximately 10 percent, the NPV calculations favor the Main Street proposal.

As Figure 6.15 also shows, if the cost of capital were as low as 6 or 8 percent, the Interstate would have the better NPV, and hence would be the choice. So, how do you determine this point of indifference? Since there is this obvious change in NPV status in the two analyses, you can solve for it by setting the cash flows equal to each other and doing a little algebra to see the trick. In these cash flows CFMS refers to the Main Street cash flow and CFIN to that of the Interstate.

Main Street cash flow = Interstate cash flow

$$\sum_{n=1}^{9} \frac{\text{CFMS}_n}{(1+r)^n} - \text{Proj} = \sum_{n=1}^{9} \frac{\text{CFIN}_n}{(1+r)^n} - \text{Proj}$$

$$\sum_{n=1}^{9} \frac{\text{CFMS}_n}{(1+r)^n} - \text{Proj} - \left(\sum_{n=1}^{9} \frac{\text{CFIN}_n}{(1+r)^n} - \text{Proj} \right) = 0$$

TABLE 6.6 ANALYSIS TABLE: MAIN STREET VERSUS INTERSTATE CENTER

Proposal	IRR%	NPV @ 12%	NPV @ 16%	NPV @ 20%
Main Street	19.2685	$155,368.58	$63,009.08	−$12,806.14
Interstate	16.0094	127,639.75	262.40	−99,362.26

$$\sum_{n=1}^{9} \frac{\text{CFMS}_n}{(1+r)^n} - \left(\sum_{n=1}^{9} \frac{\text{CFIN}_n}{(1+r)^n} \right) = 0$$

This may appear confusing, but here is what you need to know to find the rate where they both have the

Disc Rate	Main Street	Interstate
7%	$301,649.26	$341,442.82
8	269,133.97	292,724.63
9	238,359.30	247,227.14
10	209,209.83	204,697.33
11	181,579.06	164,904.84
12	155,368.58	127,639.75
13	130,487.45	92,710.54
14	106,851.50)	59,942.27
15	84,382.79	29,175.01
16	63,009.08	262.40
17	42,663.36	26,929.63
18	23,283.44	52,524.05
19	4,811.51	76,633.69
20	(12,806.14)	99,362.26
21	(29,619.52)	120,805.08

(a)

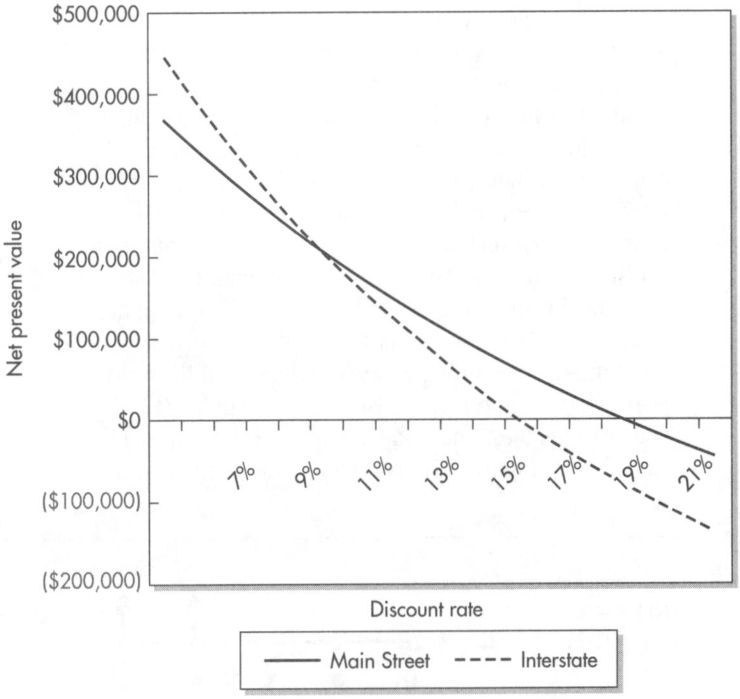

(b)

FIGURE 6.15 *Main Street versus Interstate analysis: (a) table of values, and (b) NPV curves.*

same NPV. Simply stated, carefully subtract one cash flow from the other, on a period by period basis, beginning with the difference in the cost of the project, which in this case is zero. CF_1 is $140,000 – 0, CF_2 is $150,000, CF_3 is –$40,000, and so on. You want to find that rate at which this *difference* cash flow equals zero. But isn't that exactly the definition of the internal rate of return? When you solve for this point, which is 9.6520 percent, you have found the *indifference point*—that is, the point about which one proposal is no better than the other. The graph in Figure 6.15 shows the net present values of both cash flows over a range of increasing rates. Clearly, for discount rates greater than 9.65 percent, the Main Street location is the superior investment, for it yields a greater NPV—note that its curve is above that of the Interstate Center for these rates. And just the opposite is true for rates less than 9.65 percent, and as a result, the Interstate proposal is financially more attractive.

 Dealing with Negative Cash Flows

The *Wine Spectator* has indicated that the company's 1997 Cabernet Sauvignon vintage will be outstanding, and worthy of storage for future consumption. Customers have been warned that prices will really take off, so they should buy early. This vintage will double in its value in three to four years.

Suppose you see this as an investment opportunity and decide to buy 10 cases of your Leaping Lizards cabernet sauvignon for $480 a case. Now you can't just store this in your hall closet (specifically the one near your radiator); such an investment must be stored in the safest of conditions. The local wine merchant will store the wine for an annual fee of $1 a bottle. If you sell half of the 10 cases at the end of the third year for twice their cost, and the remaining 5 cases at the end of the fourth year, what is the return on your investment? Don't forget your storage fees, and to help you see this point, see the cash flow in Figure 6.16. Note that you are not taking

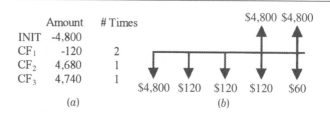

FIGURE 6.16 *The Leaping Lizards cash flow: (a) table of values, and (b) diagram.*

any for yourself; you personally do not believe in drinking any wine costing more than $8 a bottle.

This example is meant to demonstrate that when you have cash both coming in and going out in any period, it is your job to reconcile the amount for that period. Note that in periods 3 and 4 you must adjust the $4,800 selling price with the cost of storing the wine. If you got a rate of 20.077 percent, I'll bet you were surprised. You were probably thinking the answer would be 22 or 23 percent. The small fees for storage, which are entered as negative flows, have their effect.

 Bond Pricing the Easy Way with NPV

To raise capital, Cyber Vineyards is selling 10-year corporate bonds with a coupon rate of 12 percent at discount for $971.09. Should consumers be attracted to this bond if they can obtain as safe an investment yielding 14 percent?

As a potential investor, you want to determine the yield to maturity for this investment assuming you'll hold the bond for the entire 10-year period. Now that you know how to do a cash flow, working with bonds will be very easy. Set up the cash flow with annual coupon payments. Recall that when doing the cash flow you took advantage of the number of times entry when you had payments that were for the same amount and repeated for a number of years. In this case, set up the coupon payments with the coupon amount and the corresponding number of times entry. But, important to note, the final amount will be the face value plus the last coupon amount. This is similar to the point made earlier, that within any flow period it is your responsibility to consolidate the flows within a period to determine a single entry for that period. Use the internal rate of return to calculate the yield to maturity, and the NPV to determine the price with an alternative discount rate.

Once you see the cash flow in Figure 6.17 it is very easy to understand why the yield maturity is nothing more than the internal rate of return. It is the same cash flow diagram shown earlier in this chapter. Likewise, delete the initial amount value to actually solve for the

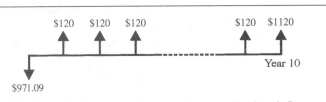

FIGURE 6.17 *The cyber vineyards 12 percent bond cash flow.*

TABLE 6.7 THE CASH FLOW ENTRIES

Cash Flow Settings for IRR		
Year or CF_n	Amount	# Times
INIT or CF_0	–$ 971.09	
CF_1	120.00	9
CF_2	1,120.00	1

Cash Flow Settings for NPV		
Year or CF_n	Amount	# Times
IIT or CF_0	–$ 971.09	
CF_1	120.00	9
CF_2	1,120.00	1
I%	14%	

price by using the current discount rate and the NPV calculation of the existing cash flow. The keystrokes shown in Table 6.7 should be employed for these values, assuming an interest rate of 14 percent for the NPV.

The yield is 12.5227 percent and the NPV at 14 percent is –$75.41, indicating that it is not as good an investment as another investment that would yield 14 percent.

Now here is another trick. Go back into the cash flow and enter 0 in the Init or CF(0) cell. Now the cash flow consists of only the positive entries, $120 to $1,120. Now calculate the NPV of the cash flow with a rate of 14 percent. The answer is $895.68, which is exactly the price of this 12 percent bond if the discount rate grew to 14 percent. Note: What is the sum of the current purchase price ($971.09) and –$75.41 from before? So, this is yet another way to find the price of a bond.

⟳ END POINT

By far, internal rate of return and net present value are the most important tools employed in financial decision making. The IRR, which is a function of the cash flow structure itself, yields a break-even return on investment percentage against which different proposals can be compared. But we also know that the discount rate changes, and companies will change their required return on any use of their funds to reflect these market conditions. The beauty of the net present value is that it assesses the cash flow against the given discount rate to yield a comparison between the value of the discounted cash flow and the cost of the investment. When this net present value is positive, the proposal represents a good investment against the projected discount rate.

PART 2

Business Statistics
Making Decisions from Data

CHAPTER 7

Organizing Your Data for Better Decision Making

The preceding chapter discussed the importance of being able to derive quality financial information in order to make decisions about potential investments. The concepts of future and present value eventually led to the key decision-making tools—internal rate of return and net present value. This chapter takes elementary statistical concepts, like the mean and standard deviation, and from them builds decision-making and estimation tools such as hypothesis testing and regression. Given a problem, you want to be able to plan the collection of data that will support your analysis, then take that data, organize it, and translate it into decision-making information.

STATISTICS IN ACTION

Because of the flood of data that is collected on every aspect of business, the use of statistical techniques has become a necessary tool for today's successful manager. And with the personal computer on every manager's desktop, you can use spreadsheets to analyze the data, thereby making it very easy to perform robust analyses without the rigors of the mathematics required for these calculations. More managers are using statistics to do even more for their business. Consider the following example.

Nike, Adidas, and Asics, among many others, are developing new shoes to meet an insatiable market demand for athletic footwear. This is an extremely competitive market and information helps determine new product initiatives. Suppose you were employed in one of these companies—how would statistics play a role in your business responsibility?

- As a *corporate manager* you need to analyze the portfolio of products and services, examine trends, and predict future market performance. You can use statistics to compare current performance, antici-pate product life cycles, and plan future initiatives.

- As the *product manager* for an individual line—for example, women's running shoes—you need to esti-mate future product activity based upon current sales, detect market sensitivity to new products, and develop new products based on customer feedback.

- As the *customer service manager* you need to assess customer satisfaction and provide feedback to prod-uct management on product performance. You would use statistics to alert you to performance problems and to determine levels of consumer dis-satisfaction or satisfaction.

- As the *financial analyst* you need to evaluate finan-cial performance of the products based on historical performance and return on investment. As well, you could use statistics to estimate corporate earnings based upon historical performance.

In each of these situations you need to analyze quan-titative data in light of the objective and make decisions based upon that data. Hence, the need for understand-ing statistics, and the ability to employ its various tools effectively to compete in businesses that are heavily dependent upon their use.

DESCRIPTIVE VERSUS INFERENTIAL STATISTICS

In light of our objective, we define *statistics* as the study of collecting and processing data to assist busi-ness managers in making informed decisions where uncertainty exists. It employs quantitative analysis; hence, it should be included with the topics in the time value of money sections. In each of the examples just cited we could break the process of using statistics (per-forming statistical analysis) into three broad phases:

1. *Data gathering or sampling.* This phase requires the design of a survey, planning a sampling strat-egy, and conducting the sample.

2. *Descriptive analysis.* This phase focuses on describing the behavior of the sample—a snapshot, if you will, of current or historical business perfor-mance levels.

3. *Inferential analysis.* This phase predicts behavior of the population based upon the results of the sample, that is, how performance will change as key variables are changed.

The Importance of Planning the Project

The descriptive and inferential phases are analytical in nature and make up most of what is covered in this study of statistics. But there is a danger. Note that there is a caution employed universally in technology—to really understand what users want from technology requires that developers spend a considerable amount of time defining what it is that should be developed to meet users' needs. History has shown very clearly that when this important phase has been neglected, the investment is a failure. There is a similar concern with statistics: You must invest time in planning the questionnaires, verifying the sources of data, understanding the characteristics of the population being measured, and then conducting the survey or gathering the data. In fact, data collection is so important that if it is not planned well, the remainder of the analysis could be worthless. You have surely heard of GIGO—garbage in, garbage out—in reference to computer programming. Well, the same applies to conducting an experiment.

The use of the term *experiment* in statistics denotes that there is an appreciation of methodology for your analysis. An appreciation of the scientific method goes a long way here. You should ensure that the collection of data is controlled, that there are no biases, that it is random, that you employ well-defined measurements for your data description, and that you use acceptable techniques to draw conclusions or make inferences. Truly, your analysis begins with knowing what to collect and how. You must get data in a form that allows decisions to be made. You may know of situations where data were collected but the critical information required for a decision was unavailable because it was not planned for at collection.

Figure 7.1 shows how the analysis proceeds from understanding the sample to making judgments about the population. You go from a historical perspective of what is, to a predictive perspective of what may be. In the *descriptive phase,* you present the sample data summary, develop some graphs to describe the general behavior, and interpret results in a way that enlightens the decision making. *Inferential statistics* is the phase in which inferences are made regarding the population from which the sample was selected. Not only can you make estimates or predictions but you can also consider the reliability with respect to these predictions. So this is your course of action: How do you plan for effective collection, describe the results of the data collection, identify general tendencies, specify consistency of the data, and infer or estimate future behaviors based upon the data?

First analytical phase
Descriptive statistics
Analyze the sample: Categorize the data, summarize it, and describe general behavior such as central tendency and variance.

Second analytical phase
Inferential statistics
Make inferences about the population based upon the sample: From the samples, estimate the behavior of the population.

FIGURE 7.1 *Purposes of the analytical phases*

Each of the chapters in Part 2 has a major objective, ranging from data organization to hypothesis testing and estimation. Each chapter focuses on applications that should address your specific business needs, including product forecasting, investment analysis, quality control, and attitudinal surveys. Chapters 7 and 8 explore descriptive statistics, from graphing to measures of central tendency and spread or dispersion. Chapters 9 to 12 explore the estimation and inferential concepts in statistics, from confidence intervals and hypothesis testing to regression.

KEY CONCEPT — Start Statistics with a Sample

Where do you start when you have a statistics problem? That is a tricky question, because you don't really have a statistics problem—what you have is a business problem whose solution and understanding will be supported by statistical tools. Before getting lost in the quantitative, make sure you've got your eye on the objective. You want to know as much as you can to minimize uncertainty. Be realistic. You'll probably never eliminate uncertainty, but you can minimize the risk of making an erroneous and costly decision by having factual information, as opposed to going with your gut feeling.

As Figure 7.2 shows, sampling is a tool that allows you to analyze a subset of a population, and provide factual information about this subset with the intent of inferring population behavior. Statistics is about analyzing a manageable number of items to tell you something about an unmanageable number. Sounds simple enough! But before going out to gather the data, you should do a little planning.

Do Your Homework

In any of these situations, you want to be able to check to verify your plan of action before going full speed into the collection of the data. Going back a second time is costly and potentially embarrassing.

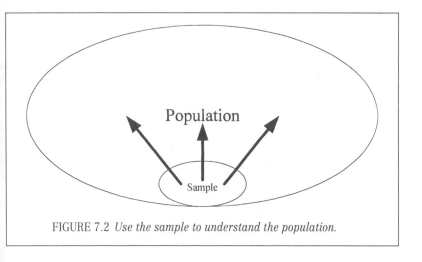

FIGURE 7.2 *Use the sample to understand the population.*

Finally, a note regarding the size of the sample. It surely makes sense that the greater the sample size, the more confidence you will have in the results and in inferring behavior of the total population. But what is the magic number—10, 50, 100? We make some suggestions on sample size later in the chapter. But you should be aware that there are cost-benefit tradeoffs in sample size. It is one thing to do random people-on-the-street sampling regarding coffee preferences, and quite another to conduct a usability test for a new pilot navigation system. Sometimes 10 participants will be sufficient because the cost of the study for any one case is very expensive. As well, when doing studies that require a successful outcome to a procedure—for example, the installation of a printer for a personal computer—you will find the critical show-stoppers in just a few cases. In situations like these, treat the test as a prototype: Test a few times, make revisions based upon the results or observations, and test again.

KEY CONCEPT — Sample versus Population

In statistics it is important to differentiate between respondents who are being surveyed and the population to which the respondents belong. We speak of *population* in terms of people, but it actually refers to the total set of objects you are studying—all students in the school, all employees with five years' or more experience, all air conditioners, all sheets of processed plywood, all bottles of wine, and so on. Most likely you will not be able to interview the entire population of people or examine the entire set of objects, so you look to a small group of them to guide you. A *sample* is a subset of your population—a small group within the desired population. You will infer behavior of the population based upon the descriptive results of your sample. You select a sample because it is usually very difficult, costly, and/or impractical to survey the entire population.

RULES REGARDING SAMPLING

Are there any rules with respect to sampling? When selecting the items for the sample, they should be representative of the population you need to assess, as well as unbiased, and random. *Bias* refers to a flaw in your study whereby the sample does not truly represent the population. Bias may occur when you not-so-randomly select a sample by convenience. For example, if you work in New York City and conduct a study of importance to the people of the State of New York by sampling people in Manhattan because they are close to your place of business, you have introduced a bias. An unbiased random strategy for this case might be to randomly select zip codes representative of all New York, and then randomly select participants from them. Understanding the population is key to selecting a successful sample. But as Paul Thurman, an outstanding adjunct professor at Columbia University, states "this is indeed the Catch-22 of statistics. You need to know something about the population just to get a good sample. The better the sample, the better the inference, and the less uncertainty. But at what point do you consider the sample 'good enough' to represent the population?" Good judgment, as well as economics, has to prevail. For more on valid methods for selecting a sample, see *Sampling Techniques,* Third Edition, by W. G. Cochran (John Wiley & Sons, 1977).

A Little Wine to Help with Statistics

How should we approach this subject? Many statistical tools for decision making are built upon some fundamental measures such as the mean and the standard deviation. It will help your learning if it is clear how they are employed in calculations, through studying a single case. Therefore, we will become vintners and discover how statistics can help in the production and marketing of wine, and, we will use this production case through much of the book so you can follow how various statistics weave their way through different stages of the analysis. So grab your galoshes and a wine glass to begin the tour.

The goal is to increase wine sales, but should you expand current wine production or do you introduce a new wine? What is the behavior of your current wine buyers? How do they assess your wines? How much wine do they purchase? Based upon these data, is there a relationship between income and the amount of wine they buy? This would certainly have an effect on how you spend your advertising dollars.

As you can see, your wine business needs to know its customers and the success of its various products. So, the goals of this analysis include assessing the quality of the various wines, determining consumption behavior, and determining ways to forge a stronger bond with customers by means of target mailings, e-mail announcements, or website access.

A Note on the Use of Technology

In Part 1, on the time value of money, we were quite happy and even thankful that the calculator was available for managing all of the calculations we had to perform. Hopefully you developed an understanding of the topics from the mathematical approach, so that you better understand how these values on the calculator came to be. In statistics the premier tool for data analysis is not the calculator but data analysis and spreadsheet tools that are available on personal computers. We continue to take the mathematical approach—that is, all the topics are developed by the formulas that define that particular statistic. Thus, if the math makes sense to you, it is easier to understand the concept and apply the technology. In applying the technology, we often refer to Microsoft Excel and present the output from that application in the text. If you have Lotus, SAS, or any other data analysis tool that performs these analyses, please feel free to use it. In fact, we would suggest that you look over your software to see if you can do some of the problems in the upcoming sections.

Your plan is to have customers fill out a short survey in your wine shop, or while ordering on your 800 number service, or while surfing your newly created website. You feel comfortable that these participants are representative of your total customer base. Assume that you took our advice and tested the survey with a few of your employees before interviewing any participants. The surveys will be collected and tallied for your data analysis.

The young person working as a summer intern has excitedly run into your office with the responses to the first few questions on your survey, "Which of our wines is your favorite?" and "How many bottles of wine are purchased in your house in a week?" You think, this data is a little rough, it's all over the place. Imagine if you had 500 or 1,000 responses. As you examine the data in Figure 7.3, it is also clear that your customers like your wine.

Look before Calculating

DANGER!

Never start calculating statistics until you are sure of the general behavior of the data. You can save yourself time (when you must redo the analysis with data

Cabernet					Chardonnay			Merlot	
2	6	8	9	6	6	6	4	7	6
5	9	5	5	5	7	7	3	7	6
7	11	4	10	4	3	5	4	12	8
3	7	6	7	6	5	6	4	8	3
7	6	5	5	6	5	6	5	6	7
6	4	7	7	4	7	5	7	9	8
6	8	2	5	3	6	8	6	7	5
8	5	7	4	6	7	6	8	5	8
5	3	8	10	5	5	5	4	6	7
6	8	6	6	7	5	6	5	4	3

FIGURE 7.3 *The wine purchase survey data.*

that are more accurate to the population) and embarrassment (when presenting statistics that are not in fact supported by the data). Reviewing each survey item is not very efficient either, so you need a way to get a high-level view of the results of your sample.

Benefits of the Frequency Distribution

When raw data are collected, they are not particularly informative, so the first step in the analysis is to organize them in a summary form that gives you some general impressions of their behavior. When you get data, it is important to have an idea as to whether your analysis is on the right track. The best way of presenting this summary is to group all the data into equal discrete classes that range over all possible values of the variable. Each class is referred to as a *frequency class* (or *class*), which is a uniform interval defined by a lower and upper bound. Once you've defined these classes, it's time to tally the data, which means to assign each item in your sample to a frequency class.

Frequency distribution is the process by which each item in the sample is assigned to a group or interval, thereby creating a tally of the data into a smaller more manageable series of groups. From this tally, the range and frequency of the data can be displayed through a graphical presentation called a *histogram*.

COMPUTER TIP

When doing a frequency distribution or histogram in your spreadsheet application, the classes used for your tallying are referred to as *bins*. Before performing the analysis, define the bins in a range of sequential cells, then identify those cells as the *bin range* when selecting the histogram tool. Since bins must be uniform in their width, you could use the Fill tool to generate the bins (see Figure 7.4). The value of predefining the bins is that you can use them as a standard for comparing other samples. If you are performing only one analysis, you can let Excel define the bins by just ignoring that range in Excel.

DETAILS REGARDING FREQUENCY CLASSES

When preparing a frequency distribution, pay attention to the following details in setting up and assigning frequency classes.

- Frequency classes should be the same width. In Figure 7.4, you determined that the width is 2. The width of each class is determined by dividing the range of the distribution (the largest score minus the smallest score) by the number of classes you think will best support your data.

- The number of classes should be more than 5 but not so numerous that you lose the summary effect (12, 15, but no more than 20.) There are two methods for determining the number of classes:

  Take the square root of the number of observations.

  Take the maximum integer value of x such that $2^x < n,$ where n is the number of observations. In the example in Figure 7.4, six classes are used, as explained in the following tip.

- There should be no ambiguity as to where to place a score. An item cannot belong to more than one class. Therefore, end points of classes should be determined in such a way that no score is on an end point.

- In selecting an end point, examine the significant digits in your data—for example, in this sample you are dealing with natural numbers—1, 2, 3, . . . To define your first end point, subtract half a unit from the minimum score, and then add the class width sequentially to create all the remaining classes. The half point assures that no value in the sample will fall on an end point; there will be no ambiguity.

Making the Frequency Table

In the case of your wine survey, the frequency classes are defined in the following manner. Note that no score can be counted twice, in two different classes. Since 6 is the maximum power of 2 less than the sample size of 100, then 6 classes should be defined.

Determining the class width (range ÷ number of bins):

Maximum score = 12   Minimum score = 2

Range = maximum – minimum = 12 – 2 = 10

Number of classes = 2^6 = 64

Weekly wine purchases										
		Cabernet				Chardonnay			Merlot	
2	6	8	9	6	6	6	4	7	6	
5	9	5	5	5	7	7	3	7	6	
7	11	4	10	4	3	5	4	12	8	
3	7	6	7	6	5	6	4	8	3	
7	6	5	5	6	5	6	5	6	7	
6	4	7	7	4	7	5	7	9	8	
6	8	2	5	3	6	8	6	7	5	
8	5	7	4	6	7	6	8	5	8	
5	3	8	10	5	5	5	4	6	7	
6	8	6	6	7	5	6	5	4	3	

Frequency
bins
1.5
3.5
5.5
7.5
9.5
11.5
13.5

FIGURE 7.4 *Spreadsheet analysis setup.*

Class width = 2   (10/6 is close enough to 2.)

Determining the end points of the first class:

Left-hand end point for first class = 2 − 0.5 = 1.5

Right-hand end point for first class = 1.5 + 2 = 3.5

First class = [1.5, 3.5]

Each remaining frequency class is found by adding 2 to each right-hand end point.

Using the steps outlined here, the frequency classes in Table 7.1 are defined and data are assigned to the respective class. This assumes that people who respond to the survey are wine drinkers. If not, you should start at −0.5 to support the class where a respondent enters 0 bottles of wine per week.

How do you use this frequency distribution? The frequency indicates the number of responses in that particular class; for example, 31 respondents in our survey indicated that they purchase 4 or 5 bottles of wine per week in their household.

Now that we have displayed the class end points in Table 7.1, it should be clear how they were determined. The key is the first left-hand end point. For example, if your data is in tenths, and the minimum value of the variable in the sample is 22.6, then the left-hand end point would be 22.55 (22.6 − 0.05.) As shown in Table 7.1, use an easy interval if you can. In this case, the choice is 2 because it will yield 6 classes. We now have

TABLE 7.1 FREQUENCY TABLE FOR WINE

Bottles per Week	Tally	Frequency	Cumulative Frequency
1.5–3.5	///// ////	9	9
3.5–5.5	///// ///// ///// ///// ///// ///// /	31	40
5.5–7.5	///// ///// ///// ///// ///// ///// ///// ///// ///// //	42	82
7.5–9.5	///// ///// ////	14	96
9.5–11.5	///	3	99
11.5–13.5	/	1	100

disjoint classes (no overlap) and every score is recorded into a class. Success! This table now tells you a lot more about the survey responses than a table of raw data.

GRAPHICALLY SPEAKING

Setting Up the Histogram

The graphical presentation of the frequency distribution is the *histogram,* which shows in vertical bar chart format the number of tallies for each class in the distribution. To construct the histogram, place the frequency classes along the horizontal axis, and set up units on the vertical axis that conform to the number of units of the category having the greatest frequency. Now, for each class in the frequency table, draw a bar rising vertically to the number that indicates its frequency or tally value. Do this for each frequency class defined by your distribution. Figure 7.5 shows the histogram for the consumption survey using Excel.

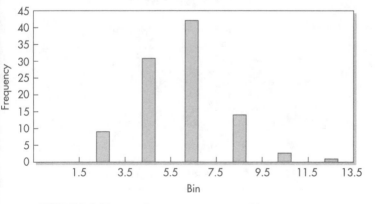

FIGURE 7.5 *The purchase survey response histogram.*

When using a spreadsheet program to perform these frequency tables and histograms, there is a slight inconsistency. Excel, for example, automatically establishes a bin for scores below the first bin and above the last bin. When graphed, this forces extra positions for columns and, unfortunately, moves the class end points between the tick marks. Although it does not affect the basic distribution of data on the histogram, its x axis may be a source of confusion.

Now you have more information about the survey. The histogram clearly shows that the 6 to 7 bottle per week class is the most frequent response. Note, as well, that the response classes adjacent to the 6 to 7 class also have high frequencies.

Different Types of Histograms Tell More Information

There are variations of the frequency chart that you may use, such as the *cumulative frequency chart* or the *Pareto chart*. The cumulative frequency chart, shown in Figure 7.6, employs the data from the last column of Table 7.1, labeled "Cumulative Frequency." The purpose of this graph is to show how many items are above or below a particular class. (Incidentally, Excel does this automatically for you if you click the Cumulative Frequency output when creating the histogram.) For example, by examining Figure 7.6 you can see that 80 percent of the distribution or approximately 80 participants purchase 7 or fewer bottles of wine per week. Examining the chart, the dot close to the top of the 5.5 to 7.5 bar indicates the 80 percent point, meaning that 80 percent of the distribution is less than that point. The chart indicates points for 20 to 100 percent of the distribution of

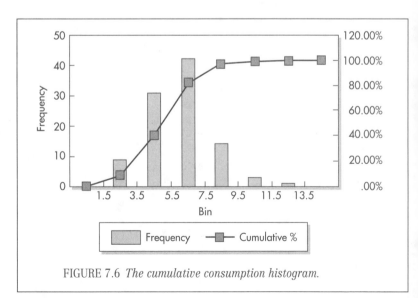

FIGURE 7.6 *The cumulative consumption histogram.*

scores. As the dot above the fourth column indicates, nearly 100 percent of the distribution has been tallied by the time you complete the 7.5 to 9.5 collection of scores. In addition, if you need to translate the frequency amounts into a percentage, you know the total number of responses in the sample—simply divide each frequency by the total.

The other important form of the histogram is the Pareto analysis, shown in Figure 7.7, which is also known as the *80/20 rule.* This famous principle states that 80 percent of your business comes from 20 percent of your customer base. For example, to analyze sales you could set up a table in your spreadsheet with customer names in one column and their corresponding annual sales in the second column. Then run a Pareto analysis. The result will rearrange the frequencies in order of total sales from the most to the least, thereby giving you a very important distribution showing your best customers as a percentage of total sales. This is why the Pareto curve is often called the 80/20 curve. It shows which 20 percent of your customers make up 80 percent of your receivables.

By examining Figure 7.7, you can see that the first two classes (4 or 5 and 6 or 7 bottles) make up 80 percent of your sample. The dot in the second column, 3.5 to 5.5, indicates that 80 percent of the scores are found in these two classes. Figure 7.7 differs from the cumulative frequency curve displayed in Figure 7.6 in that the classes have been rearranged to easily identify those classes that make the greatest contribution to consumption. The placement of the dot in the first column of the Pareto analysis indicates that the 5.5 to 7.5 class accounts for 40 percent of the distribution, and that it contains the greatest collection of scores.

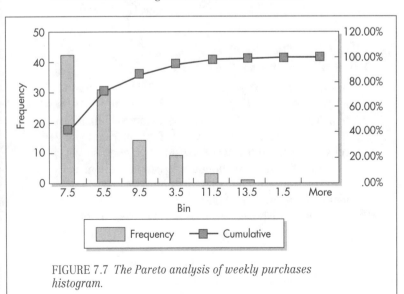

FIGURE 7.7 *The Pareto analysis of weekly purchases histogram.*

COMPUTER TIP

All of the graphs displayed in this analysis were constructed by entering the survey data into Excel as displayed in Figure 7.4. Enter the data as it is shown, in sequential rows and columns. In a range of sequential cells enter your bin assignments (end points). Then access the Tools/Data Analysis/ Histogram menu option.

The graphs are excellent summaries of all the responses. Note that you could have referenced the different bin results and constructed a single bar chart showing all three for comparative purposes. The frequency distribution clearly shows, on a visual level, the range and *clustering* (a nontechnical term to pique your curiosity for the next section) that are helpful for management to understand the dimension of the variable they are studying. The summary perspective helps validate the appropriateness of the data gathering. But these graphs are not true tools for decision making, for they lack the quantitative measures that are required to truly understand the behavior of the variable. Our next objective is to derive some of these numerical measures. Hold on—it's going to get better.

You try:

Analyzing the Three Subsets of Data

The data from the survey are actually broken into three subsets: cabernet, chardonnay, and merlot purchasers. These are interesting data that will be employed later. To better understand the differences in the three distributions, use a bin size of 2 and begin the lowest bin at 1.5. Compare the frequencies for the cabernet, chardonnay, and merlot respondents. How do they differ? Figure 7.8 provides you with the histograms for the three types.

The Significance of Central Tendency

As your wine survey shows, there is definitely a trend for the responses to cluster in the center of the distribution. The tendency of observations to increase their frequency around a particular value of the distribution is referred to as *central tendency.* It is a point about which you could say the distribution is in balance. There are three measures used to identify central tendency: the mean, the median, and the mode. Probably more than any other statistic, the mean is the first piece of information that will be asked for. People, it seems, are very content letting the mean be the representative value for the entire distribution. And, depending on the distribution of data, it may be the best representative. However, there are types of distributions where one of the other

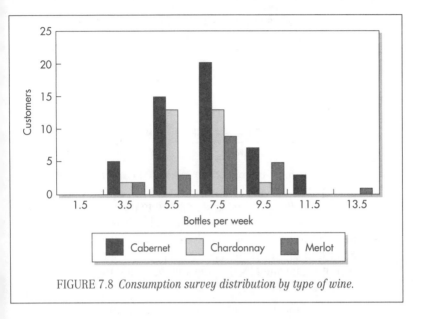

FIGURE 7.8 *Consumption survey distribution by type of wine.*

measures will be more appropriate. As we work with each of the measures we indicate those types of distributions where they are advantageous.

THE MEAN AS A MEASURE OF CENTRAL TENDENCY

CONCEPT

The mean is simply the arithmetic average. Surely you remember the simple average; it is the sum of the individual values divided by the total number of values in the study. As an example, suppose you go to a local wine store and conduct a tasting of the new merlot you are releasing. You will randomly select people entering the store, ask if they would like to try the merlot, and, if so, give them a tasting. After the tasting you will ask each of them to give you a rating based on a scale from 1 to 100, which is a very common scale for rating wine. To calculate the mean for this data, sum the values and divide by the number of values, as shown in Figure 7.9.

MATHEMATICALLY SPEAKING

Calculating the Mean

In general, we have the following notation for the mean, where n is the number of responses in your

Merlot tasting: 72, 75, 75, 79, 80, 80, 81, 81, 84, 85, 88

Sum =   Divide by: Mean =

FIGURE 7.9 *Tasting scores and finding the average.*

sample, x_i refers to the ith observation from your sample, and the symbol $\sum$ means to take the sum.

$$\text{Mean} = \bar{x} = \frac{x_1 + x_2 + \cdots + x_n}{n} = \frac{\sum\limits_{i=1}^{n} x_i}{n}$$

means

$$\frac{72 + 75 + \cdots + 88}{n} = \frac{880}{11} = 80$$

It's time for a little notation. As stated earlier, a sample is part of the population. To distinguish a mean that is calculated on a sample, as opposed to the entire population, we refer to it as $\bar{x}$ (read as "x bar"), and the number of items in the sample is indicated by a small letter n. If the calculation is for the population mean, then it is indicated by the Greek letter μ, and the number of items in the population as capital N.

For the sample:

$$\bar{x} = \frac{\sum\limits_{i=1}^{n} x_i}{n}$$

For the population:

$$\mu = \frac{\sum\limits_{i=1}^{N} x_i}{N}$$

There is an important point to note here: $\bar{x}$ is determined; it is the result of a calculation performed on a sample, where every item in the sample is used in the calculation. So what is the relationship with μ? Because μ is the mean of the population, and, in general, we do not know its value, we use $\bar{x}$ as an approximation of this value. There is more to the use of the approximation, but for now, this is the key point to know about their difference.

Now let's get back to the wine purchase survey. In examining the wine frequency distribution it would appear that the balance point of the distribution or mean is located in the vicinity of 5 to 6 bottles of wine per week. The mean $\bar{x}$ is found by taking the average of the 100 responses; in this case, sum the responses and divide by 100. But, wait—this constitutes a lot of work, even though you would most likely use a calculator to do all that adding. There must be some better way to determine central tendency. To address this dilemma we have three possible solutions:

- First, use the computer to solve for the mean (see the next computer tip).
- Second, group the data in such a way that the groups yield central tendency.
- Third, consider an alternative to the mean. Is there a measure that does not involve all this calculation yet still give us central tendency? Yes, the section on the

median discusses situations where it may be a more reliable estimator of central tendency than the mean.

COMPUTER TIP
Using Excel to Find the Mean

If necessary you can add those values, but here is how the computer can help you. Once you have entered all the data in a range, you can use the AVERAGE(range) function to determine the mean. In this case, *range* refers to the cells containing the data for which you want to find the mean. So, mathematically, the following answer for the mean of the purchase sample is 5.98 bottles per week:

$$\bar{x} = \frac{\sum_{i=1}^{n} x_i}{n} = \frac{2 + 5 + 7 \cdots + 3}{100} = \frac{598}{100} = 5.98$$

You try:

Calculating the Means for the Types of Wine

Note in the consumption survey that responses are grouped by type of wine. Determine the mean for the subgroups of cabernet, chardonnay, and merlot consumers. Hold on to these calculations; we'll use them shortly to calculate the mean by the *weighted mean* technique.

Analyzing Ungrouped versus Grouped Data

You are probably comfortable with calculating the simple or arithmetic mean in this analysis; probably the only source of discomfort might have been all that adding. Be honest now, there is no trick, you just have to add the 100 responses and be thankful we didn't employ an example with four places of precision. When data is collected, it requires some grouping strategy. To analyze *ungrouped* data you must do so on an item by item basis, which is very inefficient, and does not provide the overall view of the distribution. Because we are interested in consumption and wine-purchasing behavior we grouped the data numerically by number of bottles for future analysis. You should use a grouping principle that allows you to capture the information you need. For exercise purposes we also grouped it by preference—although we should note that if preference were an interest to management, the preference grouping would produce a very meaningful pie chart.

It is easy to see that by grouping the responses as we did in the frequency table, using the frequency tallying technique, we were able to make the initial understanding of the sample responses much easier. Therefore, it is advantageous for large samples to employ this methodology. But then, how do you calculate your central tendency measures?

Finding the Mean of Grouped Data

To find the mean of your grouped data, you need to take a representative value of each class that you have defined (for example, the midpoint of the class) and multiply it times the frequency for that class. For example, the second class defined by the interval [3.5, 5.5] has 4.5 as the midpoint. The frequency of the class is 31. Therefore, its contribution to the mean calculation is 4.5 × 31 = 139.5. Do this for each class and sum them. Then divide that sum by the total number of items in the sample—*not,* caution please, the number of classes. We will modify the original frequency table to support the derivation of this important calculation; see Table 7.2.

So, the mean $\bar{x}$ for grouped data is found by the following formula, where x_i refers to the midpoint of the frequency class and f_i refers to the number of items in that class:

$$\bar{x} = \frac{x_1 f_1 + x_2 f + \cdots + x_j f_j}{n} = \frac{\sum_{i=1}^{n} x_i f_i}{n}$$

$$= \frac{2.5 \times 9 + 4.5 \times 31 + \cdots + 12.5 \times 1}{100}$$

$$\bar{x} = \frac{\sum_{i=1}^{j} x_i f_i}{n} = \frac{598}{100} = 5.98$$

This is a very important method of calculating the mean because most likely this is exactly the way you will perform your analysis. This method of finding the mean is known as computing the *weighted average.* Each class has a weight (the number of elements in it) and a representative of the class (the midpoint). The class representative is sometimes defined as the class mark. You will

TABLE 7.2 MODIFIED FREQUENCY TABLE FOR WINE

Bottles per Week	Class Midpoint x_i	Frequency f_i	$(x_i)(f_i)$
1.5–3.5	2.5	9	22.5
3.5–5.5	4.5	31	139.5
5.5–7.5	6.5	42	273
7.5–9.5	8.5	14	119
9.5–11.5	10.5	3	31.5
11.5–13.5	12.5	1	12.5

have an opportunity to use the weighted mean method shortly when determining the mean by classes determined by the type of wine. The only caution in the following formula is that x_i refers to the class midpoint and not the individual item. And, as mentioned earlier, remember that you are dividing by the total number of items in your sample because, in actuality, the product of the midpoint x_i and frequencies f_i results in a very close estimate of the actual sum performed earlier.

Mean or Midpoint—Which Is Best?

When using the technique of the *weighted mean* or *weighted average,* the mean of the sample is determined by the proportional influence of the scores in the distribution. In this case, you are using the midpoint of a class to represent the values in the class, but you could have selected the mean of the class itself as the representative. Whatever method you use to determine the representative, it is important that it be consistent for all the classes. Once the representative is selected, multiply it by the frequency of the class. In some situations you may find that the calculation of the grouped mean varies slightly from the ungrouped mean. When using the midpoint method, there may be a slight difference between the two means due to *grouping error.* This is because the class midpoint represents the midpoint of the class interval, not necessarily its mean. If you use the mean as a representative for each of the classes, you would be consistent with your original calculation. The following exercise demonstrates this point.

You try:
Using the Weighted Mean Method

Earlier you determined the mean for the subgroups of cabernet, chardonnay, and merlot consumers. Each had, respectively, 50, 30, and 20 responses as their frequencies f_i. To demonstrate the technique of using weighted means as the class mark, multiply the means you determined earlier for each of the three types of wine with their corresponding frequencies to determine the mean of the sample, 5.98. The following equation will help you.

$$\bar{x} = \frac{\bar{x}_1 f_1 + \bar{x}_2 f + \cdots + \bar{x}_j f_j}{n} = \frac{\sum_{i=1}^{j} \bar{x}_j f_i}{n}$$

where x_i is the mean of the class

$$x = \frac{\bar{x}_{CS} f_{CS} + \bar{x}_{CH} f_{CH} + \bar{x}_{ME} f_{ME}}{n}$$

$$= \frac{\bar{x}_{CS}(50) + \bar{x}_{CH}(30) + \bar{x}_{ME}(20)}{100}$$

Now make your substitutions, multiply appropriately, sum the numerator, and divide by the sample size, 100. You should get 5.98.

Benefits of Using the Weighted Mean

The weighted or grouped mean has a number of properties that make it extremely important, other than the fact that it represents the central tendency of the distribution. First and foremost, it always exists; that is, it can always be calculated, and it is unique for the distribution. It is reliable, in that it is affected by every element in the sample, and as you conduct and compare multiple samples, you will find a consistency with respect to the mean that helps you approximate μ, the true mean of the population. As you will see shortly, other measures of central tendency do not always have these properties.

Effect of Outliers on the Mean

DANGER!

The mean has only one problem: It is influenced by extremely large or small values that may distort the representative nature of the mean, known as *outliers*. One of the best examples of this problem is in the reporting of salary or real estate information. Suppose the winery has eight employees, including yourself. When reporting the salaries, suppose your salary was initially reported as $46,000 and later changed to $110,000. How would this change effect the mean?

Original salary report, $K

50, 32, 40, 42, **46,** 36, 56, 42

Average = 43,000

when adjusted:

Adjusted salary report

50, 32, 40, 42, **110,** 36, 56, 42

Average = 51,000

This is strange. The average of the adjusted salary group, $51,000, is greater than 6 of the 8 measures of the sample. One really extreme measure has pulled the mean away from the center of the distribution. It has become a poor representative of the central tendency of this distribution. This is the sin of a small sample, and can be rectified in two ways. First is to increase the sample size—that is, when in doubt go for more. Or, eliminate the measure as one that is not representative of the population, and replace it with another randomly selected item. There is no harm in removing the item as long as you are confident that it is not, in fact, representative. This is not easily done, however, when it comes to salary data—management salaries are often outliers. But the example does demonstrate that all scores affect the mean. In such situations, a better representative of the central tendency is one that is not influenced by outliers.

THE MEDIAN—NOT INFLUENCED BY OUTLIERS

The *mean* is the average and the *median* is the score in the middle. To understand the median, think of the entire distribution arranged from the smallest value to the largest. The median of the distribution is the middle value; an equal number of values are above it and below it in the ordered list. The key here is that the list must be sorted first. If perchance the sample has an even number of items, then the median is defined by the average of the two middle values.

By example, suppose that you wanted to calculate the median salary for your company. To calculate the median, arrange the values in ascending or descending order, and determine the middle value (or mean of the two middle values if there is an even number of items in the sample).

Original salary report, $K

32, 36, 40, 42, 42, **46,** 50, 56

Average = 43,000

Median = 42,000

becomes

Adjusted salary report

32, 36, 40, 42, 42, 50, 56, **110**

Average = 51,000

Median = 42,000

If n is odd, then the median is the $(n + 1)/2$ item; if even, it is the mean of the middle scores. Hence, the median is $42,000. The median addresses the problem that arose with the mean when we encountered the outliers in the distribution. For example, consider Figure 7.10. In the original distribution the mean and the median are basically the same, hence, the same line in the figure. If you replace the $46,000 salary with the adjusted salary of $110,000 in the distribution, the median is not affected—but see what happens to the mean. This is the effect of outliers.

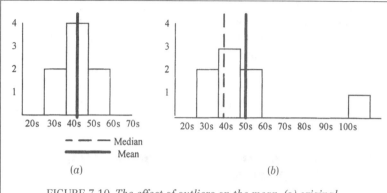

FIGURE 7.10 *The effect of outliers on the mean: (a) original distribution, and (b) revised distribution.*

GRAPHICALLY SPEAKING

Effect of the Moving Mean—Skewness

As you look at the original salary distribution in Figure 7.10 it is clear that mean and the median are close to each other and other scores distribute themselves about this center. But in the second case, the effect of the outlier is to pull the mean away from the median in its direction. When a distribution is pulled in this manner, it is said to be *skewed* in that direction. More on skewness in the next section.

This example also demonstrates why "average" salary is generally reported using the *median* as the measure of central tendency. When it comes to dollar-measured units, like salary or property values, outliers will always affect the mean; therefore, this type of data is often reported with the median because it provides a much better sense of what the central value of the distribution is.

This example also demonstrates how to determine the median when the size of the sample is an even number. In this case, the two middle items have the same value. That makes this calculation too easy! Suppose the second salary of $42,000 was replaced with a salary of $44,000. The ordering of the items would not be affected, but the median salary would be the average of $42,000 and $44,000, which is $43,000.

MEAN OR MEDIAN—WHICH IS BETTER?

The last observation regarding the mean indicated that its weakness is that in small distributions it is influenced by outliers. Again consider the salary distribution, whose median remains $42,000, which is a very good representative of the sample. It is not influenced by the unrepresentative $110,000 salary. The median certainly is a favorable statistic to use, particularly with small skewed samples. But when it comes to large samples, what should you use? Considering the wine consumption survey with 100 sample items, which should you use? Is it easier to calculate the mean or rearrange all the items in ascending order to find the median? Because the mean involves calculations it may be seen as more work than the median, which requires only an appreciation of order. The important point to know is that with large samples the effect of outliers is minimized; hence, both statistics tend to be very close in value. The median may very well be the easiest to determine if doing this manually, but if you are using a computer, the spreadsheet can calculate either—so do them both.

THE MODE—IDENTIFYING THE CLUSTERS

The mode is simply the most frequent item in the distribution, easily found by examining the items and counting individual frequencies. It is cited as a measure of central tendency because in large samples you would expect that the most frequent item would be near or contribute the most to the average. The problem is that the mode may not exist or be unique in a selected sample. Consider the following examples of responses:

Sample	Mean	Median	Mode
1, 2, 3, 4, 5	3	3	Does not exist
1, 2, 3, 3, 4, 5, 6	3.43	3	3, one mode
1, 1, 2, 3, 4, 5, 6	3.14	3	1, one mode
1, 1, 2, 3, 4, 5, 6, 6	3.5	3.5	1 and 6, bimodal

As you can see from the examples, the mode could be a poor indicator of central tendency, and, as a result, is not used extensively. However, it does give rise to the concept of *modality*—that is, the number of "humps" that exist in the distribution. If you consider the responses from the wine survey, they gather around the center; this is referred to as a *unimodal* distribution. If the survey somehow included folks who did not like merlot or drank very little wine, you might get two sections of the distribution where clustering would occur. Cases where there are two humps in the distribution are referred to as *bimodal* (see Figure 7.11).

Before making the mode sound totally useless, it does have its own special application. The mode is a very good tool to employ when conducting a survey using qualitative data such as response scales like

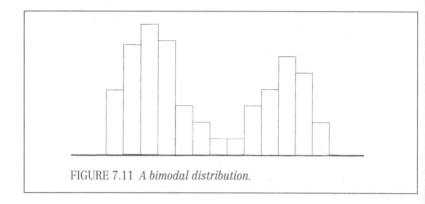

FIGURE 7.11 *A bimodal distribution.*

"Never . . . Always" or "Poor . . . Excellent". It is easy to set up a bar chart for the responses and demonstrate those categories with the greatest number of responses.

DANGER! The example shown in Figure 7.11 represents a case where the advice about making a frequency distribution and histogram is important. Recall the emphasis that you should get to know the data before jumping into calculations. Here's one reason why: Although the mean and the median will exist for this distribution, there is no central tendency; hence, relying on these two statistics for further analysis could lead to a major erroneous business decision.

SKEWNESS

Many distributions behave very much like the wine consumption survey—observations cluster at the mean and taper somewhat symmetrically as you move away from it; that is, the curve is bell-shaped. When extreme values are encountered in a distribution they have the effect of pulling the mean away from the median, toward the left or right side depending on whether the extreme value is above or below the mean. When this occurs, as it does in the salary example, the distribution is *skewed* to the side of the extreme value. *Skewness* refers to the shape of the distribution, as being positively skewed (as demonstrated in Figure 7.12) or negatively skewed.

The direction of the skewness indicates the source of the extreme observations. The extreme observation has the effect of pulling the mean in its direction, thereby causing the skewness.

APPLICATIONS OF DATA ORGANIZATION AND CENTRAL TENDENCY

This section demonstrates how the material in this chapter can be applied to investment analysis and quality-control surveys.

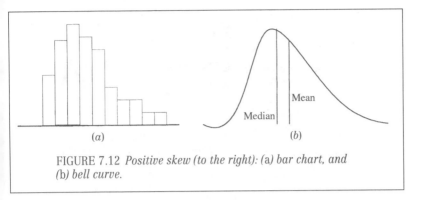

FIGURE 7.12 *Positive skew (to the right): (a) bar chart, and (b) bell curve.*

Investment Analysis

KEY CONCEPT

Your brother-in-law has been in charge of the company's pension portfolio since you instituted it two years ago. He is enamored with technology stocks and has the fund predominately invested in Internet companies. Some of your older employees are questioning this strategy and would prefer a more diversified strategy to protect the company's position in case of a downfall in this niche market.

So, how would you prepare for this kind of decision? What is the decision and what data will help you make it? Assume that the decision is the selection of a fund manager. After conducting interviews, three managers look like they could manage the pension plan. Since all three are competent fund managers, the group has determined that data should be collected to assess performance. A suggestion has been made to collect data on the S&P 500 as well, so you can benchmark the three managers with respect to general market behavior. You decide to collect the annual performance for each manager and the S&P, determined by the percentage of annual growth over each of the past 10 years. The data appears in Table 7.3.

This case is expanded in later chapters, and is fully explored to support a discussion of the efficient frontier. To prepare for this, determine the mean, median, and mode for each manager, along with the S&P 500.

| | | Portfolio Managers | | |
	S&P 500	A	B	C
Mean				
Median				
Mode				

From this basic data, who would appear to be the best choice? Examine Figure 7.13 for some assistance.

TABLE 7.3 PORTFOLIO MANAGER PERFORMANCE DATA

| Year | S&P 500 | Portfolio Managers | | |
		A	B	C
1	0.060	0.080	0.050	0.040
2	0.050	0.060	0.080	0.050
3	0.040	0.040	0.050	0.040
4	0.020	0.050	0.020	−0.030
5	0.060	0.070	0.070	0.060
6	0.070	0.080	0.070	0.060
7	0.090	0.090	0.110	0.140
8	0.110	0.110	0.100	0.120
9	0.110	0.080	0.110	0.130
10	0.120	0.090	0.140	0.140
11	0.130	0.110	0.110	0.130
12	0.170	0.140	0.170	0.230

As you look at the histograms, what additional information becomes apparent? Portfolio manager A has a very narrow interval defining his or her returns, portfolio manager B is a little wider in the returns, and portfolio manager C has a wide interval, indicating that there have been some big winners and a few losing periods as well. What you need is a way to express this numerically, and leads to the next chapter.

 Quality Control

You have been commissioned to perform a study of user satisfaction for the recently developed Cyber Cellars website, where your computer-savvy customers can obtain information about your wine, place orders, and look up recipes that feature your wines. An Internet consultant has warned you that websites can become the company to these customers. That is, they form impressions about the company based upon their interaction with the website. If a website is poorly constructed or too busy, thereby creating access and response time problems, the customers may develop a negative attitude toward your wines. The survey was set up on the website and users had the option to select the survey and complete it. The data in Table 7.4 shows the results from the first 50 respondents. Determine the mean, median, and mode for the three variables: number of attempts to access, response time, and satisfaction (1 = very good; 5 = very poor).

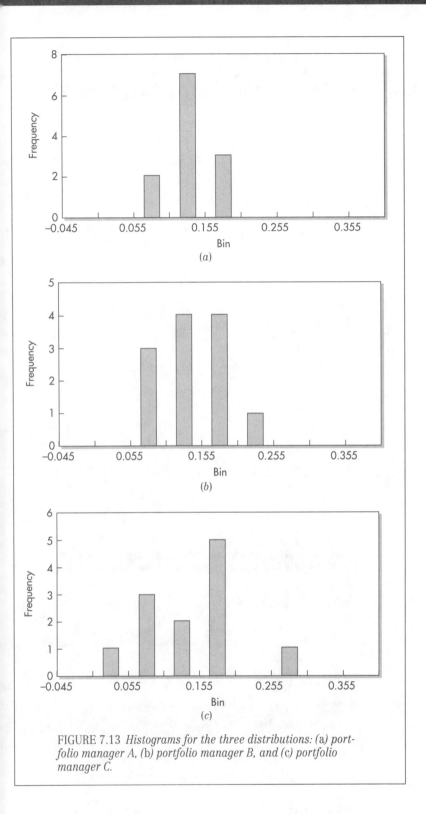

FIGURE 7.13 *Histograms for the three distributions: (a) port-folio manager A, (b) portfolio manager B, and (c) portfolio manager C.*

TABLE 7.4 WEBSITE SURVEY DATA

Item	Access Attempts	Response Time	Site Satisfaction	Item	Access Attempts	Response Time	Site Satisfaction
1	1	9	2	26	2	11	4
2	2	17	5	27	2	18	5
3	3	21	5	28	1	5	2
4	2	19	5	29	1	1	1
5	1	8	2	30	3	23	5
6	3	20	5	31	2	18	5
7	3	23	5	32	1	3	2
8	1	7	2	33	2	13	4
9	3	25	5	34	4	30	5
10	3	20	4	35	1	6	2
11	2	14	4	36	2	19	5
12	2	14	3	37	1	8	3
13	2	18	3	38	2	18	5
14	2	18	3	39	2	15	5
15	1	11	2	40	3	24	5
16	2	14	3	41	2	14	4
17	2	19	5	42	2	13	4
18	2	11	4	43	2	19	5
19	3	22	5	44	3	21	5
20	1	6	1	45	2	13	5
21	2	11	4	46	3	25	5
22	1	10	3	47	1	2	1
23	2	12	4	48	1	9	3
24	2	14	5	49	1	4	1
25	1	4	1	50	2	16	5

	Access Attempts	Response Time	Satisfaction
Mean			
Median			
Mode			

The data analysis should lead to a few of the following conclusions:

- It takes people two attempts, on average, to access the website. Mean, median, and mode are basically the same.

- Response time is a little more than 14 seconds, on average. Again, median and mode are basically the same.

- Unfortunately, people are not inclined to be satisfied with the website. The fact that the mode is 5 indicates that the most frequent response was very poor, yet the mean (3.7) and median (4.0) are close in value.

But if this data has to be explained to management, the best way to do it would be with graphs. Create a frequency distribution and histogram for each of the variables using the following class definitions. The histograms in Figure 7.14 were done using Microsoft Excel, and they are a powerful way to communicate your concerns about the website to management.

	First Class	Last Class
Access attempts	0.5–1.5	3.5–4.5
Response time	0.5–4.5	28.5–32.5
Satisfaction	0.5–1.5	4.5–5.5

On a technical note, the x axis on the satisfaction scale has values 0.5 to 5.5, which might be confusing to a reader of your chart. Once the chart is complete, you can change these values of the bins by typing over their respective values in the Bins column. In the column to the left of the corresponding frequency, type 0, 1, . . . , 5, respectively, for 0.5, 1.5, and so on. The new values will appear on the chart and will be more meaningful in understanding your data.

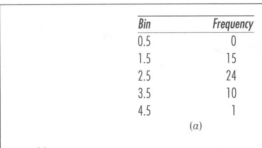

Bin	Frequency
0.5	0
1.5	15
2.5	24
3.5	10
4.5	1

(a)

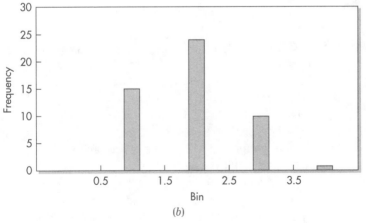

(b)

FIGURE 7.14 *Website survey: (a) values for number of access attempts and (b) histogram.*

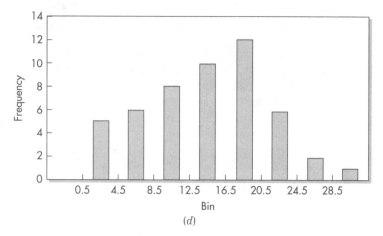

Bin	Frequency
0.5	0
4.5	5
8.5	6
12.5	8
16.5	10
20.5	12
24.5	6
28.5	2
32.5	1

(c)

(d)

FIGURE 7.14 (Continued) *Website survey: (c) values for response time in seconds and* (d) *histogram.*

END POINT

This introduction to statistics emphasizes three important points:

- First, when designing a study, be sure you understand the problem, and verify that your data gathering will produce the information that will help yield the answers. Test the data-gathering mechanism before actually doing the work with the selected sample.

- Second, samples should be free of bias, and sufficiently large that you feel comfortable extrapolating your results from the sample to the population.

- There are several measures of central tendency, but by examining the distribution you can select the best representative for your sample, whether it be the mean or the median. The arithmetic mean lends itself to individual as well as frequency class analy-

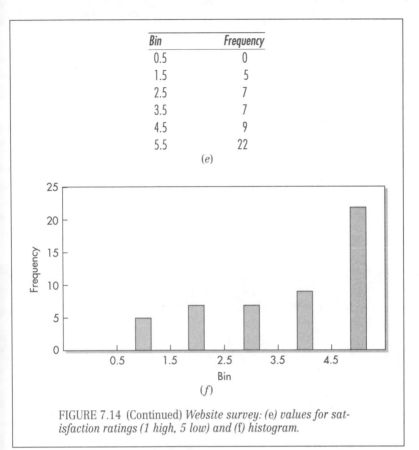

Bin	Frequency
0.5	0
1.5	5
2.5	7
3.5	7
4.5	9
5.5	22

(e)

(f)

FIGURE 7.14 (Continued) *Website survey: (e) values for satisfaction ratings (1 high, 5 low) and (f) histogram.*

sis; it always exists and is the most understood statistic in business.

● The median is applied when you detect skewness in the distribution or the sample is so large that performing all the calculations might be a problem.

So now you have representatives for central tendency. The next question is how the data distributes itself around the mean. What is the significance of a narrow or tight distribution compared to one that is really spread out?

Describing Variation

Two fundamental concepts are core to all the tools employed in descriptive statistics: central tendency and variation. The preceding chapter shows how the central tendency of a distribution can be described using the mean or the median. But how do you measure the *spread* of a distribution? It is important to have a measure, a yardstick, if you will, that can be used for identifying the spread of the data in a distribution and for comparing the degrees of spread between distributions.

For example, consider the three portfolio managers from the last chapter. Portfolio managers A and C are compared in Figure 8.1. The histograms of the distributions of annual performance show a narrow interval for returns for manager A and a wide distribution for manager C. What behavior might we infer about these managers by examining their distributions? We might infer that manager A is conservative and less risky in his or her portfolio selections; possibly there is a covenant that requires that the portfolio hold 50 percent of its assets in bonds. Compare this histogram with that of manager C, who is probably 100 percent invested in equities. He or she is not afraid to take risks for the sake of greater returns, but incurs returns that are all over the place. Sometimes he or she hits those big returns, but other times the portfolio performance is way below the performance of the other managers. This chapter is about trying to put a measure on this spread, or *variation,* and specifically about being able to compare behavior in distributions numerically as well as graphically.

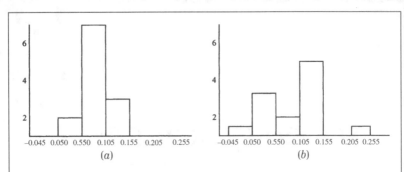

FIGURE 8.1 *Comparing portfolio managers A and C: (a) portfolio manager A, and (b) portfolio manager C.*

DEFINING VARIATION

KEY CONCEPT

If you have ever attended a wine tasting, you know it is a wonderful opportunity to see variation in action. Think about you and your friends gathered around a bottle of wine, exploring its depth, color, bouquet, and so on. Some tasters may agree on certain aspects of the wine, but most likely each will have their own opinion. People's tastes differ, and wine certainly seems to be a place where it happens with vigor. *Variation* is simply the idea that items in the sample are not all the same—they vary. The extent that they vary from the mean is an important property of the distribution, and it can be described numerically. So, with the mean or median as the primary tools for representing the behavior of a sample, we now need a quantitative tool that tells us how data behave in relation to the mean. Are the observations, scores, or responses close to the mean—that is, are they all huddled up around it—or are they spread out, exhibiting values that vary greatly from the mean? All of these questions describe the degree of dispersion or variance in a distribution.

The idea of variance has been in the press a lot recently. The strong financial market has attracted an insatiable interest on the part of small investors who want to invest their pensions in mutual funds. In this last bull market run these funds have grown enormously, primarily from contributions from this group. The variation in portfolio performance is definitely a measure these investors look for when selecting a manager—that is, how much these managers deviate from their average return or the market's.

Variance is associated with risk. If you are close to retirement, then you might not want to see a lot of variation on the part of the fund manager you're considering. This could be cause for angina. Suppose a fund manager averages 12 percent annually, which sounds pretty good for an annual return, but further research shows that the fund also had returns of –2 percent and 22 percent during the past decade (recall portfolio manager C in Chapter 8). As a person closely watching your investment, the closer you get to retirement, the less you want to invest in such an unpredictable (read *risky*) fund. Compare this fund's behavior to that of another manager that shows a 10 percent annual return and, historically, has not fallen below 8 percent, or grown more than 11 percent annually. Because there is less volatility with this conservative approach, it is probably better for your retirement objective given your age. Obviously, if you are younger you might be more attracted to the greater potential return because you can handle the additional risk. As one of the applications shows, when analyzing a fund's performance, you should examine not only the annual returns, but also the degree of variance—the risk of poorer or greater performance.

THE FIRST MEASURE OF VARIATION: RANGE

So, your task is to understand variance. In the previous chapter you used the range to help determine the width of the class intervals for setting up your frequency distribution. The *range* is a measure of the width of the distribution, defined by the difference of the maximum and minimum values in the sample. Consider two tasting samples for the new merlot and zinfandel wines, which you are about to release. Randomly selected visitors to the winery were asked to taste either the merlot or the zinfandel, whichever they preferred, and give it a score between 0 and 100. The scores have been recorded as 2 samples of 11 tasters each. It is clear from the distributions displayed in Figure 8.2 that the merlot tasters have less spread than their zinfandel cousins. This allows us to make a point: Always make a graphic of the data before doing the analytics. It is best to know the general behavior ahead of doing calculations.

Tasting scores

Merlot: 72, 75, 75, 79, 80, 80, 81, 81, 84, 85, 88
Zinfandel: 67, 73, 75, 78, 80, 81, 82, 85, 86, 90, 94

$$\text{Range} = \text{maximum} - \text{minimum}$$

$$\text{Range}_{mer} = 88 - 72 = 16$$

$$\text{Range}_{zin} = 94 - 67 = 27$$

To determine the range for these distributions, simply subtract the minimum value of the variable from the maximum value.

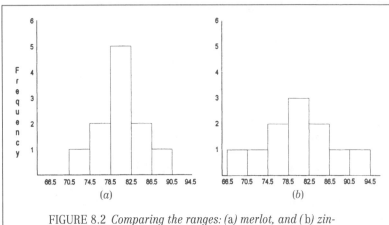

FIGURE 8.2 *Comparing the ranges: (a) merlot, and (b) zinfandel.*

COMPUTER TIP

There may not be a function for calculating the range in the spreadsheet on your software. The way in which you can calculate it is to use the MAXIMUM(range) and MINIMUM(range) functions and take the difference of their values. That is, specify the same data range and employ the maximum and minimum functions to yield the extreme values for the distribution. Then create a formula that subtracts the value in the minimum cell from the cell containing the maximum value of the range.

The merlot has a range of 16, and the zinfandel, 27. The range confirms your scan of the data that the zinfandel tasting varies more in its assessments than that for the merlot. Also, you can see in Figure 8.2 that the span of the distribution of the zinfandel is greater than that of the merlot. Since there is more *variability* with the zinfandel, you might be concerned about further production without more research. You should probably try to ascertain if the problem is in the wine or the fact that the market for zinfandel has been slow in developing.

THE SECOND MEASURE OF VARIATION: AVERAGE DEVIATION

Although you may know the range for each of these samples, the range lacks any information about how the data clusters or spreads apart—it tells us very little about what is going on between those two extreme values. Although the frequency distributions visually show central tendency and any possible symmetry, you do not as yet have a quantitative measure of variability from the mean. So you need a better tool. Certainly, one metric to consider is the distance each value is from the mean. Suppose you were to subtract the mean from each score in the distribution, and calculate the average. Might that lead to a statistic that would tell you how wide or narrow your distribution is? This statistic is called the *average deviation.* To demonstrate this calculation, continue comparing the two tasting samples for merlot and zinfandel.

As Table 8.1 shows, by calculating the individual differences with the mean $(x_i - \bar{x})$ and averaging them, you find that in both cases the value of the average deviation is 0. But wait—shouldn't this be exactly the case? Isn't the mean the exact balance point of a distribution? Therefore, when all the differences of tasting scores less than the mean are summed, they must be exactly equal to the sum of the differences of scores greater than the mean. They basically cancel each other out. So the analysis has done nothing more than confirm the very nature of the mean.

But before you grow restless, there is some insight right here. Note that the $(x_i - \bar{x})$ columns sum to 0; that is, when the mean is subtracted from each tasting score in the sample, it results in a number, and the farther the item is from the mean, the larger the number. And if you compare the $(x_i - \bar{x})$ columns from the two distributions, it is clear that you have more variation in the zinfandel sample. For example, the zinfandel score of 94 yields –13 after taking the difference with the mean, compared to the –8 associated with the maximum score of 88 from the merlot tasting.

TABLE 8.1 DERIVING THE AVERAGE DEVIATION

Merlot Score		Zinfandel Score	
$\bar{x}_{mer} = 80$	$(x_i - \bar{x})$	$\bar{x}_{zin} = 81$	$(x_i - \bar{x})$
72	–8	67	–14
75	–5	73	–8
75	–5	75	–6
79	–1	80	–1
80	0	78	–3
80	0	81	0
81	1	82	1
81	1	85	4
84	4	86	5
85	5	90	9
88	8	94	13
$\dfrac{\sum(x_i - \bar{x}_{mer})}{n} = \dfrac{-19 + 19}{11} = 0$		$\dfrac{\sum(x_i - \bar{x}_{zin})}{n} = \dfrac{-32 + 32}{11} = 0$	

Since the sign seems to be the source of the problem, you need a way to capture this variation without the sign. There are a number of possibilities available to rectify this situation, ranging from using absolute value to taking the square of the difference. Although it could be debated as to which to use, we use the technique of squaring each difference because of its implications with future statistical tools.

A BETTER MEASURE OF VARIATION: VARIANCE

Note that if we were to square each $(x_i - \bar{x})$, the sign would be eliminated as a problem. We define *variance* σ^2 to be the average of the squared deviations from the mean. It is so simple. Note how this process yields the desired analytical result. This is certainly a good test for uniformity, because the smaller the number, the less deviation, and the tighter the scores are to the mean. Take an example from the two distributions. The greatest deviations in the merlot tasting are the scores 72 and 88, which yield a difference with the mean of –8 and +8, respectively. But in the zinfandel tasting the two scores with the greatest deviation are 67 and 94, which yield a difference of –14 and +13, respectively. Now, instead of these scores offsetting each other, they get squared, and the greatest difference still yields the greatest squared value.

Calculation Differences between Samples and Populations

There is a slight difference between the calculation used on a sample from that on the population. The following two equations for the variance of the sample and populations are the squares of the average deviation, but with slightly different variables for the size, n and N. Small n refers to a sample size, and capital N is an indication of the size of the population.

$$s^2 = \frac{1}{n-1} \sum_{i=1}^{n} (x_i - \bar{x})^2 \qquad \sigma^2 = \frac{1}{N} \sum_{i=1}^{N} (x_i - \mu)^2$$

Everything has seemed so logical until this distinction in how to calculate variance. As you look closely, you are probably surprised to see that the sample formula has $(n - 1)$ in the denominator, and not n. This may seem upsetting or even illogical. In sampling, you use the mean from the sample $\bar{x}$, which may be very close to the real mean of the population μ. But the whole point of sampling is that you do not know. Statisticians compensate for this variation from the true mean by calculating the average squared variation with $(n - 1)$ in the denominator. By dividing by a slightly smaller quantity you have a slightly larger variance to compensate for the fact that you are analyzing a sample. Incidentally, if this disturbs you, take comfort in knowing that if your sample is large enough, dividing by n or $(n - 1)$ will not make much of a difference in the result. Think about it—but not too long. Maybe a glass of wine will help. Verify the calculations for the sample variance.

MATHEMATICALLY SPEAKING

Calculating the Variance

The formula is very straightforward, and the key point is whether you divide by N for the population or $(n - 1)$ for a sample.

Table 8.2 and its accompanying calculations display the difference of each score with the mean, the square of that difference, and the respective sums at the bottom of the columns. When calculating the average variation, however, you must make the distinction: Is the set of items being analyzed a sample or the entire population? If you are analyzing the entire population, then you will calculate the true average squared deviation—that is, you will divide by N, the number of items in the entire population.

TABLE 8.2 DERIVING THE VARIANCE

Merlot Score	$(x_i - \overline{x})$	$(x_i - \overline{x})^2$	Zinfandel Score	$(x_i - \overline{x})$	$(x_i - \overline{x})^2$
72	−8	64	67	−14	196
75	−5	25	73	−8	64
75	−5	25	75	−6	36
79	−1	1	78	−3	9
80	0	0	80	−1	1
80	0	0	81	0	0
81	1	1	82	1	1
81	1	1	85	4	16
84	4	16	86	5	25
85	5	25	90	9	81
88	8	64	94	13	169
Sum	0	222	Sum	0	598

$$s_{mer}^2 = \frac{1}{n-1} \sum_{i=1}^{n} (x_i - \overline{x})^2 = \frac{1}{11-1} \sum_{i=1}^{11} (x_i - 80)^2 = \frac{222}{10} = 22.2$$

$$s_{zin}^2 = \frac{1}{n-1} \sum_{i=1}^{n} (x_i - \overline{x})^2 = \frac{1}{11-1} \sum_{i=1}^{11} (x_i - 81)^2 = \frac{598}{10} = 59.8$$

COMPUTER TIP

When calculating the variance of the range of data of your sample, use the VAR (range) function. If the data is the population use the VARP (range) function. They will be slightly different because of the $(n - 1)$ denominator. Make sure you have entered the data in adjacent columns and rows before accessing the function. Do not leave any blank cells in the data range. You might want to use the Function Wizard to select the desired function, and when prompted, highlight the range of data cells to be analyzed.

What Variance Tells You

What do variances of 22.2 and 59.8 tell you about the behaviors in your samples? As you examine the histograms of the two samples in Figure 8.2, you can see that the merlot tasters were fairly consistent in their assessment of the wine. But this is not the case with the zinfandel tasters. Although some of the scores are around the mean, there were a few tasters who really loved it, as evidenced by the high scores, and some who absolutely didn't like it. There is more variability and less consistency in the zinfandel tasting. The tail values (67 and 94) have a greater effect on the variance than those found in the merlot tastings, thereby producing a higher value for the variance.

Variance appears to satisfy your information requirements—it is positive, it employs every item in the distribution, it is unique, and it increases as the distribution spreads out with values further from the mean. Its one deficiency is a rather subtle one; it is in units of the sample squared. For example, if you are analyzing regional sales in dollars, then the variance would be in dollars squared; or, in units of production, it would be bottles of wine squared. In this case, the variance is in units of squared wine-tasting scores. Since the measures of central tendency are all in units of wine scores, then it would be convenient (for reasons you'll toast to later) if the measures of dispersion could be defined in terms of these units as well.

THE ALMIGHTY STANDARD DEVIATION

The standard deviation sounds like a very sophisticated term, but it is a very simple concept and is important at this point in our development of statistics. Simply stated, the *standard deviation* of a distribution is nothing more than the square root of the variance. In taking the square root, you maintain all the analytical and comparative capabilities of the variance that were mentioned previously, but you gain by the fact that the measure is now in units of the original distribution. And it is important to note that when you take the square roots, order is preserved; that is, if $x_1 \leq x_2$ then $\sqrt{x_1} \leq \sqrt{x_2}$. So, for either a sample or the population, you need only take the square root of the variance to reach the success of the standard deviation.

For a sample:

$$s = \sqrt{\frac{1}{n-1} \sum_{i=1}^{n} (x_i - \overline{x})^2}$$

For the population:

$$\sigma = \sqrt{\frac{1}{N} \sum_{i=1}^{N} (x_i - \mu)^2}$$

In the case of the merlot and zinfandel tasting samples, you can calculate the respective standard deviations by taking the square root of the variance calculations performed earlier.

$$s_{\text{mer}} = \sqrt{\frac{222}{10}} = 4.712 \qquad s_{\text{zin}} = \sqrt{\frac{598}{10}} = 7.733$$

Do you get any new information here? Since you have only taken the square root of the variance, the core relationship of dispersion is maintained; that is, the merlot tasters are more tightly clustered around the mean than their zinfandel-tasting brethren. But the beauty of using the standard deviation is that it is an important metric employed in sampling distributions: It can be used to make estimations of the behavior of the population itself based upon what you find from your sample.

COMPUTER TIP

When calculating the standard deviation of the range of data of your sample, use the STDEV(range) function. If the data is the population, use the STDEVP(range) function. As stated earlier with the use of other functions, it is important that the data be located in a range of continuous cells. When using the function you are specifying the entire range for the data, not just referencing the variance cell. To use the functions, access the desired one, then highlight the range of data cells for the range.

A Little Insight, Thanks to Chebyshev

What can you say about the behaviors of the population of merlot and zinfandel consumers based on your samples? There is an intimate relationship between the mean and standard deviation that allows you to estimate the behaviors of the population of merlot and zinfandel. Recall that the means are 80 and 81, and the standard deviations are 4.7 and 7.7, respectively, for merlot and zinfandel.

Note that in Figure 8.3, the merlot distribution ($s = 4.7$) is narrower than that of the zinfandel ($s = 7.7$). You

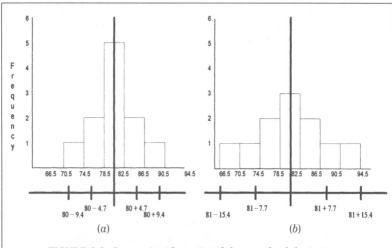

FIGURE 8.3 *Comparing the units of the standard deviation:*
(a) merlot, and (b) zinfandel.

can enhance your understanding of the standard deviation, and appreciate its capability, by considering it a
unit of measure along the horizontal axis. The larger
the standard deviation, as for zinfandel, the wider the
unit and, therefore, the wider the distribution. Each
unit to the left or right of the mean is defined by the
relationship $\bar{x} \pm (n)s$, where s is the sample standard
deviation and $n = \pm1, \pm2, \pm3$, and so on. Remember
that within these units, tasting scores are being collected. Now here's the fascinating part. A Russian
mathematician, P. L. Chebyshev (1821–1895) showed
that in any kind of distribution (skewed or whatever):

- At least 75 percent (or 3/4) of the items in the sample or population will fall within 2 standard deviations of the mean $\bar{x} \pm (2)s$, or $\mu \pm 2\sigma$.

- At least 89 percent (or 8/9) of the items in the sample or population will fall within 3 standard deviations of the mean $\bar{x} \pm (3)s$, or $\mu \pm 3\sigma$.

Continuing with this observation, Chebyshev's rule
can now make a statement about how a randomly
selected taster will evaluate the wine. In the case of the
merlot we could say that at least 75 percent of the
tasters will give the merlot a score between 70.6 and
89.4 [$80 \pm 2(4.7)$]. Because the zinfandel has a larger
standard deviation, we would expect that at least 75 percent of the tasters will give a score between 65.6 and
96.4 [$81 \pm 2(7.7)$]. Although the next chapter covers
probability, it is interesting to note Chebyshev's actual
theorem: The probability that a score will be within k
standard deviations of the mean is $100(1 - 1/k^2)$ percent,
assuming $k > 1$. So, what is so important about all this?

The bridge to probability lies before you. With the
help of Chebyshev's theorem, we can say—with com-

plete independence of the type of distribution—that the behavior of the variable can be predicted. Consider three deviations with the merlot study. We can say that 8/9 or 89 percent of the tasters will give it a score between 66 and 94, derived by 80 ± 3(4.7). Or, the probability that a taster will give the merlot a score between 66 and 94 is approximately 90 percent.

KEY CONCEPT · Dispersion for Grouped Data

Often your analyses will be performed on grouped data, as in the wine purchase survey from the last chapter. How do each of these calculations change when using grouped data? The answer is, very little.

- First, as in the preceding process, you must determine the group or weighted mean.

- Once the mean is found, determine the difference of the group mean with the class mark (midpoint or mean) of each frequency class.

- Square the difference, and then multiply by the frequency of that class f_i.

- The sum of these products yields the grouped variance.

MATHEMATICALLY SPEAKING

Determining Dispersion with Grouped Data

To demonstrate this process, consider the purchase analysis performed earlier, where you determined that the average weekly number of bottles of wine purchased in your sample was 5.98. In Table 8.3, the column f_i refers to the number of observations within that frequency class. The class midpoint is used as the *class mark* x_i. The equation used for this calculation is very similar to the original equation for calculating the variance. But here k refers to the number of frequency classes employed in the distribution and x_i, the class mark.

$$\text{Variance for grouped data} = s^2 = \frac{1}{n-1} \sum_{i=1}^{k} f_i(x_i - \bar{x})^2$$

where $\bar{x}$ is 5.98

The variance for the wine purchase survey is 3.8481 bottles of wine purchased per week, squared. Recall that you have divided by 99 (the 100 total sample items – 1), because this is a sample. To determine the standard deviation for this survey, simply take the square root of the variance.

TABLE 8.3 GROUPED FREQUENCY ANALYSIS FOR VARIANCE

Bottles per Week	Class Mark	$(x_i - \bar{x})$	$(x_i - \bar{x})^2$	f_i	$f_i(x_i - \bar{x})^2$
1.5–3.5	2.5	−3.480	12.110	9	108.990
3.5–5.5	4.5	−1.480	2.190	31	67.902
5.5–7.5	8.5	0.520	0.270	42	11.357
7.5–9.5	10.5	2.520	6.350	14	88.906
9.5–11.5	12.5	4.520	20.430	3	61.291
11.5–13.5	12.5	6.520	42.510	1	42.510

$$s^2 = \frac{1}{n-1}\sum_{i=1}^{k} f_i(x_i - \bar{x})^2 = \frac{1}{99}\sum_{i=1}^{6} f_i(x_i - 5.98)^2 = \frac{380.96}{99} = 3.8481$$

$$s = \sqrt{\frac{1}{n-1}\sum_{i=1}^{k} f_i(x_i - \bar{x})^2} = \sqrt{3.8481} = 1.9617$$

So, the question may occur to you, how do these two statistics compare to the variance and standard deviation if you had not grouped the data? The answer to this question is quite simple now that software can perform the labor-intensive operation. But that is exactly the point as to why you group the data in the first place, so you don't have to do all those extra calculations. The spreadsheet analysis derives 3.41 and 1.85 for the variance and standard deviation, respectively, for the ungrouped analysis. If the means were used as the class marks, the two sets of values would be very close, differing only by rounding.

KEY CONCEPT **THE COEFFICIENT OF VARIATION**

The *coefficient of variation* (CV) is defined to be the ratio of the standard deviation (risk) to the mean (average return), expressed as a percentage. It gives us a way to express the spread of a distribution in terms of central tendency and allows us to compare the variation of different distributions. The advantage of this statistic is that it is a pure number—that is, there are no units—and as a result, it can be used to compare distributions even if they are not samples from the same population. It is a pure dispersion ratio that shows the average in terms of the standard deviation, as defined here:

For a sample

$$CV = \frac{s}{\bar{x}} \cdot 100$$

For the population

$$CV = \frac{\sigma}{\mu} \cdot 100$$

The coefficients of variation for the merlot and zinfandel tasting samples are calculated here:

$$CV_{mer} = \frac{4.712}{80} \cdot 100 = 5.89\%$$

$$CV_{zin} = \frac{7.733}{81} \cdot 100 = 9.55\%$$

So, what does this mean? Since the denominators are approximately the same, the factor that is driving the different CVs is the numerator, the standard deviation. Recall that the zinfandel has more spread in its sample, while the merlot is far more uniform in its assessments. You can see that compared to the merlot tasting, the zinfandel tasting is extremely diverse. One might conclude that the merlot tasters have come to know their wine, whereas with zinfandel, the population is quite mixed in its appreciation relative to the merlot tasters. Hence, there may be more risk in expanding production into the zinfandel market than into the merlot market.

There is a slightly different way of using these two statistics, mean and standard deviation, with the concept of risk and reward. Instead of looking at their ratio, consider them as a set of ordered pairs on a two-dimensional axis. This exciting interpretation of reward to risk has been applied to portfolio management—comparing different portfolios to determine a ranking with respect to units of return to risk. This is the subject of one of the applications later in this chapter.

APPLICATIONS OF DATA VARIATION

This section demonstrates how the material in this chapter can be applied to investment analysis, portfolio management, and quality control analysis.

KEY CONCEPT — Investment Analysis

Upon further analysis, each of the portfolio managers has given you more information on how they construct their portfolios. Specifically, portfolio manager A keeps 50 percent of the portfolio's assets in bonds, portfolio manager B requires that only 25 percent of the portfolio be invested in bonds, and portfolio manager C invests totally in equities. Some of the employees are concerned about risk and would like to make sure that whoever is selected will be more risk averse to protect the pension portfolio. How will the mean and standard deviation help?

So now risk is part of the decision. Based on the analysis of central tendency from the previous chapter, you could have selected portfolio manager C because he or she returned the best average return over the 12 years in which data was collected. But how will the decision change if performance is measured with respect to risk? The data and the means appear in Table 8.4.

To better understand risk, and be able to make comparisons, determine the variance and standard deviation for each manager, along with the S&P 500. The results are provided to help you check your work, particularly if you are working these problems with a calculator.

		Portfolio Manager		
	S&P 500	A	B	C
Variance	0.001881	0.00077	0.001745	0.004675
Standard deviation	0.04337	0.02774	0.04178	0.06837
Coefficient of variation	50.53%	33.29%	46.42%	73.92%

As you examine your data, you might want to review the three distributions as displayed in Figure 7.13. It is pretty clear from your calculations and Figure 8.4 that the widest distribution is portfolio manager C's, with a standard deviation of 0.06837, and the narrowest, showing the greatest consistency, is portfolio manager A's, with a deviation of only 0.02774. So, when the objective of analysis is risk, portfolio manager A has a

TABLE 8.4 PORTFOLIO MANAGERS DATA AND MEANS

		Portfolio Managers		
Year	S&P 500	A	B	C
1	0.060	0.080	0.050	0.040
2	0.050	0.060	0.080	0.050
3	0.040	0.040	0.050	0.040
4	0.020	0.050	0.020	−0.030
5	0.060	0.070	0.070	0.060
6	0.070	0.080	0.070	0.060
7	0.090	0.090	0.110	0.140
8	0.110	0.110	0.100	0.120
9	0.110	0.080	0.110	0.130
10	0.120	0.090	0.140	0.140
11	0.130	0.110	0.110	0.130
12	0.170	0.140	0.170	0.230
$\bar{x}$	0.0858	0.0833	0.0900	0.0925

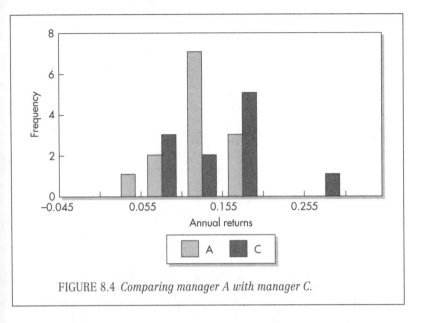

FIGURE 8.4 *Comparing manager A with manager C.*

tighter distribution, thereby displaying behavior that might be termed risk aversive or conservative.

But how can their behaviors be judged against the benchmark of the S&P 500? Consider the calculations from the coefficient of variation. Again, it would seem portfolio manager A is conservative with respect to risk, probably due to the high investment in bonds. Portfolio manager B exhibits the same level of risk as the S&P 500, and portfolio manager C takes on almost 50 percent additional risk. Now a serious question could be posed: Is the size of the return from portfolio manager C worth the additional risk exhibited by his or her performance?

 Risk, Return, and Portfolio Management

One of the more exciting applications of the mean and standard deviation is the concept of risk and reward as applied to portfolio management. Specifically, for a particular collection of securities, what is the graphical relationship of risk to return for each of the three portfolios? (Although this chapter examines only the elementary mathematics of this incredibly interesting theory about risk, it is highly recommended that any reader interested in how risk applies to investment analysis read the entertaining book, *Against the Gods: The Remarkable Story of Risk,* by Peter L. Bernstein [John Wiley & Sons, 1996]. Particularly see Chapter 15, "Efficient Frontier," highlighting the work of Nobel Prize–winning economist Harry Markowitz.) To display the relationship between risk and reward, create an axis as in Figure 8.5, where the horizontal values are

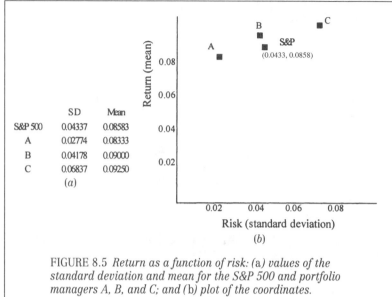

	SD	Mean
S&P 500	0.04337	0.08583
A	0.02774	0.08333
B	0.04178	0.09000
C	0.06837	0.09250

(a)

Risk (standard deviation)

(b)

FIGURE 8.5 *Return as a function of risk: (a) values of the standard deviation and mean for the S&P 500 and portfolio managers A, B, and C; and (b) plot of the coordinates.*

units in risk (the standard deviation) and the vertical values are units of return (the mean). On this axis, graph the three ordered pairs determined by your analysis of the three portfolio managers. To help reference the points, plot the S&P coordinates as well.

How does this simple but insightful representation help you? Use the S&P as a literal benchmark on the graph. Points that plot to the right of the S&P position represent additional risk due to a greater value of the standard deviation. Points to the left represent values where portfolios display less risk. But what is the meaning for positions above or below this point? If a portfolio is above the point representing the S&P, it indicates an average return greater than that determined by the S&P; below, an average that is less. So where do you want your portfolio to lie relative to the S&P or any other portfolio? Right—the answer is northwest—or, for Cary Grant and Alfred Hitchcock fans at least, *North by Northwest.* You want more gain with less risk. But another way to look at it is that if you take on additional risk—that is, you move to the right—then you had better be compensated with a sufficient return to justify that risk. So, to complete this analysis, you might be attracted to portfolio manager B because he or she has a gain greater than the S&P, and at the same time has less risk. So when doing this type of analysis, northwest is the direction you should pursue.

KEY CONCEPT — Quality Control

Response time is always mentioned as a criterion for assessing the interactivity of a website. Poor log-on response time just kills the remainder of the online experience. What is important about this piece of information is that unless product interest is high for the content of the website, the person logging on will kill the inquiry and go to another choice from the search engine. That could be critical to online growth if new users get frustrated before they even get to your site. You've decided to randomly select 25 responses to analyze the behavior of this variable with the intent of making recommendations to management.

Once given the data, you set up a spreadsheet and perform the appropriate analysis. The mean and median response times are 19 and 18 seconds, respectively. There is a positive skew effect because of the extreme values of 32, 33, and 40 seconds. (If this does not make sense to you, go back to Chapter 7 and read about the effect that outliers have on the mean.) But what can you determine from a standard deviation of 7.78 seconds and a mean of 19 seconds?

You collect the data and set up two columns in your spreadsheet applications and secure the descriptive statistics you need.

END POINT

By far the most important measure of dispersion is the standard deviation. Not only is it an indication of the variability of the distribution, but it always exists, is unique to the distribution, is easily applied to both grouped and ungrouped data, and plays an important role in making inferences about the population from the sample data. Once calculated, it can be used to infer the behavior of the population with the use of Chebyshev's rule.

Fundamentals of Probability Distributions

This is a transition chapter in the development of statistics. It is important for a number of reasons.

- First, we change direction from the objective of describing the sample to inferring behavior of the population from the sample.
- Second, we develop the relationship between the frequency of an event and the probability of its occurrence.
- Last, we address the fundamentals of probability with discrete variables to set up the work with continuous variables in the next chapter.

The end of the last chapter stole a peek at probability by applying Chebyshev's theorem to your surveys. But to better understand probability, you need to cover the fundamentals, and the best way to present them is by analyzing the behavior of a discrete variable. We show by means of a simple binomial experiment how a frequency distribution leads to a probability distribution, which, in turn, defines the probability of the events in the distribution. As well, we use the binomial distribution to introduce another important concept, similar to the mean, the expected value of a distribution.

Before getting into probability, you need a better understanding of random variables—by which is meant the things you are measuring in your survey or study—and, in particular how the two types of random variables, discrete and continuous, generate their probabilities. Then we build on the work from the last two chapters to help you understand the basics of a probability distribution.

THE NATURE OF RANDOM VARIABLES

When you conduct a study, experiment, or some analytical procedure, you need to collect data in order to gain information. What do the data look like? If you are doing a financial analysis you may collect data on the closing prices of the security or the S&P 500 index. If you are studying wine vintage quality, you might collect weather characteristics such as temperature, air pressure, and amount of rainfall. The entity or subject on which you are collecting data is termed a *random variable,* such as number of cases of wine sold, number of seconds response time, number of hours billed by temporary workers, or the amount of rainfall on any given day during the growing season. Statisticians use the term *random* to indicate that the outcome, from a set of all possible outcomes, cannot be predicted with certainty.

Let's explore this last statement for a little more understanding. What is interesting is that sometimes you know all the possible outcomes of the variable—for example, rolling a die has six possible outcomes, and a stock price will either go up, go down, or remain unchanged. And sometimes you do not know—for example, the monthly Consumer Price Index, the amount of rainfall on a given day, the true width of a sheet of plywood, or the true amount of wine found in a standard 750-ml bottle. Not only is variability human nature, it is also the nature of machinery. This means when you consider a variable, sometimes the outcomes are clearly known and other times you have to classify the outcomes in sets or classes of potential outcomes. And if the thought of frequency classes comes to your mind right now, your intuition is working just fine.

DISCRETE AND CONTINUOUS VARIABLES

As the examples suggest, statisticians differentiate between two types of random variables: discrete and continuous. Sometimes measuring the variable is a simple exercise in counting, such as the following:

- The number of votes in an election
- The number of even outcomes in tossing a die
- The number of defective units in a given production period

In these situations, the behavior of the variable is defined by counting units, such as votes, cases, or defective units. These variables only take on integer values, 1, 2, 3, . . . ; hence, the variable is termed a *discrete* variable.

Continuous variables, on the other hand, are variables that usually require some kind of measure to determine their value, not necessarily simple counting. As a result, these variables are considered continuous because in reality they can take on any value in some predefined interval—for example, the closing value for the S&P index, or the amount of rainfall for the growing season. There is an important reason for appreciating the difference between these types of variables, and that is that continuous variables lead to distributions that are curves, and probabilities are expressed as areas under those curves. It is easier to understand how this occurs if you first study how probability and frequency distributions behave in the discrete, countable case.

KEY CONCEPT

INTRODUCING PROBABILITY

Probability is related to statistics inasmuch as statistics is used to describe the behavior of a variable—that is, to determine frequencies of events, the average and variance—whereas probability is used to determine the likelihood that an event or set of events will occur from a "universe" of possible events or outcomes. There is a natural relationship between describing the behavior of a variable and asking the probability that a particular value of the variable will occur. Here's a survey that will help you understand the nature of probability.

Based on the merlot–zinfandel tastings, the data for which follow here, which has the higher probability of occurring: a merlot taster giving the merlot a score of 79, 80, 81, or 82; or a zinfandel taster giving the zinfandel a score of 79, 80, 81, or 82?

Tasting scores
Merlot: 72, 75, 75, 79, 80, 80, 81, 81, 84, 85, 88
Zinfandel: 67, 73, 75, 78, 80, 81, 82, 85, 86, 90, 94

Recall from your analysis in the previous two chapters that you defined a frequency class that contained just those tasting values, 78.5 to 82.5. As done in earlier chapters, the first step is to make a frequency distribution and histogram of the data. See Figure 9.1 to compare the two distributions.

Examining the frequencies in Figure 9.1 for the merlot distribution, you see that 5 tasting scores fall in the interval [78.5, 82.5], while the zinfandel has 3 scores. So, how does this translate into probability? What does your intuition say? First, although you may not get an exact probability, hopefully your intuition says that it is more likely that a randomly selected merlot taster will

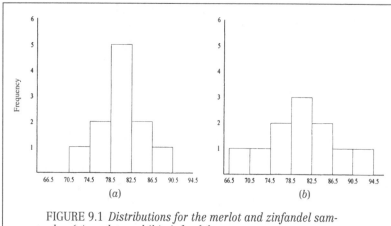

FIGURE 9.1 *Distributions for the merlot and zinfandel samples: (a) merlot, and (b) zinfandel.*

give the merlot a score in that interval than would a randomly selected zinfandel taster. In that you are correct. But can you assign an actual value to the occurrence of each, and then compare?

Defining Probability

A good friend and a highly praised statistics teacher, Professor Donald Pardew of Columbia University, says, "Although there are certain probabilities that are conceptually remote, or even counterintuitive, the majority of probability is just common sense." Hopefully, you are using just that capacity in the problem just posed. We treat it with respect and from the commonsense perspective.

There are a number of ways in which probabilities can be defined. In this first case, we use the *relative frequency* definition. We can define the *probability* of an event to be the ratio of the number of favorable outcomes—that is, a score of 79 to 82—to the total number of possible outcomes. The total number of outcomes that is possible for a given experiment or sample is sometimes referred to as the *sample space*. Since both samples as seen in Figure 9.1 consist of 11 tasters, the probability of getting 79, 80, 81, or 82 for the Merlot tasting is 5/11, which is .4545. Viewing the frequency table, it is pretty clear that the interval containing those scores has the highest frequency, so we would expect it to have a high probability of occurrence, particularly when compared to the zinfandel. In the case of the zinfandel, it is more spread out, with fewer scores in that interval, so common sense would suggest a smaller probability. Indeed, only 3 tasters rated it one of those 4 scores, resulting in a probability of 3/11 or .2727.

Probability of a Discrete Random Variable

Since the behavior of a variable can be either discrete or continuous, it is natural to ask how probabilities are determined as a function of the type of variable. Our method: Consider the probability of the discrete variable, learn from it, and enjoy the continuous case after. You might have encountered probability and counting events back when you were in elementary school, when you flipped coins or rolled a die with a group of friends. (By the way, this is not meant to be any reflection on your childhood.) As you figured out very quickly, probability is found by counting the favorable outcomes in the sample space and dividing by the total number of outcomes. You never used that terminology, but that is what your experience told you. So, by examining the relative frequency of success, the probability of that event can be determined by the following equation. Note that by the nature of dividing by the universe of events, the probability that event A occurs, $P(A)$, must be less than or equal to 1 and greater than or equal to 0, as seen in the examples in Table 9.1.

$$P(A) = \frac{\text{Outcomes favorable for } A}{\text{Total number of outcomes}}$$

You could ask questions such as, "If the coin is flipped three times, what is the probability that you would get all heads or all tails?" Examining the sample space, you see that there are 2 events out of 8, yielding a probability of 1/4.

From Sample Space to Subjective Probability

When you have a discrete variable, as in number of heads when flipping a coin, you know the outcomes; therefore, you can determine probabilities for each of

TABLE 9.1 EXAMPLES OF PROBABILITIES

Occurrence of Event	All Events— Sample Space	Probability of Event
Flipping a head	Head(H), Tail(T)	1/2
Flipping two heads	HH, HT, TH, TT	1/4
Flipping three heads	HHH, HHT, HTH, HTT, THH, TTH, THT, TTT	1/8
Rolling a 3	1, 2, 3, 4, 5, 6	1/6
Rolling an even number	1, 2, 3, 4, 5, 6	$3/6 = 1/2$

the events. Sometimes the probabilities are determined by the sample space, as shown in the examples, or by experience and counting, such as in determining the probability of a part on an assembly line being defective. For example, suppose that a glassmaker knows that on any given day he usually produces 10 defective wine glasses ("seconds") out of 200. So, the probability of a defect is 10 out of 200, or 5 percent, which is based on experience. When probabilities are defined this way it is referred to as *subjective* probability.

Determining Probability from a Frequency Table

But how do you work with a sample? As you saw in the merlot and zinfandel wine tastings, there is a distribution of survey results, which should, in some manner, relate to the probability that a tasting will receive a certain score. In either case it should be unlikely that a taster would give either wine a score of 100 (although possible), and far more likely that the taster would give a score in the low 80s. As you will see shortly, there is an intimate relationship between the frequency distribution of the variable and probabilities of the values belonging to that variable. Just as a frequency distribution counts the number of occurrences for each value of the variable, so a probability distribution defines the relationship between the values of the variable and their corresponding probability. This can best be explained with a coin example and an understanding of a binary variable.

 The Discrete Binomial Variable

CONCEPT   A binomial random variable is a discrete random variable where there are only two outcomes: success or failure, acceptable or defective, like or dislike, yes or no, and so on. Sometimes these experiments are referred to as *binomial* or *Bernoulli trials,* named after Jakob Bernoulli (1654–1705), who, like the other Bernoullis, was fascinated by games of chance—that is, probability. The use of the word *trials* in this sense indicates that the experiment is repeated often. This tool is often used to test a product's acceptance in the market. In marketing you may conduct preference surveys, asking participants whether they watch a particular television episode, use a certain dishwashing product, or prefer a particular wine to another. In this type of experiment you create a sample by repeating the same trial with many participants. There are four requirements for using a binomial model:

● Each trial is identical, and there are only two outcomes.

- The outcome is random.
- If one of the outcomes occurs, then the other cannot. This is the mutually exclusive rule—they can't possibly occur together.
- The probability is the same for each trial. This is the independence rule—the result of one trial does not affect another.

How do these requirements actually translate to a business situation? Certainly, preference surveys are obvious. On an operations level, this model might be used in acceptance testing where, based on a sample, a supplier's shipment will either be accepted or rejected (the two mutually exclusive outcomes). When judging a shipment's suitability from the supplier, you may randomly select items from the shipment, determine if each one is defective or not, and, based upon the number of defects, accept or reject the shipment. We explore this usage through hypothesis testing.

Setting Up the Experiment

The objective of the next few sections is to explain the binomial distribution and use it to define and explain the use of the term *distribution*. To help, we return to our experiment in coin flipping. Suppose you flip a coin and record the outcome as a head or a tail (this is your trial). You then repeat this experiment four times. The random variable is the number of heads observed. It is binomial in nature because each individual trial has the same probability of being a head, namely 1/2—the result can only be a head or a tail, and the result of one flip does not alter the probability of occurrence on any sequential flip. So the conditions are satisfied.

Determining Probability from Frequency Analysis

As you did this earlier, you could determine the sample space and solve for favorable occurrences. If you spend a moment you will determine that there are 16 possible events in this sample space, ranging from 4 heads (HHHH) to 4 tails (TTTT). Hence, the outcomes are known and probabilities can be determined by the relative frequency of the particular outcome to the total number of outcomes.

In examining the sample space or using your common sense, you can see that the most likely value of the random variable "number of heads showing in a flip of 4 coins" is 2. Figure 9.2 shows the frequency distribution, and verifies that even with a small number of flips there is some central tendency, which implies that mean and variance lie ahead.

Event	Possible Outcomes	Frequency
0 heads	TTTT	1
1 head	HTTT, THTT, TTHT, TTTH	4
2 heads	HTTH, HTHT, HHTT, THTH, THHT, TTHH	6
3 heads	HHHT, HHTH, HTHH, THHH	4
4 heads	HHHH	1

Since you have the frequency data available, how do you determine the probability of a particular outcome? The probability of getting 2 heads out of 4 trials is 6 favorable events divided by 16, resulting in 6/16 or .375.

Determining Probability from the Binomial Distribution

By means of counting from the total number of outcomes, you have determined the probability of 2 heads to be .375, but now we want to introduce the concept of a *function*—that is, a relationship between an outcome and its probability of occurring. There are 5 outcomes for this experiment, namely, 0 (no heads) to 4 (all heads). Now this is important; the use of the term *distribution* in statistics means that the collection of events defined by it satisfies two requirements:

● First, the set consists of events representing all the possible outcomes of the discrete variable—in this case, the number of heads when flipping a coin four times.

● Second, for each outcome in the set there exists the corresponding probability of its occurring.

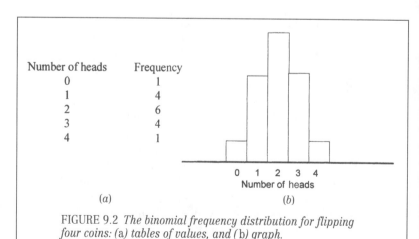

Number of heads	Frequency
0	1
1	4
2	6
3	4
4	1

(a)

(b)

FIGURE 9.2 *The binomial frequency distribution for flipping four coins:* (a) *tables of values, and* (b) *graph.*

How the Distribution Leads to Probability

Here is where it gets interesting: The binomial distribution has its own unique way of generating the outcomes and their corresponding probabilities that allows us to solve the problem of showing only two heads. There is a mathematical way of finding the probability of a number of successes x_i out of n repeated trials, given the probability p of success on a single trial and the probability of nonsuccess $q = 1 - p$. This equation makes use of factorials and some simple calculations with exponents. See Chapter 13 if you're not sure how to use either of these calculations.

The probability of x occurring in n trials is

$$p(x) = \binom{n}{x} p^x (1 - p)^{n - x}$$

$$\text{where} \quad \binom{n}{x} = \frac{n!}{x!(n - x)!}$$

We refer to this function as $p(x)$, and use it to define the *probability* of the occurrence, as opposed to the *frequency* of the occurrence as noted in the frequency distribution $f(x)$ in previous chapters. To see how this equation $p(x)$ works, find the probability of showing 2 heads out of 4 repeated flips (trials). You know that the probability p of success on any one flip is 1/2, $(1 - p)$ is also 1/2, and the total number of trials n is 4. Now, success is 2 heads; therefore, $x = 2$. Here we go:

$$p(x) = \binom{n}{x} p^x (1 - p)^{n - x}$$

$$\text{becomes} \quad p(2) = \binom{4}{2} .5^2 (1 - .5)^{4 - 2}$$

$$p(2) = \frac{4!}{2!2!} .5^2 .5^2 = \frac{4 \times 3 \times 2 \times 1}{2 \times 1 \times 2 \times 1} (.25)(.25)$$

$$= 6 \times .0625 = .375$$

The probability of showing 2 heads from 4 flips is .375, which, in fact, you found earlier by examining the frequency table. But here is the fascinating part: Don't look at the equation as just a number, try to think of it as a generator. And what will this *generate,* you ask? It generates the distribution of probabilities for all the values of the variable, from 0 to 4 heads. Here's how. Consider the results of Table 9.2, which assumes four flips of the coin.

You can verify with the classical definition that all these values are exactly correct and were generated by this special relationship $p(x)$, called the *binomial probability function.* Table 9.2 shows why this relationship is

TABLE 9.2 BINOMIAL DISTRIBUTION FOR $N = 4$ AND $P = 1/2$

Outcome x heads	Formula	Simplified	$p(x)$
$p(0)$	$f(0) = \binom{4}{0}.5^0(1 - .5)^4$	$(1)(.5)^0(.5)^4$	.0625
$p(1)$	$f(1) = \binom{4}{1}.5^1(1 - .5)^3$	$(4)(.5)^1(.5)^3$	.2500
$p(2)$	$f(2) = \binom{4}{2}.5^2(1 - .5)^{4-2}$	$(6)(.5)^2(.5)^2$	.3250
$p(3)$	$f(3) = \binom{4}{3}.5^3(1 - .5)^1$	$(4)(.5)^3(.5)^1$	.2500
$p(4)$	$f(4) = \binom{4}{4}.5^4(1 - .5)^0$	$(4)(.5)^4(.5)^0$	.0625

called a *probability distribution,* because the probabilities are distributed across all the different values of the success variable, from 0 to 4 heads.

Relationship between the Frequency and Probability Distributions

A *probability distribution* is defined as a relationship that shows the correspondence between the outcome and its probability (see Table 9.2 for the table format or Figure 9.3 for the graph format). The points on the graph correspond to the probability that a particular event will occur. Since it is a correspondence, it is often referred to as a *probability function.* Note the difference in the vertical axis of the two graphs in Figure 9.3: The frequency distribution measures outcomes, and the probability distribution measures the likelihood of occurrence. You should see a consistency. These are just two different views of the same idea.

Both Table 9.2 and Figure 9.3 clearly show the two requirements for a probability distribution, which is sometimes referred to as the mathematical definition of discrete probability distribution.

- $\sum p(x_i) = 1$ By adding the probabilities in the last column of Table 9.2, it should be clear that the sum of the probabilities for all possible outcomes of the variable is 1.

- $0 \leq p(x_i) \leq 1$ Individual probabilities take on a value between 1 and 0.

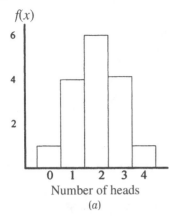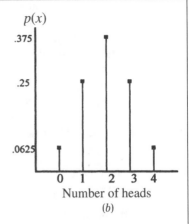

FIGURE 9.3 *Frequency distribution and probability distribution for flipping four coins: (a) frequency distribution, and (b) probability distribution.*

Observe that the "impossible event," such as rolling a 7 with a single standard die, has a probability of 0. If the probability of an impossible event is 0, then the probability of the certain event, such as flipping a head or a tail, is 1. Although this last point is probably obvious, it requires stating because we want to relate all this back to the normal curve, which to be a valid model must satisfy the requirements of a probability distribution—namely, the total area under the curve must be equal to 1. If this can be shown, then a partial area under the curve can be interpreted as the probability of an event—that is, a value between 1 and 0 with the normal distribution.

KEY CONCEPT

EXPECTED VALUE AND THE MEAN

As you can see from Figure 9.3, the greatest probability (the value .375 of the $p(x)$ axis) is found at the value of $x = 2$, which corresponds to the event of showing 2 heads. The corresponding frequency is the greatest at that point, and therefore it is a point of *central tendency*. Might there be some significance of this value of the variable with respect to the distribution?

Suppose you were asked to repeat this experiment many times—what would you conclude would be the most frequent solution? The question is very simple: "In counting heads, what is the most likely outcome for the four flips?" There is an expectation that the most frequent score over the period of flipping and recording would be 2 heads.

How does this relate to the concept of the mean? The mean of a discrete random variable is termed *expected value $E(x)$*—it is what you expected—and is calculated by summing the products of each outcome in the distribution and its corresponding probability of occurrence. This may sound strange, but recall that when introducing the mean in the descriptive sense earlier, you added each item to calculate the average. So it must be here as well, that each value in the distribution must be accounted for in calculating the mean. For the sake of simplification, you can omit the index on the summation with the understanding that all events x_i will be calculated.

$$\text{Expected value (outcome } x) = E(x) = \sum x_i p(x_i)$$

Since discrete variables are countable variables, you can construct a product relationship with the value of the variable and its probability. In the equation for $E(x)$, x_i refers to each value of the variable (outcome), and $p(x_i)$ is its corresponding probability. For example, for the occurrence of only 1 head, x_i is 1 and $p(x_i)$ is .25. The trick to remember is that this product must be performed for all values of the variable. Also, note the use of μ instead of $\bar{x}$ in some of the equations. The population mean is used because you are working with a discrete random variable and, hence, know all the outcomes in this experiment; it is not a sample.

What will help enormously right now is for you to remember what you observed earlier when asked about what you thought would be the most frequent occurrence when flipping the four coins. Recall that you answered two heads. Now watch as we derive the expected value for the four-coin problem, which mathematically is very similar procedurally to calculating the weighted mean.

MATHEMATICALLY SPEAKING

Calculating Expected Value (the Mean)

$$\mu = E(x) = \sum_{i=1}^{n} x_i p(x_i) \quad \text{becomes} \quad \mu = E(x) = \sum_{i=1}^{4} x_i p(x_i)$$

$$\mu = E(x) = 0(.0625) + 1(.25) + 2(.375) + 3(.25) + 4(.0625)$$

$$\mu = E(x) = 0 + .25 + .75 + .75 + .25$$

$$\mu = E(x) = 2$$

In other words, the expected value of the number of heads when flipping four coins over a long period of time is the average or mean value of two heads. Isn't this the answer you expected? It is the value of the variable at which central tendency occurs. It is the variable with the highest probability of occurring, .375.

And what of variance, you ask? Recall from the previous chapter that variance is found by squaring the difference between the mean and each item in the distribution. Here again, it is related to the average square of the deviations from the mean, but in the following manner. As before, the standard deviation σ is the square root of the variance.

For variance:

$$\sigma^2 = E(x - E(x))^2 = \sum_{i=1}^{n} (x_i - \mu)^2 \, p(x_i)$$

For standard deviation:

$$\sqrt{\sigma^2} = \sigma$$

MATHEMATICALLY SPEAKING

Calculating the Variance and Standard Deviation

Table 9.3, generated with the use of Excel, demonstrates the process whereby the variance and standard deviation are calculated for the experiment of flipping four coins. Note that the fourth column determines the mean $\mu = 2.00$, which is then used for the calculation for variance in the last column, $\sigma^2 = 1.0000$.

$$\sigma^2 = E(x - \mu)^2 = \sum (x_i - \mu)^2 \, p(x_i)$$

$$= .25 + .25 + 0 + .25 + .25 = 1$$

$$\sigma = 1$$

Shortcuts for Binomial Distribution

Now that you have used the general methods for finding expected value and variance for the distribution of a discrete variable, here are a few shortcuts that are employed later when we show how the binomial distribution can be approximated with the normal curve. The variables are defined as they were originally; n is the number of trials, p is the probability of success on

TABLE 9.3 CALCULATING VARIANCE AND STANDARD DEVIATION

Number of heads x_i	Frequency of event	$p(x_i)$	$x_i p(x_i)$	$(x_i - \mu)^2 p(x_i)$
0	1	0.0625	0.00	0.2500
1	4	0.2500	0.25	0.2500
2	6	0.3750	0.75	0.0000
3	4	0.2500	0.75	0.2500
4	1	0.0625	0.25	0.2500
sum	16	1.0000	$\mu = 2.00$	$\sigma^2 = 1.0000$

a single trial, and $q = (1 - p)$ is the probability that there won't be success. Recall that in the example you flipped the coin 4 times and had probability of success equal to .5.

Mean	*Standard deviation*
$\mu = np$	$\sigma = \sqrt{npq}$
$\mu = 4(.5)$	$\sigma = \sqrt{4(.5)(.5)}$
$\mu = 2$	$\sigma = \sqrt{1} = 1$

APPLICATIONS OF THE BINOMIAL DISTRIBUTION

This section demonstrates how the material in this chapter can be applied to estimating customer volume or event attendance.

 Estimating Customer Volume

Here's how the expected value approach to a problem can be helpful. Suppose you manage a computer training center at Micro Memories, and every month you produce a mailing that goes to the top 100 businesses (in terms of number of employees) in your area. At the end of the month you tally the number of attendees for your sessions. Instead of listing all the numbers of attendees for each day, you create a table that displays the same information but in slightly different manner (see Table 9.4).

The grouping methodology is by number of trainees. To create a frequency distribution, you count the number of days that x number of trainees attended. For example, twice over the 20 days there were 6 attendees. The probabilities for the values of the variable,

TABLE 9.4 ANALYZING COMPUTER TRAINING ATTENDANCE

Trainees/ days	Frequency, days	$p(x_i)$	$x_i p(x_i)$	$(x_i - \mu)^2 p(x_i)$
6	2	0.100	0.60	0.4623
7	3	0.150	1.05	0.1984
8	6	0.300	2.40	0.0068
9	8	0.400	3.60	0.2890
10	1	0.050	0.50	0.1711
Σ	20	1.000	$E(x) = 8.15$	$\sigma^2 = 1.1275$

Standard deviation of the sample:
$$\sigma = \sqrt{\sigma^2} = \sqrt{1.1275} = 1.0618$$

trainees/day, is determined by the ratio of the frequency to the total number of days, 20. From the analysis you can see that the expected value—in this case, the number of attendees in a training session on any given day—is 8.15 attendees, with a standard deviation of 1.0618 persons. This process is not that different from making frequency distributions as you did in earlier chapters.

As Figure 9.4 shows, these calculations do not require that you have nice symmetrical distributions. In fact, knowing the information that you have just derived, you could use Chebyshev's rule to determine characteristics of anticipated class sizes. For example, you know that at least 75 percent of class sizes will fall within 2 standard deviations of the mean. To make sure you can support at least 75 percent of the class sizes, then how many PCs must be in the room, assuming 1 microcomputer per participant?

Estimated attendance for at least 75% of the class sizes

$$\mu + 2\sigma = 8.15 \pm 2(1.0618)$$

$$= 8.15 \pm 2.1236 = 6.02 \quad \text{to} \quad 10.27$$

Since the mean is 8.15, then the interval where at least 75 percent of the activity will fall is class sizes between 6.02 and 10.27. So, to make sure people aren't turned away, there must be at least 11 microcomputers in the classroom. If you wanted to assure at least 89 percent, then Chebyshev would tell you to go out three standard deviations from either side of the mean. The point is that despite the lack of symmetry in your distribution,

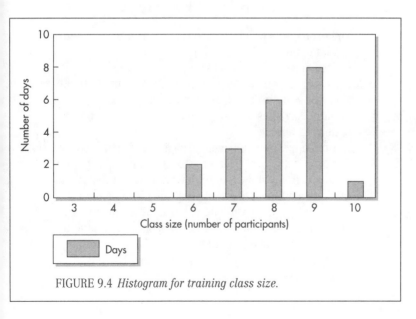

FIGURE 9.4 *Histogram for training class size.*

you are still able to apply probability to the problem. That is, on any given day, there is at least a 75 percent chance that at a minimum 6 to 11 people will show up for classes.

This "crazy" value 8.15 warrants a cautionary note: The expected value is defined by the distribution and is not necessarily an element in the sample space. In this case, you will not see 8.15 people one day in the classroom, yet for planning purposes it is a perfectly acceptable number from which to estimate.

Binomial Experiment—Tasters to Purchasers

Suppose you know from experience that at any given tasting the probability that any one person will buy your wine after tasting it is 80 percent. On a Saturday afternoon 10 people stand around your table tasting the wine. What is the probability that 8 out of the 10 participants will purchase a bottle of your wine? In determining the probability, consider the general formula, make your substitutions, and calculate. Oh, yes—you will need your calculator. What is p, the probability of success on a single trial, and $q = 1 - p$, the probability for nonsuccess?

$$p(x) = \binom{n}{x} p^x (1 - p)^{n - x}$$

$$\text{becomes} \quad p(8) = \binom{10}{8} .8^8 (1 - .8)^{10 - 8}$$

$$p(8) = \frac{10!}{8!2!} .8^8 (.2^2) = \frac{10 \times 9 \times 8!}{8! \times 2 \times 1} (.1678)(.04)$$

$$= 45 \times .006712 = .302$$

The probability of 8 wine tasters purchasing your wine is a little more than 30 percent.

If the probability falls to 60 percent, then what does that say about the probability that 8 out of 10 participants will purchase your wine? What does your intuition say? Yes, it should be less—a lot less, approximately 12 percent.

But suppose the problem is slightly different. If there is a probability of 80 percent that any participant in the tasting will buy the wine, then what is the probability that at least 8 people out of 10 at the tasting will buy the wine? We do not intend to solve this problem right here, but instead mean to show that solving it could be a very quantitatively cumbersome problem. It requires that you solve for 8, 9, and 10 successes. There is a better way—look to the next chapter.

END POINT

Although this is a short chapter, it serves a very important purpose in your understanding of probability. It establishes the important connection between descriptive and inferential statistics by showing that frequency distributions and probability distributions are really the same thing. You have seen the importance of a probability function or distribution as a generator of the probabilities. The important characteristics of a probability function are that the probabilities must sum to 1 and each individual occurrence has a probability between 0 and 1. But what would happen if the binomial distribution had a very large n? In the next chapter you learn that when the binomial sample is large, you are able to use the normal distribution to approximate the behavior of the variable, thus making calculations easier and less time consuming. Finally, you have seen the concept of expected value, a new way of thinking about the mean.

CHAPTER 10

Probability and the Normal Distribution

This is the most important chapter in the development of statistics because so much of the decision making in statistics is based on the normal distribution. The previous chapter developed probability from the perspective of the discrete variable, in order to define the relationship called the probability distribution. Now we take this to the next level, to the continuous variable. Although there are many distributions defined with continuous variables, we concentrate on the normal curve because we can get a lot of business decision making from it and still maintain a general approach.

What makes the normal distribution so special? Is there some benefit that requires your attention to this most famous of probability distributions? Of course, the answer is *yes*—but *why?* This chapter is where you will learn to take the mean and standard deviation from descriptive statistics and use them to make inferences about the behavior of the population. That is, the mean and standard deviation not only describe behavior of the sample; they define the very characteristics of the normal distribution, allowing us to infer behavior to the entire population. Yes, this chapter is about inference. Based on the work of the preceding three chapters we turn fully to inference—what can be said of the population, and with what level of confidence. The normal distribution is the vehicle for this analysis, including hypothesis testing, acceptance sampling, confidence intervals, and more.

PERSPECTIVE ON THE NORMAL DISTRIBUTION

It was somewhere in one of your educational experiences or in dealing with the company's human resources group that you first encountered the famous bell-shaped curve, also known as the *normal curve* or *normal distribution,* the pillar of statistics and inference. In education, you might have heard in a class that "the grades in this course are normally distributed," which might not have made much sense to you in the beginning of the class but might have upset you by the end of the class. In business, you might have heard that the number of sick days a person takes, employee productivity, or numbers of returned units are normally distributed. What are the characteristics of a normal distribution? Simply that the distribution is unimodal— that is, there is a single hump, there is an average for the activity, and most grades, customer returns, wine preferences, and so on, cluster somewhat *symmetrically* around that average. As you move away from the average in either a positive direction (greater than the average) or negative direction (less than the average) there are fewer items—that is, it's leaner out in the tails of the distribution. Now, to be clear, other distributions do this as well, but the study of their various applications is beyond the scope of this book.

 The Evolution of the Normal Curve

Let's demonstrate how the normal distribution fits with our current analyses. Suppose you conduct another wine tasting experiment consisting of 30 participants in another location to determine their assessment of the new merlot. The first task is to group the data and look at how it is distributed. It certainly could be "normal." So, we make the assumption that wine tasting is normally distributed. The increased sample size allows us to show in Figure 10.1 how the frequency table leads to the normal curve. It is unusual that the data would be so *perfectly* symmetrical, but we permit that to happen so that we can show how the normal curve evolves. Because of the increased sample size of 30, the class width was reduced from 4 units to 3.

The histogram of this frequency distribution shows that the mean is in the middle class and that that there is less frequency as you examine tasting scores away from the mean. If you construct a *smooth* curve by connecting the midpoints of each of the frequency classes, the result would look like the famous bell-shaped curve, or normal curve (see Figure 10.2).

As you conduct studies in business, often the data

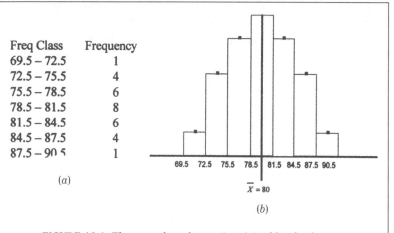

Freq Class	Frequency
69.5 – 72.5	1
72.5 – 75.5	4
75.5 – 78.5	6
78.5 – 81.5	8
81.5 – 84.5	6
84.5 – 87.5	4
87.5 – 90.5	1

(a)

(b)

FIGURE 10.1 *The second merlot tasting:* (a) *table of values, and* (b) *frequency distribution histogram.*

will behave like this. They may not be nicely symmetrical, but they will be unimodal, and frequencies will increase around the mean and decrease away from it. Accept on faith that you are allowed to "connect the dots" and smooth out the curve, hence making it look like a normal distribution.

But where is the connection with continuous variables? Recall that values of continuous variables occur as a result of measure, not of counting, and therefore have an infinite range of potential values. The nature of the infinite number of values within the range defined by the distribution produces a curve and, therefore, a continuous distribution. One of the reasons we focus on the *normal distribution* is that when distributions appear bell-like, you can use the analytical procedures from this distribution, even if the variable is not continuous itself. What we show next is that even discrete distributions can be "normal-like," and, as a result, analyzed with the normal distribution.

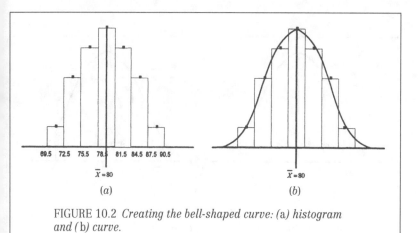

FIGURE 10.2 *Creating the bell-shaped curve:* (a) *histogram and* (b) *curve.*

How the Normal Curve Model Works

The beauty of the normal curve is that it is a model which explains in a percentage form how many scores, observations, and so on, lie between intervals defined by the standard deviation with respect to the mean. Many probability distributions do this, but the normal distribution ripples through so much of statistics that you must have a good understanding of it.

Here's how the model works. For the sake of the example, what could you say about the population of merlot drinkers based upon this sample? First, what do you know about the normal curve? As seen in Figure 10.3, it is symmetrical and has units defined in terms of the standard deviation. Essentially, it translates a frequency distribution into a scale where units are expressed in multiples of the standard deviation. When data can be approximated by a normal distribution, predefined percentages of the data are located in an interval whose end points are one or more standard deviations on either side of the mean. For example, 68 percent of the data are defined in an interval 1 standard deviation on either side of the mean, $(\bar{x} \pm 1s)$. Going one additional deviation from the mean, $(\bar{x} \pm 2s)$, determines an interval where a little more than 95 percent of your data are located. Both of these approximations are a major improvement over Chebyshev's rule.

Figure 10.3 shows how to apply the model to your wine tasting survey. The results from the sample indicate a mean score of 80 with a standard deviation of 4.5. Because you assume that merlot tasting approximates a normal distribution, you can estimate that 68 percent of people tasting your Merlot gave it a score between 75.5 and 84.5, defined by $80 \pm (1)4.5$; or 95 percent gave it a score between 71 and 89, defined by

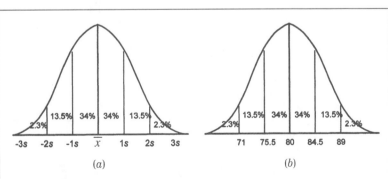

FIGURE 10.3 *Creating the bell-shaped curve:* (a) *standard normal distribution, and* (b) *merlot tasting distribution.*

80 ± (2)4.5. Now that you have an understanding of how this will be used, we'll relate it to probability.

There is a natural question at this point in your understanding: If 68 percent of the scores will be in the interval between 75.5 and 84.5, what is the probability that a randomly selected score will be in that interval? Hopefully, your intuition says 68 percent, or 68 chances out of 100. Or, what is the probability that a score will be in the frequency class [78.5, 81.5] defined earlier in the frequency table found in Figure 10.3? Or, since there are fewer scores out in the tails, what is the probability that an individual will give the merlot a score of 85, 86, or 87, which is defined in the frequency class [84.5, 87.5]? These are not quite so obvious as the first question, but the point should be clear: There is a natural relationship between the statistical frequency of occurrence and the probability of that event. Now you need to develop greater flexibility with it.

MATHEMATICALLY SPEAKING

Plotting the Normal Distribution

The equation that produces the normal curve is pretty complicated and beyond the general scope of our study. But you should realize that, as a function, it behaves as we have stated when given a mean and standard deviation. In any calculation of the normal curve these two values, the mean and the standard deviation, define the characteristics of the curve. The purpose of this section is to prove that, so you will feel comfortable employing it to determine probabilities.

Consider as an example the merlot wine-tasting analysis of the 30 participants, where the mean of the population is 80, and the standard deviation is 4.5. We want to show that by knowing only these two pieces of information, you can generate the curve. We limit the values for x to between 70 and 90 to verify our observations about the nature of the function and behavior of the variable. The function for the curve specified by the normal distribution whose mean and standard deviation are given was developed by a young mathematician, Carl Gauss (1777–1855). As a result, the curve and distribution are also known as the *gaussian distribution.*

As you did earlier, suppose you needed to find the probability that a taster would give the merlot a score of 79, 80, or 81 (i.e, a score in the interval [78.5, 81.5]). To determine the value of $f(x)$ for a given outcome of the variable $x,$ you make the substitution in the following equation:

$$f(x) = \frac{1}{\sigma\sqrt{2\pi}}\, e^{-(x-\mu)^2/2\sigma^2}$$

$$\text{where} \quad \pi = 3.1416$$
$$e = 2.71828$$

For the merlot example, you would substitute the mean (80) and standard deviation (4.5) from your sample into the general equation. You now have the probability function that will generate probability for a value of x. Actually, for a continuous variable you are concerned with ranges and not individual points—for example, the probability that someone will rate the merlot between 78 and 81. More on this after you generate the curve.

$$f(x) = \frac{1}{\sigma\sqrt{2\pi}}\, e^{-(x-\mu)^2/2\sigma^2}$$

becomes

$$f(x) = \frac{1}{4.5\sqrt{2\pi}}\, e^{-(x-80)^2/2(4.5^2)}$$

This may seem very abstract, so let's do a demonstration of how this function becomes a probability function. First, you have been given the two key variables, a mean of 80 with a standard deviation of 4.5. Suppose you want to find the value of $f(x)$ for a score of 82. This could be considered an approximation for the discrete probability case.

$$p(x) = \frac{1}{4.5\sqrt{2\pi}}\, e^{-(x-80)^2/2(4.5^2)}$$

becomes

$$p(82) = \frac{1}{4.5(2.5066)}\, e^{-2/(20.25)}$$

$$p(82) = \frac{1}{11.2798}\, e^{-.0988}$$

$$p(82) = \frac{.9060}{11.2798} = .0803$$

In statistics you would not use the normal curve in this manner; you do not use a continuous function to determine the probability of a discrete event. The purpose of this demonstration is to show you that in fact this curve is real and can be generated from only two parameters, a mean and a standard deviation. Table 10.1 shows the integer values of the variable for the function $f(x)$ between 70 and 90. Don't get upset thinking you should reproduce the data in the table; they were done using a spreadsheet program on a microcomputer. Even doing these on a calculator would be no fun. However, you might try to show that the calcu-

TABLE 10.1 SELECTED VALUES OF THE NORMAL DISTRIBUTION

Score, x	f(x)	Score, x	f(x)	Score, x	f(x)
70	0.007505	80	0.088447	81	0.086492
71	0.011998			82	0.080317
72	0.018256			83	0.070989
73	0.026440			84	0.059721
74	0.036447			85	0.047821
75	0.047821			86	0.036447
76	0.059721			87	0.026440
77	0.070989			88	0.018256
78	0.080317			89	0.011998
79	0.086492			90	0.007505
Sum	0.445985			Sum	0.445985

lation for the mean of 80 is close to .9 as an exercise to verify these values for yourself.

When these values are graphed in Figure 10.4 they show the characteristics of a probability distribution, and this is the main purpose of the exercise. These values were generated by substituting the mean of 80 and standard deviation of 4.5 in the normal equation.

From the data you can ask questions such as, "What is the likelihood that a randomly selected wine taster will give the merlot a score of 79, 80, or 81?" Now, since these scores represent the frequency tallies for the class defined by [78.5–81.5] in the sample, you can look up the distribution and see that 8 scores were tallied in that category. Therefore, by frequency there is a likelihood of 8/30 or .2667. But what of the preceding analysis? Now, for the excitement of what you have done with this normal curve equation, add the results of $f(x)$ for the values 79, 80, and 81:

$$f(79) + f(80) + f(81) = .08649 + .08865 + .08649$$
$$= .26163$$

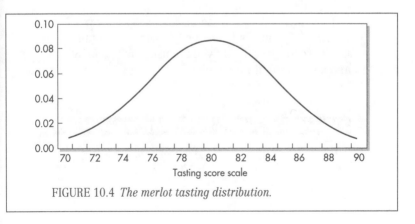

FIGURE 10.4 *The merlot tasting distribution.*

Although this value does not exactly equal the value of .2667, it is close enough to give confidence that you are on the right track to discovering how to apply probability to the frequency distribution of a continuous variable. The real probability is the area under the curve of the probability function between 79 and 81. This is the difference between a continuous distribution (a curve) and a discrete distribution. From this sample you can then estimate that there is approximately a 1 in 4 chance that the entire population will give your merlot a similar positive assessment—and, in turn, possibly buy more of the wine.

The points in Table 10.1 were used in an Excel spreadsheet to create the graph in Figure 10.4. When those points are graphed, the result is a normal curve and you can finally live the joy of the moment—the normal curve really does exist, and you can easily see that it has the following important properties that support its interpretation as a probability distribution:

- The total area under the curve and above the x axis is 1.
- Any individual value of $f(x)$ is between 0 and 1.
- The curve is symmetrical about the mean.
- Frequency decreases as you move away from the mean.
- The characteristics of the curve are determined solely by the mean $\bar{x}$ and standard deviation s.

The importance of the last observation will become evident as you consider more examples and become familiar with the standard deviation as a unit of measure. Earlier it was stated that a percentage of the area under the curve is determined by units of the standard deviation on the x axis. Specifically, you can expect 34 percent of the distribution's scores, observations, and so on to lie in an interval defined by the mean and 1 positive unit of the standard deviation. In turn, because of symmetry, you would expect 68 percent of the observations to lie between 1 and −1 deviations around the mean. Think of two vertical lines at the $\pm s$ points on either side of the mean.

By applying the model to the sample as shown in Figure 10.5, you would get the following distribution of merlot scores (recall that you are using a mean of 80 and a standard deviation of 4.5).

Interval	Score Interval	%
$0 \leq \bar{X} \leq s$	80–84.5	34
$-s \leq \bar{X} \leq s$	75.5–84.5	68
$-2s \leq \bar{X} \leq 2s$	71–89	95

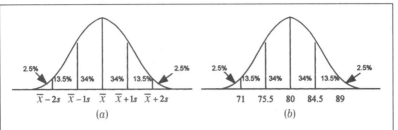

FIGURE 10.5 *Applying the normal distribution: (a) standard distribution, and (b) merlot tasting distribution.*

As the model shows, you can expect 95 percent of the variable's activity to be defined within 2 standard deviations of either side of the mean. You can spin the concept around and say then that 95 percent of the tasters from this sample gave your merlot a score between 71 and 89. Or, what is the chance that a randomly selected tasting of merlot from this sample was below 71 and above 89? This is starting to sound like probability.

Determining the probability that a score will be in an interval defined by the two deviations on either side of the mean is very important in testing, which comes up later in this chapter and the remaining two chapters. You use this tool when asked to assess the significance of a hypothesis, or confidence in a score—for example, you have a 95 percent confidence interval. The next section explains how to use this tool.

 ## FINDING PROBABILITIES WITH THE NORMAL DISTRIBUTION

Consider another example to develop the concept of probability of a continuous variable: Suppose the consultants who designed your website have indicated that you should get, on average, 500 visits per day to your virtual tasting room. The system that they have installed to support your website will easily maintain that level of activity. But the Internet is a funny place, so the activity could vary greatly from day to day. Did someone say *variance?* A standard deviation of 100 is rather high because of the flaky nature of the Internet. If the random variable is number of visits to the website per day, then what percentage of days will have calls between 500 and 600? For the sake of the example, assume that the behavior of this variable is normally distributed.

THE IMPORTANCE OF SKETCHING

When attacking a problem such as this, how should you proceed? First, make a simple sketch, as in Figure 10.6.

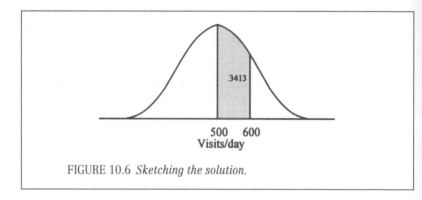

FIGURE 10.6 *Sketching the solution.*

This helps set up the problem—determine what this distribution looks like by identifying the mean, marking off units of the standard deviation, and highlighting the area representing the favorable events. The solution is the area under the curve defined by the end points, 500 (the mean) and 600.

To find the probability that you will, on any given day, receive between 500 and 600 visits requires that you determine the area under the curve determined by the 2 end-point values 500 and 600. This is the essence of a continuous variable—you no longer count occurrences, but use the concept of area under the curve defined by two values of the variable (end points). Specifically, the probability of any given point—for example, $x = 500$ or $x = 600$—is 0. You only analyze intervals. This is why it is important to sketch the area before performing the calculations.

Determine the area, then relate it to probability. Since 500 is the mean and 600 is actually 1 positive deviation from the mean in the positive direction, the shaded area is .3413. You have been accustomed to seeing 34 percent as representing the area determined by 1 standard deviation to the right or left. As an actual area, however, it is .3413. This first example is intentionally convenient, with one standard deviation to ensure that you have the right idea. What would happen if the right end point of the interval was 650? This would not be so easy, because it is not an integer multiple of the standard deviation. So, you need a tool that will free you of this restriction.

 USING THE STANDARD NORMAL CONCEPT DISTRIBUTION

Since all these normal distributions have the same characteristics, differing only by the respective mean and standard deviation used to create them, they can be translated into a *standardized* form where the mean is 0 and the unit of the standard deviation is 1. This standardizing of the distribution (displayed in Figure 10.7) is called the *standard normal distribution.* The following illustrates this translation, relative to the website visits per day analysis. Again, assume the data is normally distributed.

Mathematically, this translation into standardized form is performed by defining standardized values for each data point by dividing the distance between the end point and the mean by the standard deviation. The resultant value, called a Z *score* or Z-*scale value,* can be referenced in a table to determine the area under the normal curve. Try it for the problem you had before. In performing the translation, the Z scores can be found by the following equation, which then creates a new version of the distribution with a mean $\mu = 0$ and $\sigma = 1$. Using the following translation equation, you can translate the x values of 500 and 600 into their corresponding standardized score (Z score):

$$Z_x = \frac{x - \mu}{\sigma}$$

where x is the value to be standardized.

Determine the Z score for the mean 500:

$$Z_{500} = \frac{x - \mu}{\sigma} = \frac{500 - 500}{100} = 0$$

Determine the Z score for the value 600:

$$Z_{600} = \frac{x - \mu}{\sigma} = \frac{600 - 500}{100} = \frac{100}{100} = 1$$

For the sake of the example, Z_{500} is used to indicate the standardized score for the mean 500, and Z_{600} to reference the right end point (see Figure 10.8). The calculation of the area is found by determining the Z value and looking it up in Table A.5 in the appendix. To look up the Z-scale value, look in the left column for 1.0, and

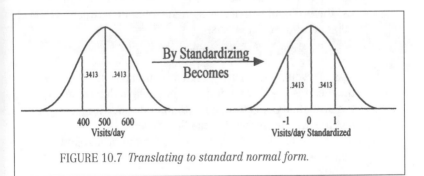

FIGURE 10.7 *Translating to standard normal form.*

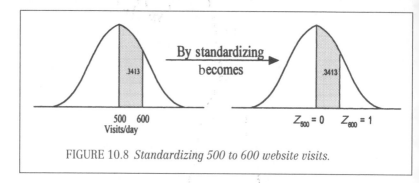

FIGURE 10.8 *Standardizing 500 to 600 website visits.*

then look to the right for the corresponding Z value, .3414. This represents the area to the right of the mean up to the value $Z_{600} = 1$, and the area represents the probability of this event. This probability is expressed in the following equation, which begins with the initial definition of the probability, the interval of site visits between 500 and 600, and then translates that into Z scores.

$$P(500 < x < 600) = P(0 < Z < 1) = P(Z = 1) - P(Z = 0)$$
$$= .3413 - 0 = .3413$$

This equation defines the area for solution, demonstrates the translation to Z scores, and then indicates the operation required to solve for the required probability. The Z-scale value for 1.0 is .3413, and for 0, standardized value of the mean, the value is 0. It is important to note that these measures are all relative to the mean, which is why the last scale value is 0. There is no difference between $<$ and $\leq$ relationships on the Z scale. The table values represent the area under the curve formed by the mean and the point x to the right of the mean. As you scan this table you will see that the values range from 0 (at the mean) to .5, representing half of the area under the curve. Now for the final step, since the area under the curve is 1, it must be that the probability of a day having visits between 500 and 600, represented by the shaded area under the curve, is .3413. You express this in the following equation, read as "the probability that x lies on the interval between 500 and 600 website visits."

$$P(500 < x < 600) = P(0 < Z < 1) = .3413$$

Since you know that the total area to the right of the mean is .5000, then it is also possible to determine the probability of getting more than 600 visits. It is just the area to the right of the line $X = 600$, or in terms of the standardized Z scale, $Z > 1$. Then the probability that more than 600 visits would hit the website is .5000 − .3413 or .1587.

What about the area for a point to the left of the mean? To solve for a point $-x$, you use the Z value for x (in the positive direction), and take advantage of the symmetry of the normal curve—that is, it produces the same area under the curve to the left of the mean as it does to the right. For example, if you needed to determine the probability that you will receive between 400 and 500 visits on any given day, you would be determining the area from the mean to the point 1 standard deviation to the left, which is .3413 as it was before (see Figure 10.9).

So, the key to determining these areas is to find the corresponding Z value by using standardized form and then looking up the values in the Table A.5 in the appendix. The problem now is how you do this when you do not have multiples of the standard deviation.

Solving in the Positive Direction

What is the probability that you will have between 500 and 550 website visits in a day? Set up a diagram like Figure 10.10. Be careful of your intuition; the probability will not be .3413/2. To solve the problem, you need to find the area swept from the mean of 500, or Z_{500}, to the point 550, or Z_{550}. As in all these problems it is a good idea to sketch what you believe is the solution area, then begin your Z-score translations.

$$Z_{500} = \frac{500 - 500}{100} = \frac{0}{100} = 0$$

$$Z_{550} = \frac{550 - 500}{100} = \frac{50}{100} = .5$$

$$P(500 < X < 550) = P(0 < Z < .5) = P(Z = .5) - P(Z = 0)$$
$$= .1915 - 0 = .1915$$

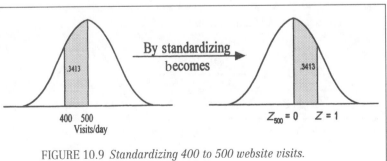

FIGURE 10.9 *Standardizing 400 to 500 website visits.*

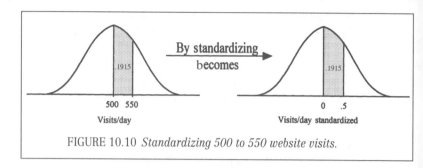

FIGURE 10.10 *Standardizing 500 to 550 website visits.*

Solving in the Negative Direction

Suppose you were asked to determine the probability of between 450 and 500 visits on a given day. It would be the exact same probability as before (500 to 550 visits) because of the symmetry of the normal distribution. Set up a diagram like Figure 10.11, and notice the similarity to the previous problem.

$$P(450 < x < 500) = P(-.5 < Z < 0) = P(0 < Z < .5) = .1915$$

Solving for an Area on the Same Side of the Mean

Suppose the interval did not include the mean as one of the end points—for example, what is the probability that you could have between 600 and 750 website visits? Set up a diagram that sketches the solution, as in Figure 10.12. In this example, the area representing the solution is an interval above the mean. To determine the area for the Z score, subtract the area swept by 600 from the area swept by 750. This yields the desired probability.

$$P(600 < x < 750) = P(500 < x < 750) - P(500 < x < 600)$$

$$Z_{750} = \frac{750 - 500}{100} = \frac{100}{100} = 2.5$$

$$Z_{600} = \frac{600 - 500}{100} = \frac{100}{100} = 1$$

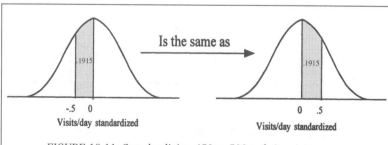

FIGURE 10.11 *Standardizing 450 to 500 website visits.*

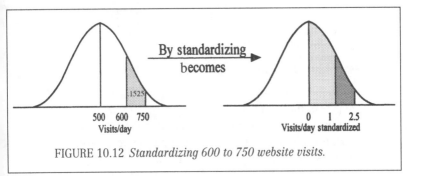

FIGURE 10.12 *Standardizing 600 to 750 website visits.*

$$P(600 < x < 750) = P(1 < Z < 2.5)$$
$$= .4938 - .3413 = .1525$$

Since .1525 of the area is determined by the interval from the points 600 to 750, then the probability that a given day will yield website visits in that range is 15.25 percent.

Solving for Areas on Both Sides of the Mean

Now consider the case where the interval is defined by points on both sides of the mean—for example, what is the probability that you could have between 450 and 550 visits? In this problem the probability is represented by the sum of the areas swept from either side of the mean, as demonstrated in Figure 10.13.

$$P(450 < x < 550) = P(450 < x < 500) + P(500 < x < 550)$$

$$Z_{450} = \frac{450 - 500}{100} = \frac{-50}{100} = -.5$$

$$Z_{550} = \frac{550 - 500}{100} = \frac{50}{100} = .5$$

$$P(450 < x < 550) = P(-.5 < Z < .5)$$
$$= .1915 + .1915 = .3830$$

This last equation shows symmetry once again. You could have seen that 450 and 550 visits are both 50

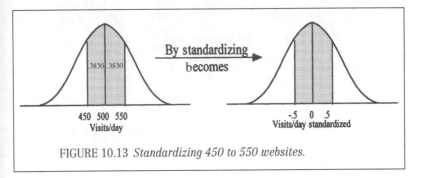

FIGURE 10.13 *Standardizing 450 to 550 websites.*

visits from the mean. The probability could be determined by finding the probability for 500 to 550 visits and multiplying by 2.

$$P(450 < x < 550) = 2P(0 < Z < .5) = 2(.1915) = .3830$$

Remember that although the point on the horizontal axis is in the negative direction, you are interested in the probability, which is an area and, hence, becomes a positive number. The important point to understand is what is being done with the areas; that is, are they being added or subtracted. As has been stated all through these examples, it is very important to make a sketch of the area you are trying to determine.

You try:

Working with Standard Scores

What is the probability that a selected day will have between 400 and 600 visits? Now, what would your intuition say? You really do not need the tables for this one (68 percent). Try one requiring a little more thought and table usage: What is the probability that any selected day will have between 350 and 650 visits?

Answer: $2 \times .4332 = .8664$ or 86.64 percent.

Solving for Areas on the Tails

The last type of Z score is one that has infinity as one of its end points—for example, what is the probability that a selected day will have fewer than 200 visits? To solve this type of problem, it is important to define the area under the curve that represents the solution, which is the shaded area to the left of the value $x = 200$ in Figure 10.14. The solution is found by determining the area swept from the mean to $x = 200$, and then subtracting that area from .5, which is the total area less than the mean.

$$P(x < 200) = P(x < 500) - P(200 < x < 500)$$

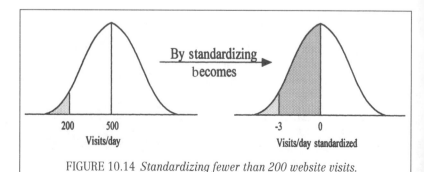

FIGURE 10.14 *Standardizing fewer than 200 website visits.*

$$Z_{200} = \frac{500 - 200}{100} = \frac{300}{100} = 3$$

$$P(x < 200) = .5000 - P(0 < Z < 3)$$
$$= .5000 - .4987 = .0013$$

This last problem demonstrates an important technique when referencing intervals such as fewer than 200 visits or greater than 1,000 visits. Since you know that half the area, indicated by all the values less than the mean or greater than the mean, will be .5, then determining the solution is just subtracting out the interval defined by the mean and the end point, in this case the value $x = 200$.

You try:

Working with Standard Scores

What is the probability that a selected day will have more than 800 website visits?
Answer: .5 − .4987 = .0013.

KEY CONCEPT

THE IMPORTANCE OF SAMPLE MEANS

So is this distinction between the types of variables important? In your real-world applications, possibly not. But that is no reason to skip this paragraph. Here is the reason why, at least theoretically, the distinction is important. Earlier you sampled a set of randomly selected individuals to determine how well people like the merlot on a scale of 100 points. From this survey you derived an average score of 80. Although the tasting scores are most likely integer in nature, the value of any sample mean can really take on any value in the interval you are studying, for example, 70 to 100. It was for the convenience of this introduction that it was 80, exactly. Upon further sampling, you could have other samples yielding means of 80.15, 82.72, 79.53, and so on, where the means could be rounded or carried to any number of positions. Here is where the discussion gets interesting. Suppose you conducted many samples and created a distribution of their respective means (not the data, but the means). Since the means can take on any value, you have the behavior of a continuous variable. What would that distribution look like? Since the means will cluster within a smaller interval, the frequency classes will be smaller, and with more concentration, as shown in Figure 10.15.

Here is an important question: What is the objective of performing all these samples? The objective is to infer the true mean μ. By conducting many samples with 30 participants tasting the merlot, there would be more sample means $\bar{x}_1, \bar{x}_2, \bar{x}_3$, and so on. All these sam-

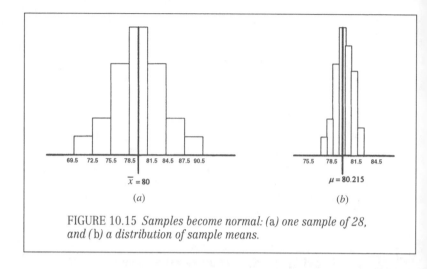

FIGURE 10.15 *Samples become normal:* (a) *one sample of 28, and* (b) *a distribution of sample means.*

ple means $\bar{x}_i$ will, in fact, begin to cluster around the true mean of the population μ. This is formally known as the *central limit theorem,* an important theorem in statistics, which asserts that even if the data themselves are not normally distributed, their distribution of sample means will be. Recall that your population is all merlot drinkers. It stands to reason that the more tastings you conduct, the better the cluster of sample means will concentrate around the true population mean (the "mean of means," if you will). This is an important point to understand about sampling: The means of the samples will themselves produce a normal distribution, from which you can infer, with some confidence, the true mean of the population. Again, this central tendency to the real mean applies not only to populations that are themselves normally distributed, but even to those that aren't. This is an important point about sampling and leads to the very famous theorem stated earlier, the central limit theorem.

But will you ever sample an entire population—that is, will you survey everyone in the world who likes merlot, so that you achieve nirvana and truly determine μ? It is unlikely, and truth be told, you may not even do multiple samples. So you are left with the question of how good the mean from your sample $\bar{x}$ is. And the answer is, good enough as long as the n is large enough. The rule of thumb is that n should be at least 30. Now to see why.

One last observation: What do you think is the behavior of the standard deviation for a collection of sample means? Because the sample means all hover around the true mean, the standard deviation of the distribution of sample means will be quite small relative to the standard deviation of any one sample. This deviation is referred to as the *standard error of the mean,* denoted by $\sigma_{\bar{x}}$. This is an important statistic because it measures the variability of the sample means themselves—that is, how much they fluctuate away from the true mean. It makes sense that the smaller $\sigma_{\bar{x}}$, the better the estimate will be of the true mean. By using the following formula you can obtain the deviation of the sample means without in fact performing all those samples. In this equation, s is the standard deviation of the sample and n is the size of the sample. That's right, you have not actually performed multiple samples to gain the significance of the deviation of the means.

Standard error of the mean:

$$\sigma_{\bar{x}} = \frac{s}{\sqrt{n}}$$

As you examine this equation, it is clear that it will be less than the standard deviation of the data in the sample. And this is as it should be, since you are analyzing a collection of means. And upon closer observation, it becomes apparent that this number actually is made smaller by increasing the sample size. You'll have the pleasure of exploring the significance of this deviation when you encounter hypothesis testing.

APPLICATIONS OF THE NORMAL DISTRIBUTION

This section demonstrates how the material in this chapter can be applied to estimating construction time, future sales, break-even points, and response to direct mailings.

 Estimating Construction Time

You have negotiated with some of the owners of the vineyards near you to supply the grapes for the new wine you'll introduce next year. Producing the wine will require an expansion of the current facility to support the additional processing required for pinot noir. The construction firm selected to build the extension has estimated that the time required to complete the job is 100 days. However, because of weather and demands from completing other jobs, there is a standard deviation (very impressive terminology for a construction company) of 20 days stipulated in their contract proposal. (The industry standard is 20 percent.) Failure to complete the construction in 125 days would cause severe logistical problems with respect to harvesting the grapes. What is the probability that the construction team will complete the job within 125 days?

In solving this problem, assume that the mean is the proposed number of days for completing the work, and the standard deviation is the 20 days stipulated in the contract. As well, assume that the variable, days to complete, is normally distributed. Your first step should be to sketch the area that represents completing the job within 125 days. Then compare your sketch to Figure 10.16.

The solution is the area under the curve less than the critical point of 125 days. The next step is to determine the Z-scale value.

$$Z_{125} = \frac{125 - 100}{20} = \frac{25}{20} = 1.25$$

$$P(0 < x < 125) = P(Z < 1.25) = P(Z < 0) + P(0 < Z < 1.25)$$
$$= .5 + .3944$$

$$P(0 < x < 125) = .5 + .3944 = .8944$$

Remember when calculating the area that it is always relative to the mean—that is, the values you look up in appendix Table A.5 refer to the area swept out from the mean to the Z value. Hence, $P(Z < 1.25)$ will produce the value of the area from the mean to $Z = 1.25$ or $x = 125$. Since the area under the curve less than or equal to the 125 days is .8944, then the probability that the construction company will complete the job in less than 125 days is 89.44 percent. Incidentally, the probability that they will take longer than the 125 days, thus incurring the penalty, is 10.56 percent $(1 - .8944)$.

Alternatively, look at a variation of this work plan. Suppose the construction company gets a 5 percent bonus on the job if they complete the building within 80 days. What is the probability that they will receive the bonus? Again, what is the area that represents completing the job in less than 80 days (see Figure 10.17)?

The solution is the area under the curve less than the bonus point of 80 days. The next steps are to determine the Z-scale value, look up the value in appendix Table A.5, and calculate the bonus probability.

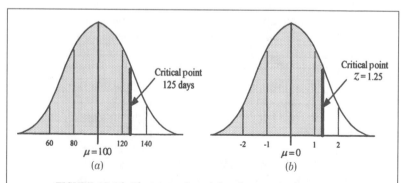

FIGURE 10.16 *The general model and area of solution: (a) days to complete construction, and (b) days to complete construction, standardized.*

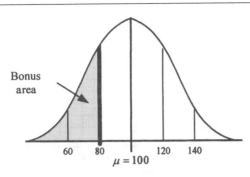

FIGURE 10.17 *Area of the solution for less than 80 days to complete construction.*

$$Z_{80} = \frac{80 - 100}{20} = -\frac{20}{20} = -1$$

$$P(0 < x < 80) = P(0 < Z < -1) = P(0 < Z) - P(Z < 1)$$
$$= .5 - .3413 = .1587$$

Because the area under the curve is .1587, the probability that they will finish the job in 80 days or less, thus qualifying for the bonus, is 15.87 percent.

You try: **Finishing between 110 to 125 Days**

Show your skill by determining the probability that they will finish the job late, but not late enough to be penalized, like most contractors. Determine the probability that they will finish the job in 110 to 125 days.

Answer: approximately 20 percent probability (.3944 − .1915 = .2029).

 Estimating Future Sales

Can the normal curve help estimate the future demand for your new wine? Suppose that you think the demand for the new wine will be 7,200 cases. Assume that demand is normally distributed. The marketing analyst you have consulted has researched other new wine offerings with approximately the same volume projection as yours and found that new wine introductions have a standard deviation of 1,200 cases during their rollout. What is the probability that you will sell at least 9,000 cases?

In this situation, assume that the demand of 7,200 cases will be the mean and the 1,200 cases will be the standard deviation. Your first step should be to sketch the area that represents sales greater than 9,000 cases. Then check your solution diagram with Figure 10.18.

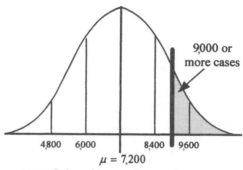

FIGURE 10.18 *Solution for sales of 9,000 cases or more.*

The solution is the area under the curve greater than the point of 9,000 cases. The next step is to determine the Z-scale value.

$$Z_{9,000} = \frac{9,000 - 7,200}{1,200} = \frac{1,800}{1,200} = 1.5$$

$$P(x > 9,000) = P(Z > 1.5) = P(Z > 0) - P(Z < 1.5)$$
$$= .5 - .4332$$

$$P(x > 9,000) = .0668$$

Since the area under the curve greater than or equal to the optimistic 9,000 cases is .0668, then the probability that you will meet or exceed that sales goal is 6.68 percent. Indeed, very optimistic.

But optimistic is better than pessimistic. Suppose the wine sales fall on the poorer side: What is the probability that you will sell 5,000 to 6,000 cases (see Figure 10.19)?

The solution is the area under the curve less than 6,000 cases but greater than 5,000 cases. This solution definitely requires a sketch. The next steps are to deter-

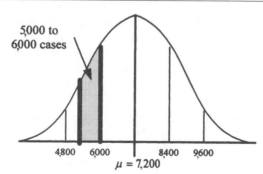

FIGURE 10.19 *Area of solution for sales of 5,000 to 6,000 cases.*

mine the Z-scale values, look them up in appendix Table A.5, and calculate the probability.

$$Z_{6,000} = \frac{6,000 - 7,200}{1,200} = -\frac{1,200}{1,200} = -1$$

$$Z_{5,000} = \frac{5,000 - 7,200}{1,200} = -\frac{2,200}{1,200} = -1.83$$

$$P(5,000 < x < 6,000) = P(-1.83 < Z < -1.0)$$
$$= P(Z < 1.83) - P(Z < 1)$$

$$P(Z < 1.83) - P(Z < 1) = .4664 - .3413 = .1251$$

 Approximating the Binomial with the Normal Distribution

We want to show that the binomial distribution can be approximated with the normal distribution. There are two benefits to taking this direction: First, you need to know this important distribution anyway; and second, if it can approximate others, then you really need to know only one (for this level of learning). With all pun intended, we can ask what does this mean; where are we going with this? Well, hopefully, it shows that you should be able to use the normal distribution for these types of problems, assuming you can get your hands on the mean and standard deviation (remember, that's all you need for using the normal distribution).

MATHEMATICALLY SPEAKING

The Easy Way to Find the Mean and Standard Deviation for the Binomial Case

Recall the coin-flipping exercise where you recorded the results of four repeated trials. You showed through that example that indeed the binomial distribution has the appearance of being "normal." You were able to determine the expected value of 2 and a standard deviation of 1. Knowing these two pieces of information, you can generate the normal distribution.

As the previous chapter shows, the *mean for the binomial distribution* can be defined alternatively as the product of the number of trials n and the probability of the successful outcome for any occurrence p, since the probability is the same across all trials. This makes sense—if you flip a coin 10 times, and success of a head is .5, then the mean for number of heads is 10(.5). A successful outcome might be the occurrence of a head in coin flipping; or in general, success could be the lack of a defect, the acceptance of a product, or the viewing of a certain television program. The *standard deviation* is determined by the square root of the product of the probability of success p, the number of trials n, and the probability that the successful event will not occur $1 - p$. In the example, the probability of a success (head) is $1/2$ and the number of trials (flips) in the experiment is 4.

Mean	Standard Deviation
$\mu = np$	$\sigma = \sqrt{npq}$ where $q = (1 - p)$
$\mu = 4(.5)$	$\sigma = \sqrt{4(.5)(.5)}$
$\mu = 2$	$\sigma = \sqrt{1} = 1$

Criteria for Using the Approximation

DANGER!

The preceding demonstration verifies that these two formulas for determining the mean and the standard deviation, which we use with the normal distribution, in fact produce similar results as when we analyzed this variable earlier in the binomial distribution section. But can we use the normal distribution as an approximation to the binomial all the time? The *criteria* for using this approximation is that the products np and $n(1 - p)$ should both be greater than 5. This is clearly a function of n, the sample size. This approximation is valid when the number of trials is sufficiently large to accommodate these criteria. The only other potential problem in meeting this criteria is if either p or $1 - p$ is so small that its product with n produces a value less than 5. As a careful reader may note, the approximation we used for the example would not in fact satisfy our criteria [both np and $n(1 - p)$ equal 2]. Let's get back to the wine business for a more realistic example.

Back to Merlot

For a business example, suppose you decide to launch your new merlot wine with a free tasting at the local wine merchant. The probability that someone will buy a bottle of your new Merlot based upon the tasting is .6, so says your marketing consultant and the wine merchant. This is a binomial model because the customer will either buy the wine or not. And each customer is independent—one customer does not influence another's assessment and purchase. The wine merchant has indicated that Saturday afternoon has the most traffic and at least 100 people will taste your wine. What is the expected number of bottles to be sold and the standard deviation? And how does this information help you?

$\mu = np$ $\mu = 100(.6) = 60$

$\sigma = \sqrt{npq}$ $\sigma = \sqrt{100(.6)(.4)} = \sqrt{24} = 4.9$

Validity check:

$$np = 100(.6) = 60 \quad \text{which is greater than 5}$$

$$n(1 - p) = 100(.4) = 40 \quad \text{which is greater than 5}$$

Since the mean is 60, you can expect to sell 60 bottles, but now here is what is interesting. Because we can use the normal distribution as an approximation of a binomial model, we can also ask what the probability is that you will sell at least 70 bottles. As recommended earlier, always make a sketch of the area that represents the probability for the success, as in Figure 10.20.

The probability that you will sell 70 bottles or more is the area to the right of the bold line. This is found by subtracting the area between the mean and the 70 bottles end point from .5000.

$$Z_{70} = \frac{X - \mu}{\sigma} = \frac{70 - 60}{4.9} = \frac{10}{4.9} = 2.04$$

$$P(X > 70) = .5000 - P(0 < Z < 2.04)$$
$$= .5000 - .4793 = .0207$$

What the normal approximation of this binomial event shows is that there is a 2.07 percent chance that you will sell 70 or more bottles of merlot at this tasting, given the mean and standard deviation as stated.

You know the expected value or mean is 60 bottles. What other information can be derived? Determine with 95 percent confidence the range of the number of bottles of wine you will sell at the tasting. From the normal distribution you know that approximately 95 percent of observations, scores, and so on will fall within $\pm 2\sigma$ of the mean.

$$\mu \pm 2\sigma = 60 \pm 2(4.9) = 60 \pm 9.8 = [50.2, 69.8]$$

You can be 95 percent confident that you will sell between 51 and 69 bottles of your new merlot, based on this data. So to satisfy potential demand, you'd better have at least 70 bottles with you at the tasting.

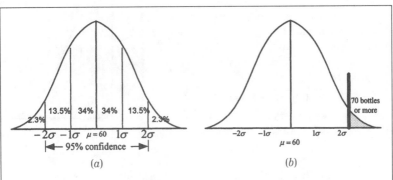

FIGURE 10.20 *Probability of selling at least 70 bottles:* (a) *general distribution, and* (b) *probability of selling 70 or more.*

Marketing by Direct Mail

One of the ways you anticipate marketing the new wine is to conduct a direct-mail campaign to the subscribers of a well-known wine magazine. The magazine has indicated that similar initiatives have had an average response rate of 18 percent from its reader base. To test the readership's interest in your products you have decided to conduct a sample of 500 randomly selected readers. You will be happy if there is a return of 15 percent. What is the probability that you will get at least a 15 percent return on the direct-mail piece?

Remember that p is the standard of success (a successful response), and for this case, the magazine has established the standard of 18 percent. Since you feel the marketing group has inflated expectations, you think they will be very lucky to achieve the goal. Check it out.

Looking at the curve in Figure 10.21, it appears that the interval begins a little below the 75-unit point. In fact, you have to make a technical adjustment for the following reason. Recall that discrete variables are those variables whose values are determined by counting the number of occurrences; hence, they are expressed as whole numbers—for example, 15 bottles. In developing an understanding of the normal curve we pointed out that it is used with continuous variables; hence, the ability to create a curve from the histogram. In essence, you are approximating the behavior of a discrete variable with an instrument designed for continuous variables. To correct for this minor inconsistency, you start the interval a half a unit to the left or right, whichever yields the greater solution area. Note then that defining the interval at 74.5 gives a little more area to the interval defined by 75 or more responses.

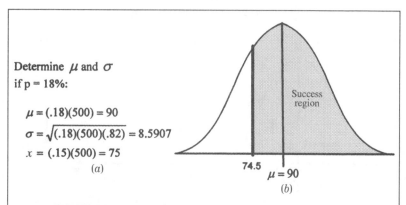

Determine μ and σ
if p = 18%:

$\mu = (.18)(500) = 90$
$\sigma = \sqrt{(.18)(500)(.82)} = 8.5907$
$x = (.15)(500) = 75$
(a)

Success region

74.5 $\mu = 90$
(b)

FIGURE 10.21 *Area of solution for probability of 15 percent direct-mail response: (a) calculation of values, and (b) curve of response distribution.*

The success region for this problem is the area to the right of the line $X = 74.5$. The end point of 74.5 is determined by 15 percent of 500 mailings, which is a return of 75. But this must be adjusted to the value of 74.5.

The probability is defined by the following equation:

$$P(x > 74.5) = P(X > 90) + P(74.5 < x < 90)$$

Now determine the Z value:

$$Z = \frac{74.5 - 90}{8.5907} = \frac{15.5}{8.5907} = -1.804$$

$$P(X \geq 74.5) = P(X > 90) + P(74.5 < X < 90)$$
$$= .5000 + .4645 = .9645$$

The conclusion is that there is a 96.45 percent probability that you will achieve the goal of seeing a return of better than 15 percent on the mailing initiative.

END POINT

Without a doubt, this is the most robust chapter thus far in statistics. It establishes the important connection between descriptive and inferential statistics by showing that frequency distributions and probability distributions are really the same thing. The importance of a probability function or distribution, as a generator of the probabilities, leads to the normal distribution. The important normal distribution is explained, explored, and exploited for the important opportunities it affords. Not only can the normal distribution describe the behavior of a continuous variable, but it is shown to be a very good approximation of some of the discrete functions, such as the binomial. When the binomial sample is large, you can use the normal distribution to approximate the behavior of the variable, thus making calculations easier and less time consuming (See the application "Approximating the Binomial with the Normal Distribution.") And the distribution of sample means will be normal, even if the distribution of the population from which it is drawn is not. And finally, you must live with the results of our sample, so the key is to make the sample large, at least 30, so that the standard error of the mean is as small as possible. Now on to the application of hypothesis testing.

Hypothesis Testing

E very day you make decisions based upon what you believe is true; for example, consider what you do when you hear the morning weather forecast. If there is a probability of rain that afternoon, what do you wear? Suppose you are concerned about ruining a pair of good shoes due to rain, shoes that obviously go with your pants. So you accept the forecast and wear a pair of boots that, although dry, do not go nicely with the day's outfit. Now if it rains you've made the right decision, but if you accept the forecast by wearing the boots and it does not rain, you risk ridicule at your office. Or, alternatively, you reject the meteorologist's assessment and do not wear the boots. If it does not rain, you are okay, but if the monsoon hits, you ruin a very good pair of shoes, and will require a sizeable amount of money to purchase a new pair. This chapter is about creating a hypothesis, such as "It will rain," and using probability to determine the likelihood that you may look foolish wearing boots to the office or that you may ruin your good shoes in the rain. Which option will cost you more?

In business, there is economic risk in making decisions that parallels this little example. Often decisions are based on your experience or what you believe to be true of the population you are working with. But how do you actually test whether results of your sample are valid with respect to some standard or predefined level of performance or behavior? Take an example from your wine business.

HYPOTHESIS TESTING AND QUALITY CONTROL—A CASE

You have a machine that pumps wine from fermentation tanks into wine bottles. The maker of the bottling machine has it calibrated such that it will pump on the average 750 ml per bottle, with a standard deviation of 10 ml. The machine is relatively new, and has been operating without any performance problems. As you watch the bottling process one day, it strikes you that you don't have any procedure in place to check the accuracy of the machine; essentially, you are taking this process on faith. If too much wine is being pumped into the bottle, you are giving away wine that eventually will reduce the total number of bottles that can be sold. On the other hand, if the process pumps too little wine into the bottle, the result could be customer dissatisfaction and/or legal action against the winery.

After meeting with the machine operator and the manufacturer of the equipment, you decide to institute a quality-control program whereby every day you will randomly select 25 bottles, measure their contents, and apply the following rule: If the volume is either below 745 or above 755 ml, you will stop the machine, correct its settings, verify that it is again operating within standard, and resume operation.

In conducting a sample you do not know the population mean, that is, the mean fill level of all bottles. But employing the central limit theorem, you know that sample means (not necessarily the fill levels themselves) are normally distributed around the true population mean. If you could survey everyone in your population—or every bottle, in this case—then you would know the population mean and have perfect information for decision making. Hypothesis testing is a tool that helps you analyze your sample data with respect to some critical value of the mean. It helps you determine the probability that your sample is representative of the population, or that your operation is within standard. Or, on the other hand, hypothesis testing can help you show that the process is operating outside acceptable limits and, as a result, has potentially severe economic consequences to production and overall business.

DEFINING THE NULL HYPOTHESIS SETUP

The process of conducting hypothesis testing requires that you set up two opposing hypotheses, the *null hypothesis* and the *alternative hypothesis*. The null hypothesis is the one that will be tested to report that the process is working properly or not, thereby requiring some action. It often takes on the role of status quo—that is, the *null* assumption is made that there is no real difference between the results of the sample and those of the true population. Statisticians use the term *population mean* to refer to a prespecified performance mean that defines performance within standard. Other sample parameters could be tested as well, for example, the standard deviation. But we confine our attention to the most often analyzed parameter, the mean. When testing on the mean, you are asking if your sample value of the mean is representative or if it is rare, and therefore questionable. The trick is that you use the data from your sample to determine the likelihood that the null hypothesis is true or false.

- The *null hypothesis H_O* represents the case where you believe that there is no real difference between the sample mean and the true mean of the population µ; that is, any acceptable difference is the result of sampling error. If the sample mean is 752 ml, you should not be that concerned, and should make the decision to accept the null hypothesis.

- The *alternative hypothesis H_A* represents the situation where the occurrence of that value of the mean must be considered improbable and the difference must be considered real (and unacceptable) and not necessarily due to sampling error. If the sample mean is 740 ml, then you should be concerned, and should make the decision to reject the null hypothesis, thus believing that the process as it is currently performing is out of control.

CREATING A NULL HYPOTHESIS

The *objective* of testing the null hypothesis is to show statistically that there is no appreciable difference between the sample and normal operation. You therefore need a rule or criterion by which that assessment can be judged. In your case, create a null hypothesis that assumes everything is fine, that the mean will be as expected, 750 ml per bottle, and that there will be *no significant difference* with the means derived from the samples. Because the strategy rests on no appreciable difference with the population mean, µ = 750, it is referred to as *null*. As professors Don Pardeu and Paul Thurman always say, "Think about the null hypothesis as conventional wisdom—that is, all samples will behave as expected." Now, the criterion: If the mean of the sample is greater than 755 ml or less than 745 ml, then this would represent an abnormal occurrence, an *appreciable difference* if you will, resulting in rejection of the null hypothesis. Remember, rejecting the null hypothesis will mean shutting the process down.

TABLE 11.1 SETTING UP THE NULL HYPOTHESIS

H_0: $\mu = 750$ The null hypothesis states that the mean of the sample will not be significantly different from 750. You can only reject the null hypothesis if you obtain a value from your sample that is improbable, for example, $\bar{x} \leq 745$ or $\bar{x} \geq 755$. Rejection of the null hypothesis implies acceptance of the alternative.

H_A: $\mu \neq 750$ The alternative hypothesis represents the situation where the occurrence of that value of the mean must be considered improbable based upon the sample characteristics; hence, the machine is not operating within standard and must be shut down for maintenance.

Table 11.1 and Figure 11.1 display the two situations in our testing: The sample mean is either in the acceptable interval $745 < \bar{x} < 755$, or it is outside this interval, indicating that the process is out of control and needs adjustment.

DECISION OPTIONS IN HYPOTHESIS TESTING

What is the range of decisions based on your sample analysis? Table 11.2 shows that there are four possible outcomes based upon the null hypothesis testing model. If the null hypothesis is *true* (meaning that the process is within standard) and you decide, based upon the sample, to *accept* the null hypothesis, then you have made the right decision. For your production problem this indicates that the mean of the sample is sufficiently close to $\mu = 750$ that you accept the null hypothesis and keep the machine running.

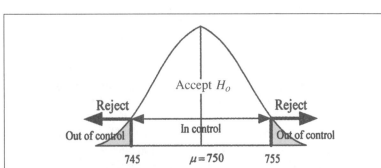

FIGURE 11.1 *Acceptance and rejection regions.*

TABLE 11.2 DECISION MATRIX FOR THE NULL HYPOTHESIS

True State of Operation	Your Decision	
	Accept H_0	Reject H_0
Process within standard: H_0 true	Right decision	Type I error α
Process not within standard: H_0 false	Type II error β	Right decision $1 - \beta$ = power of the test

Type I Error α

This gives rise to the first of two types of errors that can occur as result of this testing. In the first case, suppose that the sample produces a mean that causes you to believe that the machine is out of control, and to reject the null hypothesis when, in fact, the processing is within standard; that is, H_0 is true. To be clear, the machine is operating within standard, but you got a once in a lifetime sample that indicates otherwise. As a result, you unnecessarily shut the machine down, thereby halting production, waiting while the operator recalibrates it, then testing to verify, and finally resuming operation. This adjustment delays shipments, causing potential customer dissatisfaction and increased labor costs. Rejecting the null hypothesis when it is actually true is termed a *Type I error,* and the probability of its occurrence is referred to as α (alpha). *The key to employing hypothesis testing is using the normal distribution to decide, based on business tradeoffs, the maximum probability that just such an uncharacteristic mean could occur.*

Type II Error β

On the other hand, suppose the null hypothesis is false; that is, the actual state of the machine is not within standard. When it is false and you decide to reject the null hypothesis (accepting the alternative), you have made the right decision: You halt the operation because you suspect the machine is not filling the bottles properly. But suppose the null hypothesis is false (the true state of the machine is not within standard), and you, in fact, accept the null hypothesis as true; that is, you don't think there is any real difference based upon your sample. This results in a *Type II error,* and the probability of its occurrence is referred to as β (beta). Since the idea in this testing process is to minimize the possibility of just such a situation occurring, $1 - \beta$, the probability of making the right decision, is referred to as the *power* of the test.

DETERMINING RISK WITH TYPE I AND TYPE II ERRORS

What do these errors mean to your operation? Either error could be very costly indeed because the machine is filling bottles with either too much wine (giving away product) or too little (setting you up for consumer fraud). Either of these events could cause severe market reactions that will affect your company's financial well being. But now it's time for an important point regarding hypothesis testing: This process will not eliminate the risk of the errors occurring, but it does help you assign a *tolerance level* or probability that either of these errors will occur, based on your sample data and the null hypothesis criterion. Knowing the probability of the occurrence helps management make informed decisions based on data, not feelings, and, as a consequence, implement procedures that increase the effectiveness of the process.

Since both α and β are probabilities, they have a range from 0 to 100 percent; the greater the percentage, the greater the risk that the error will occur. Think about these two errors: Is one more serious than the other? If you are going to make a mistake, are you better off stopping the process when it is really not flawed (α), or allowing the process to continue when it really is flawed (β)? Consider this example, which, although serious, displays the difference between these two errors. A person is arrested for theft. The null hypothesis is that the person is presumed innocent until proven guilty. Suppose the person is innocent. If the judicial system convicts an innocent person, that is a Type I error. On the other hand, suppose the person is actually guilty. If it frees a person who is guilty, that is a Type II error. If anything, our justice system tends to minimize Type I errors, and the tradeoff is to live with Type II errors. Unfortunately, like the justice system, you can't eliminate both, and there are tradeoffs you must consider.

Setting Up the Error Test

A Type I error occurs when the null hypothesis is true; that is, the operation is actually running within standard, but you reject it. Solving for this type of error requires that you determine the probability of its occurrence. In your sample, you need to determine the probability that the sample will yield a mean that is less than 745 ml or more than 755 ml (see Figure 11.2).

When examining the criterion associated with the null hypothesis or its alternative, you will need to perform one of two types of tests: *one-tailed tests* and

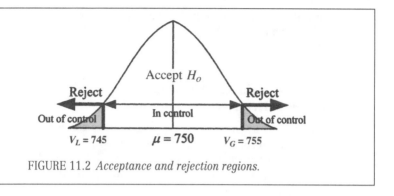

FIGURE 11.2 *Acceptance and rejection regions.*

two-tailed tests. When the projected values of the mean are less than or equal to the value V_L, or greater than or equal to V_G, then construct your hypothesis test as a two-tailed test. Figure 11.3 shows how the test is constructed, and provides insight as to how the normal distribution is used. Recalling the use of Z scores in Chapter 10, the value of α (probability that the process is out of control) is the probability that a mean will fall anywhere to the left of 745 ml or to the right of 755 ml.

Two-tailed tests are perfect designs for quality interval testing where quality issues surface when a machine's critical performance is at or below the value V_L or at or above the value V_G. But some designs are concerned with maintaining a minimum or maximum value—that is, a critical standard, values below or above which can't be allowed. For example, suppose you did not care about overflow but concentrated only on making sure each bottle contains at least 745 ml. In this case you are concerned with only one end of the distribution—the mean is greater than or equal to the value V_M. So, you construct your hypothesis test as a one-tailed

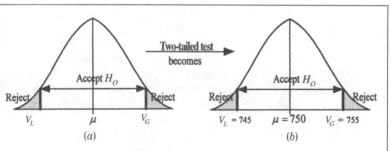

FIGURE 11.3 *Acceptance and rejection regions of the two-tailed test. (a) Reject* H₀ *when sample mean exceeds* V_G *or falls below* V_L. *(b) Reject* H₀ *when volume of the sample mean exceeds 755 ml or falls below 745 ml.*

test. If you will, a one-tailed test is one directional, whereas a two-tailed test is two directional. Figure 11.4 shows how a one-tailed test is used.

Critical Values versus Levels of Significance

As you look at either of these types of tests you will note that there are critical values and regions that define acceptance and rejection of the null hypothesis. The critical values, in units of the sample, can be defined for the hypothesis test in one of two ways: from experience or from statistical levels of signifi-cance. Here's the difference. Critical minimum or maximum values of acceptance are based upon the experience of the managers of the process—for exam-ple, a weight, volume, or temperature. In the example we have used this approach—we have stated that the volume cannot be less than 745 ml or greater than 755 ml. These are referred to as *critical values* or *action points*. We like the term *critical value* because it conveys the meaning that a decision must be addressed; the process is operating in a critical state. When given the values, you can solve for the probabil-ity or likelihood of occurrence.

For some experiments it is necessary to use another method termed *levels of significance*—for example, to set the limits of the acceptance region so that the null hypothesis will be accepted 95 or 99 per-cent of the time. In this situation, you want to set the critical value in such a way that you are assured that the null hypothesis will be rejected at a level of 95 or 99 percent probability. But isn't that just α? We ex-plain more on this as you work through the example. Figure 11.5 shows a comparison between the two methods. So, when presented with a percentage level of significance, solve for the values in the distribution that yield those probabilities—that is, the significance

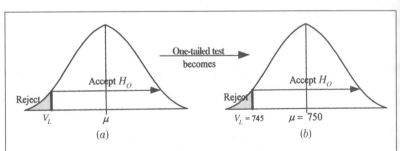

FIGURE 11.4 *Acceptance and rejection regions of the one-tailed test. (a) Reject* H$_0$ *when sample mean falls below* V$_L$. *(b) Reject* H$_0$ *when volume of the sample mean falls below 745 ml.*

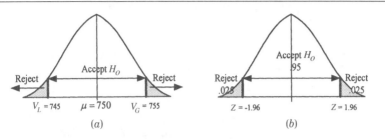

FIGURE 11.5 *Comparison of methods for defining critical values. (a) Reject H_0 when volume of the sample mean exceeds 755 ml or falls below 745 ml. (b) Reject H_0 when there is a probability of 2.5 percent or less of getting a fill level above or below 750 ml.*

of the Z values of ± 1.96 (but more on this later). In order to maintain the concept of a defined acceptance region, we show how to translate these percentage requirements into the corresponding critical values in units of the variable.

Calculating the Probability α (Type I Error)

Let's get back to the quality-control experiment with the wine-bottling process. What constitutes a Type I error? You have a Type I error if the sample mean falls outside the acceptance region, as shown in Figure 11.6. Because this is a two-tailed test, it requires that you find the probability that the sample mean will fall in either one of two areas of the distribution, below 745 or above 755. The acceptance region is defined by the critical values 745 and 755.

Recall the data provided for the sample and test: 25 bottles are going to be randomly selected, the critical measures of the sample are 745 and 755 ml, respectively, and the mean for the machine, as provided by the operator, is 750 ml, with a standard deviation of 10 ml. The next step is to determine the Z scores and

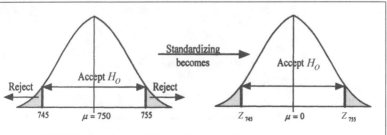

FIGURE 11.6 *Standardizing the two-tailed test.*

related probabilities. Figure 11.6 shows the sketch for translating to the Z scale.

DANGER!

As you begin to perform the calculations there is an important point to note: You are dealing with sample means; that is, hypothesis testing assumes a distribution of means. As noted at the end of the last chapter, a distribution of means results in a tighter distribution, implying a smaller standard deviation. To approximate this smaller standard deviation, you use the standard error of the mean, which is the standard deviation of the sample divided by the square root of the number of items in the sample n. As the equation for the standard error of the mean shows, as you increase the number of items sampled, you will decrease the amount of variation used for the hypothesis testing, hence the benefit of a larger sample.

The first step is to determine the standard error of the mean and then use it in the calculations of the corresponding Z values.

$$\sigma_{\bar{x}} = \frac{\sigma}{\sqrt{n}} = \frac{10}{\sqrt{25}} = 2$$

$$Z_{745} = \frac{745 - 750}{\sigma_{\bar{x}}} = \frac{-5}{2} = -2.5$$

$$Z_{755} = \frac{755 - 750}{\sigma_{\bar{x}}} = \frac{5}{2} = 2.5$$

Now that you have the Z scores, each of the probabilities can be determined by their areas.

$$P(\bar{x} \le 745) = P(Z_{745} \le 2.5) = .5000 - .4938 = .0062$$

$$P(\bar{x} \ge 755) = P(Z_{755} \ge 2.5) = .5000 - .4938 = .0062$$

$$\alpha = P(Z_{745} \le 2.5) + P(Z_{755} \ge 2.5)$$

$$= .0062 + .0062 = .0124$$

Therefore α, the probability that $\bar{x}$ will be less than 745 or greater than 755, can be calculated by adding the two areas/probabilities (see Figure 11.7). This represents the probability that you will reject the null

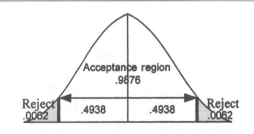

FIGURE 11.7 *Determining the probability of α.*

hypothesis when it is true, that is, when the process is within standard. There is approximately 1 chance in 100 that you will shut the bottling machine down and call for maintenance when it is not in fact needed.

Defining the Level of Significance

Using the diagram in Figure 11.7 we have an opportunity to make an observation about α. Since you got a probability of 1.24 percent, then there is a very small likelihood that this event (a sample mean outside the interval $745 < X < 755$) will occur. Consider the complement of that probability, namely $1 - \alpha$, or $1 - .0124$, which is .9876. This represents the area of the acceptance region, namely the probability that the sample mean will fall within that interval. This is referred to as the *level of significance* for this test. If you were considering levels of significance for the acceptance region based on this sample with $\mu = 750$, you could make the following observation: The critical values of 745 and 755 would yield acceptance more than 95 percent of the time but not quite 99 percent.

Calculating the Probability β (Type II Error)

But in reality machines do go out of control, workers get tired and make mistakes, and suppliers send defective material, all of which lead to processes that yield defective units. So you need to assess the quality of the process and halt it before defective units reach the consumer. These are the conditions for a Type II error, that essentially all conditions regarding the operation are the same, but the population mean, $\mu = 750$ (the standard for the processing), has changed to the point that the true state of the process being tested by the null hypothesis is false. Essentially, the population mean is taking on values outside the acceptance region.

If the null hypothesis is no longer true, what are the decision options? If you detect the change and reject the null hypothesis, thereby shutting the machine down because it is out of standard, you have done the right thing. But what if you accept the null hypothesis under these conditions? This means that the machine is not functioning properly and you have not detected it—a Type II error.

Since you know the null hypothesis $\mu = 750$ is not true in this situation, assume that a new mean exists that is not within standard, for example, $\mu = 740$. Figure 11.8 visualizes what is to happen. First, the population mean shifts down from the position of $\mu = 750$ to the new position $\mu = 740$. Second, since the standard

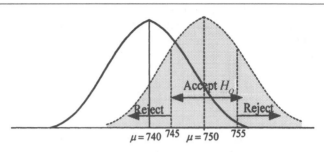

FIGURE 11.8 *The distribution shift. When the process falls out of control, the distribution of average fill rates, which is normal, shifts, but the standards for acceptance or rejection do not.*

deviation $\sigma = 10$ is still valid, the normal curve shifts to the left with the population mean, which results in shifting the critical values to the right. The area representing the Type II error should now be apparent. The probability of a Type II error—that is, deciding that H_O is true when it is actually false—is determined by solving for the area between the two decision points relative to the new mean. That is, what is the probability that a sample mean will be greater than 745 and less than 755, with a population mean of 740?

The first step is to determine the Z scores and use them to determine the related probabilities. The standard error of the mean, which acts as the standard deviation of the sample means, remains the same.

$$\sigma_{\bar{x}} = \frac{\sigma}{\sqrt{n}} = \frac{10}{\sqrt{25}} = \frac{10}{5} = 2$$

Now determine the Z values and the areas under the curve for the acceptance region, as noted in Figure 11.9. But be careful when performing your Z calculations; you are using the new shifted population mean of 740, and not 750. (Remember, the machine is actually not working properly.)

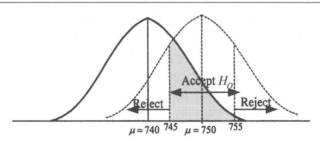

FIGURE 11.9 *Solving for β. Beta is represented by the area under the shifted curve between the acceptable limits from the original curve, 745 to 755 ml.*

$$z_{745} = \frac{745 - 740}{\sigma_{\bar{x}}} = \frac{5}{2} = 2.50$$

$$z_{755} = \frac{755 - 740}{\sigma_{\bar{x}}} = \frac{15}{2} = 7.5$$

$$P(745 \leq \bar{x} \leq 755) = P(\bar{x} \leq 755) - P(\bar{x} \leq 745)$$

$$P(\bar{x} \leq 745) = P(Z_{745} \leq 2.5) = .4938$$

$$P(\bar{x} \leq 755) = P(Z_{755} \leq 7.5) = .5000$$

$$\beta = P(x \leq 755) - P(x \leq 745) = .0062$$

As you solve for the probability of $P(\bar{x} \leq 755) = P(Z_{755} \leq 7.5)$ you will see that the table only goes as far as 4 or 5, depending on the table you use. Once you get Z scores that far out in the distribution, the area under the curve is negligible. As a result, the actual area under the curve from the mean to $Z_{755} = 7.5$ is .5000.

The Significance of β and the Power of the Hypothesis Test

So what does β tell you? Since β—the probability that $\bar{x}$ will be greater than 745 and less than 755, knowing that the true mean of the population is 740—is very small, namely .0062, there is less than 1 chance in 100 that you will continue running the bottling machine when the null hypothesis is false, that is, when $\mu = 740$. Another way to interpret this result is through the power of the test, which is defined as the complement of β, namely $1 - \beta = 99.38$ percent. The closer this number is to 100 percent, the stronger or more powerful your test. Why so? Because the smaller the value of β, the less chance that you will commit the Type II error—accepting the process as acceptable when in actuality it is not. This is one probability, a Type II error, that you want to be as low as possible. Hence, the greater the power of the test, the more secure you will be in catching a defective situation and halting the operation. Now you see why a Type II error is the more important error to avoid.

The Significance of a Changing β

You may be a little skeptical about the method of arriving at the probability for the Type II error. There is nothing wrong with a little skepticism, but what is it about the method that bothers you? Probably it is the choice of another value of the mean. The first requirement is that the value of the new mean should be outside the acceptance interval defined in the initial specification, because a Type II error, as you recall, assumes that the true state of the operation is not within standard. But suppose the selection were a value closer to that interval, for example, 744, or a value farther away, for example 730—how should β behave? After some thought, you should arrive at the following conclusions. As μ takes on a value of the mean closer to the original assumption—for example, $\mu = 744$ or 748—β gets closer to 1, because you would decide to accept the null hypothesis (equivalent to keeping the machine running). On the other hand, suppose you select values of the mean that are farther away from 750—for example, 730, or 770 for that matter. Shouldn't the values of β get smaller, and how might you interpret those values?

Consider this: If the machine gets so out of order that it truly produces bottles with 730 or 770 ml of wine in them, shouldn't you take that as an extraordinary outcome? It would certainly seem to be an unrepresentative value of the mean in light of what the operator has programmed for the machine, and you would most likely decide to reject the null hypothesis, and rarely, if ever, would accept it. Hence, in this last situation, β would become very small. The following exercise makes these last points come alive.

You try:

Analyzing β

In the following table there is a range of values of μ from 735 to 765. Use appendix Table A.5 to determine the corresponding probability of Type II errors β and the power of the test. What you should notice is that the values of β increase and approach 1 as you get to the mean, 750. For $\mu > 750$, you should see the values of β fall dramatically. This is saying that the farther μ wanders from either side of the acceptance region, the lower the probability is that you will erroneously accept the null hypothesis.

μ	β	Power 1 − β
735		
740		
745		
748		
752		
755		
760		
765		

USING LEVEL OF SIGNIFICANCE TO DEFINE DECISION LIMITS OR CRITICAL VALUES

In the previous analysis you defined, by experience of the operators, the acceptance interval in units of the variable, a lower limit of 745 and an upper limit of 755. Once you were given these limits you were able to determine β and α. Often you will not know the limits of the acceptance region; instead, you will want to set a percentage of samples as the standard—for example, that 95 percent of the samples will fall within an acceptable range. This percentage is referred to as the *level of significance or confidence interval,* that is, 95 percent acceptance. To compare these two techniques, refer back to Figure 11.5.

Given a 95 percent level of significance, you need to find the critical values of the sample mean that assure you of 95 percent successful operation. This implies that you are willing to accept a level of risk—that is, that 5 percent of the time you will reject a hypothesis when it is actually true. (Does this sound like α?) You want to determine the limit points, based on a level of significance, that are equal to a certain prespecified level of performance—a percentage, for example, to the .05 or .01 significance levels (which is, in fact, α). Therefore, you derive your confidence level by determining α and subtracting from 1. Here's a demonstration of how this works for the two-tailed model, since you are asking for an upper and lower level of volume. The model that satisfies this approach is displayed in Figure 11.10.

When you look at the figure you are probably wondering, "Where in the world did 1.96 come from?" Not only is that a good question, it is the essence of understanding how to solve this type of problem. Here's how it's determined. Since you want to achieve 95 percent acceptance, the rejection percentage of 5 percent must

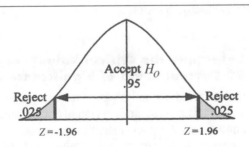

FIGURE 11.10 *Solving for critical values that satisfy 95 percent acceptance. Reject* H_0 *when a sample mean falls outside of an interval set by 95 percent acceptance. Confidence level = 95 percent = 1 − .05.*

be halved (because of the symmetry of the normal curve and the fact that this is a two-tailed test) and distributed to both sides of the distribution. Therefore, your problem is to find the values of Z that will yield an area under the curve of .025 for the rejection areas. This means there must be a value of Z that yields that percentage. If you scan appendix Table A.5, values for the area under the normal curve, look for the value of Z that yields .4750. Why .4750, you ask? Recall that the values in the table refer to the area swept from the mean to the left or right; hence, the value you seek is .5000 − .025. The value of Z that produces this area is 1.96. So, the area for the two-tailed model is found by determining the values of the variable that yield Z scores equal to ±1.96, as shown in Figure 11.10. So that is where the 1.96 comes from.

Now your problem is simply to find the values of the variable that are solutions to the following two equations, where the sample consists of 25 bottles, a population mean of $\mu = 750$, and a standard deviation of 10 ml. Remember, you use the standard error of the mean as the divisor because you are working with a distribution of sample means, that is, average fill rates.

$$z = \frac{\bar{x} - \mu}{\sigma_{\bar{x}}} = \pm 1.96 \quad \text{where } \sigma_{\bar{x}} = \frac{\sigma}{\sqrt{n}} = \frac{10}{\sqrt{25}} = 2$$

$$z_1 = \frac{\bar{x} - 750}{2} = -1.96 \qquad z_2 = \frac{\bar{x} - 750}{2} = 1.96$$

$$\bar{x} - 750 = -3.92 \qquad\qquad \bar{x} - 750 = 3.92$$

$$\bar{x} = 746.08 \qquad\qquad \bar{x} = 753.92$$

So what have you solved? If you define the critical values of the acceptance region as 746.08 and 753.92 ml, the null hypothesis will be accepted 95 percent of the time. Or, stated another way, you are at risk of rejecting H_0 and committing a Type I error 5 percent of the time. You have found the upper and lower limits to the interval that yields an α of 5 percent.

You try:

Determine the Critical Values for a 99 Percent Level of Significance

In the preceding analysis you found the action points for an acceptance region of 95 percent. Show that if the level of significance were increased to 99 percent, the Z value would be 2.575 and the new critical values of the acceptance region would be 744.85 and 755.15, respectively.

APPLYING HYPOTHESIS TESTING

This section demonstrates how the material in this chapter can be applied to one-tailed testing.

Performing a One-Tailed Test

Being an ex-lawyer (how else would you be able to afford a vineyard), you are more concerned with being accused of fraud with respect to your bottling operation than you are with overfilling bottles. As a result you want to set up a test that focuses only on insufficient filling. Set up the null hypothesis and determine the minimum level of fill volume that will satisfy this requirement. You have been advised to apply a level of significance $\alpha = .01$ to this process.

Assume that the data from the original sample is used for this test and that the acceptance region is no longer the interval defined by 745 and 755 ml, respectively, but the entire region less than the critical value that would assure an acceptance region of 99 percent. A one-tailed test is different from the two-tailed test in that it focuses only on one direction. In this case, any sample mean greater than the critical value is an acceptable mean, as Figure 11.11 shows.

Defining the Null Hypothesis for a One-Tailed Test

Assume that the current process will be modified to support a new standard, and establish an alternative hypothesis that specifies the area below Z_{min} as the reject area for the null hypothesis. In a one-tailed test, either of the tails of the distribution will contain the reject region, but not both. Therefore, the reject region will account for the total rejection percentage. Table 11.3 sets up the null hypothesis.

Since you want to achieve 99 percent acceptance, the rejection percentage of 1 percent will be the area to

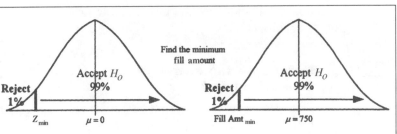

FIGURE 11.11 *Solving for the critical value that satisfies 99 percent acceptance.*

TABLE 11.3 SETTING UP THE NULL HYPOTHESIS

$H_0: \mu \geq Z_{min}$ The null hypothesis states that the fill level of the sample will be greater than or equal to a critical value Z_{min} determined by 99% acceptance.

$H_A: \mu < Z_{min}$ The alternative hypothesis represents the situation where the fill level will be less than Z_{min}.

the left of the critical value in the distribution. Now find the standard unit that will yield an area under the partial acceptance region of the curve equal to .4900 (.5000 – .01). The Z_{min} value that yields an area of .4900 is $Z = 2.33$. (It is not exact, but close enough for this analysis.) Now solve for the value of the sample mean. Note that 2.33 is used because the area representing the rejection region is to the left of the mean.

$$\text{Since } Z_{min} = -2.33$$

$$\text{Then } z_{min} = \frac{\overline{X} - 750}{2} = -2.33$$

$$\overline{X} - 750 = -4.66$$

$$\overline{X} = 745.34$$

Solving the equation yields 745.34 ml as the critical value for the sample mean. What does the critical value of 745.34 ml represent? Now you can restate the null hypothesis in terms of units of the distribution. You have redefined the critical values to units of the variable, as opposed to a significance percentage of 99 percent. And you have introduced a level of significance resulting in a probability for α of 1 percent. You have found the critical value of the sample mean that assures you of 99 percent on average successful operation. You have found the value of the mean that would set off the alarm that there could be a problem with underfilling the bottles of wine. This case focuses on minimizing α and not β. But this does lead to an interesting observation.

You try:

Determine the Power of a One-Tailed Test

What is the power $1 - \beta$ of this test, assuming that the mean of this test fell to $\overline{x}_{new} = 745.34$? The interesting characteristic here is that the new operating mean has fallen exactly to the 99 percent significance point. That means half the time your score will be above the mean, giving you a β of .5.

END POINT

All of the statistical chapters work their way toward hypothesis testing. This chapter puts together descriptive and inferential statistics, probability, the normal curve, the mean, and standard deviation into one major business decision-making tool. It all happens in hypothesis testing. Businesswise, it is one of the most important tools you can apply to processes. It is indispensable in quality control for analyzing the process by setting up the null hypothesis, determining the acceptable limits to the process or establishing confidence levels, and then analyzing the results to determine the occurrence of Type I and Type II errors. And what are the tradeoffs? What are the economic consequences due to a failed process that continues to produce defects, or due to shutting down equipment when the operation is actually under control? This chapter shows how to use statistics in a very methodical way to minimize Type II errors β and maximize the power of the test $1 - β$.

Regression and Estimation

Up to now, this excursion through statistics has concentrated on describing the behavior of a single variable, whether it was the wine tasting scores or the weekly wine purchase survey. When analyzing the activity of a single variable such as these you are performing what is termed a *univariate* analysis. But suppose you wanted to know if there is a relationship between the amount of wine purchased and household annual income? Since wine drinking has always been portrayed in theater and films as a folly of the rich, it suggests that people who have more disposable income might well be inclined to consume more wine. It would seem to be a reasonable study for marketing. You might even infer that the more income a household earns, the more wine it will purchase and consume. Such is the nature of inference or prediction—or, for that matter of wine and disposable income.

Observations like these and those that follow are found every day in newspapers and conversation. One that we hear all the time asserts that there exists a positive relationship between the number of years of education and a person's annual salary. This positive relationship has been highly documented and proven. *Correlation* refers to the measure of the degree or strength of the relationship between the two variables. Assuming there is a relationship, *regression* refers to the creation of a model or equation that is used to predict the behavior in one variable as a function of the behavior in another variable. Consider the following examples of correlation and regression.

- There is a positive relationship between performance of the stock market and restaurant volume—as the market goes up, restaurant volume increases, particularly in high-priced restaurants. It is possible to create a model to describe this relationship.

- There is an inverse relationship between the number of flu shots administered to the elderly in any cold season and the number of their reported flu cases.

- Another inverse relationship—if interest rates go up, new housing starts go down. This is surely modeled by a number of financial institutions.

- Stock analysts use this one all the time. If a security is benchmarked to the S&P 500, then an equation can be determined that will predict the security's performance based on the performance of the S&P.

CORRELATION AND CAUSATION

In each of these examples, the variables could be studied individually in a univariate analysis, but in this case, we are interested in their relationship with each other. It is important to remember that despite a strong correlation between the variables, correlation does not imply causation. On Wall Street it has been observed that, historically, the performance of the stock market is very strong when an NFC team wins the Super Bowl. Hardly causation—but interestingly, the data support this observation. However, one of the greatest years on Wall Street was 1998, and the Denver Broncos (an AFC team) won the Super Bowl. Correlation does not imply causation!

 **THE DIFFERENCE BETWEEN REGRESSION AND CORRELATION**

When analyzing the joint behavior of two variables, the study is termed *bivariate* analysis (or *multivariate,* when more than two variables are being analyzed). Specifically, we would like to know if there is a relationship between household income and the amount of wine purchased weekly. In studying the relationship we first assume that the variables being analyzed are independent—that is, that behavior in one does not influence behavior in the other. There are two phases in performing a bivariate analysis: the creation of the model and a test of its strength. When using personal computers armed with spreadsheet software, the output of the regression analysis consists of both an equation and the correlation statistic. In order to understand them both, and to emphasize that they are really two distinct processes, they are treated separately here.

- *Phase 1: correlation analysis.* The part of the study that determines how strong the relationship is between the variables. The result of this analysis is a value between –1 and +1. A value of 1 represents perfect positive correlation; –1, a perfect inverse relationship. The closer to 0 a correlation, the less the relationship.

- *Phase 2: regression analysis.* The part of the study that builds the estimating function, between the dependent variable and at least one independent variable. The result of this analysis is an equation used for predicting the activity of the dependent variable based on activity of the independent variable(s). It may be sales revenue as a function of advertising, grape production as a function of rainfall and temperature, or wine sales as a function of stock market performance.

TYPES OF REGRESSION MODELS

In performing a regression analysis you will be required to select the type of function or model assumed in your data. That is, how do your variables respond—are they related linearly, exponentially, or how? A little background on these models will prove beneficial. In business, most often people select linear models, but depending on assumptions you make about the behavior of the relationship, you could select others, as displayed in the tables and figures following. Selecting these options is particularly easy to do when employing spreadsheets on a microcomputer. But there is also the problem with microcomputers of jumping into the analysis too soon. As has been mentioned many times, it is very important to sketch the data so you can visually assess the relationship. If you make incorrect assumptions, you may waste resources, or appear to be unknowledgeable. By looking at the data and assessing the correlation between the variables, you could determine one of the following models to be appropriate.

Linear and Quadratic Models

The *linear model* of the form $Y = a + bX$ assumes a constant trend (slope is b in statistical models) over some defined interval of the independent variable(s), for example, annual income and years of education. Relationships whose values behave arithmetically assume this model (see Figure 12.1).

The *quadratic model* of the form $Y = aX^2 + bX + c$ is used when optimization is assumed regarding the behavior of a variable; that is, there is a maximum or

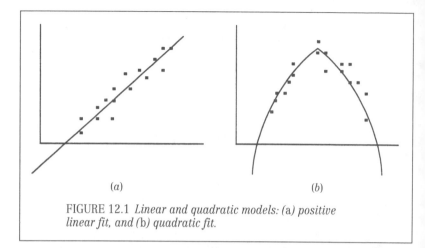

FIGURE 12.1 *Linear and quadratic models: (a) positive linear fit, and (b) quadratic fit.*

minimum to estimate. Examples are revenue optimization and the phenomenon of diminishing returns—that is, as units get closer to maximum, total revenue begins to level, and the revenue derived from each successive unit decreases (see Figure 12.1).

Exponential and Logarithmic Models

The *exponential model* of the form $Y = ab^X$, often used in financial analyses, assumes that there exists a rate or compounding factor b that predicts future valuations based upon that rate. This is the soul of the time value of money. Relationships whose values behave geometrically may assume this model (see Figure 12.2).

The *logarithmic model* of the form $Y = a \log X$ assumes a more dramatic growth in the initial phase of a product's life cycle and then levels off to some limiting value. These models are often employed with advertising expenditures and resultant revenues (see Figure 12.2).

We concentrate on linear models, because they are used most frequently to describe relationships between one dependent variable and one independent variable. Pedagogically, it is easier to understand the theory behind this analysis by working with the geometrical presentation of the relationship. This is easily done with just two variables. Multiple regression and correlation, although analytically similar to the linear case, do not have as easy an interpretation. We explore multiple regression for the linear case in the application section of this chapter.

KEY CONCEPT **CONDUCTING A BIVARIATE STUDY**

Having provided some of the background and theory about the process, now do the case where you want to determine the relationship between household

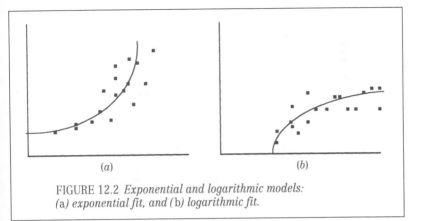

FIGURE 12.2 *Exponential and logarithmic models:*
(a) exponential fit, and (b) logarithmic fit.

income and wine purchases. Before performing the
analysis, it will be beneficial to have a map of the
process. The first two steps really have been discussed
in earlier analyses, but are briefly reviewed in light of
their application to regression and correlation. The real
content of this chapter is focused on the last two steps.
If you are not totally comfortable with the algebra of
the functions, particularly the linear function, you may
want to review these types of functions in Chapter 13
before getting into the regression analysis.

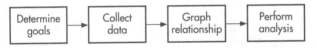

Getting Started: Know the Goal

In beginning your research, set a clear goal: Is there a
relationship between family income as indicated by
your survey participants and the amount of wine they
purchase in a week? The marketing department has
suggested that targeting future advertising to those
households with higher incomes should increase volume, and hence, revenue. Earlier it was mentioned that
the two variables in the analysis must be independent,
in the sense that they do not affect each other's outcomes. Yet, it should be clear from the preceding models that one of the variables must be selected as the
independent variable (the horizontal axis), and the
other, the dependent. Choose as the independent variable the one that is the basis of your decision making—
in this case, household income. In this way, if a
household has a certain income, you can then estimate
the corresponding amount of wine purchased in a
week. In manufacturing and operations the independent variable is usually a variable you control, and the
dependent variable may be the amount or level of production or quality factors. See Table 12.1 for examples
of relationships.

TABLE 12.1 EXAMPLES OF INDEPENDENT AND DEPENDENT VARIABLE RELATIONSHIPS

Variables You Control	Dependent Variables
Number of hours in workshift	Number of defective units produced
Hours of overtime	Units of production
Number of programmers	Lines of code
Number of days training	Staff productivity
Width of training manual	Total number of pages read by trainees

Most of the examples displayed in Table 12.1 convey a positive relationship between the two variables. We tend to think from that perspective when approaching correlation and regression. But variables may be inversely related as well—for example, demand curves. Or, as the information technology joke goes, there is an inverse relationship between the width of a training manual and its success with end users. Those who work in systems or with technology can appreciate the humor, but it serves as a reminder that relationships can be inversely or negatively correlated, as well.

Data Collection: Know the Intended Relationship

When collecting the data, you must record corresponding values of the variables as ordered pairs. Each pair of values occurs together. For example, when family income is $50,000, only 4 bottles of wine are purchased per week, but if the income is $140,000, then 8 bottles are purchased per week. These values become ordered pairs in the analysis. What is the relationship between amount of wine purchased and family income? Is it positive—that is, as income increases or decreases, does the amount of wine purchased increase or decrease? Is it strong—that is, how well do they correlate? With these two objectives in mind, take the first 10 surveys as a sample to explore this potential relationship (see Table 12.2).

 MAPPING THE STEPS IN REGRESSION ANALYSIS

There is a strategy to pursue in conducting this analysis:

- Before performing the quantitative crunching, create a visual relationship between the two variables in what is called a *scatter chart*. If there is no visual relationship between the variables, there is no sense

TABLE 12.2 INCOME AND PURCHASE SURVEY DATA

Income, $K	Consumption
50	4
70	5
75	6
80	5
100	6
110	5
120	8
130	7
140	8
160	9

in wasting your time by going any further. Read this carefully; don't jump into the analysis without having a picture of the relationship. There's an old saying that a picture is worth 1,000 words. In this case, a picture can save you 1,000 calculations as well as a lot of time and embarrassment.

- Based upon the scattergram you can sense the type of relationship, but what is the strength of the relationship between the variables? Correlation measures how well the two variables behave together. Are they related positively, negatively, or poorly?

- Assuming they are correlated, the next step is to select the type of regression model from the scatter chart and then proceed to perform the regression analysis. The result of this analysis is the estimating function.

- Once the key coefficients have been determined for the model, you will determine the coefficient of determination, which assesses the "goodness of fit" of the equation to the data.

- Finally, you can use the standard error to determine confidence intervals around the estimator—that is, what intervals give 95 or 99 percent confidence to your estimation.

First Step: Constructing a Scatter Chart—Sensing the Relationship

A *scatter chart* (also known as a *scatter plot* or an *XY plot*) is a mapping of each of the points on a coordinate system in which the independent variable is measured on the horizontal axis, and the corresponding behavior of the dependent variable on the vertical axis. Points are identified; then the strength and type of relationship is judged—linear, quadratic, and so on. The beauty of creating the scatter chart is that you are quickly able to see if you have good fit between the two variables before proceeding into heavy analysis.

A good fit is when the model fulfills the estimation relationship. When this occurs, you would expect a strong correlation—that is, close to 1. The good fit does not necessarily mean that points are in perfect alignment, as much as that the data adhere to the general conformity of the model. Note in Figure 12.3 that although the points do not follow a perfect alignment in the good relationship cases, they are reasonably close and display the necessary linear pattern. Although there are many models that can be used, this text employs the linear case, because it is readily available in spreadsheet applications.

The data yield the scatter chart in Figure 12.4. Note that the data are linear in nature and positively sloped. Therefore, there exists an equation of the form $y = mx + b$, which represents the relationship between these variables. Household income is the base variable (the x or independent variable along the horizontal axis), because you would like to predict a family's wine purchases based upon its income.

In statistics there is a slightly different version of the linear form, namely $y = \beta x + \alpha$, where β (beta) is the slope and α (alpha) is the intercept. These alphas and betas do not refer to the probability statistics employed in hypothesis testing. Leave it to statisticians to get confused—they should have stuck with $y = mx + b!$

 Second Step: Measuring the Strength of the Relationship

Since the scattergram definitely shows a somewhat linear pattern, indicating that household income can be used as a predictor of weekly wine purchases, the

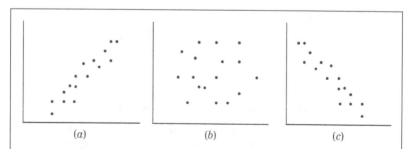

FIGURE 12.3 *Strong relationships versus weak relationship: (a) strong linear relationship, correlation close to 1; (b) weak relationship, correlation close to 0; and (c) strong linear relationship, correlation close to −1.*

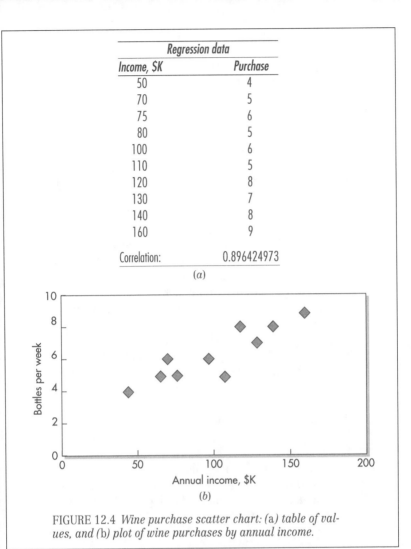

Regression data	
Income, $K	Purchase
50	4
70	5
75	6
80	5
100	6
110	5
120	8
130	7
140	8
160	9
Correlation:	0.896424973

(a)

(b)

FIGURE 12.4 *Wine purchase scatter chart:* (a) *table of values, and* (b) *plot of wine purchases by annual income.*

problem now becomes, how well are these two variables related? This brings us to correlation analysis.

Figure 12.4 includes the result of the CORREL function in Excel. The function asks you to identify the two ranges (in correlation, you are only measuring the strength of the relationship between the variables; hence, it does not matter which variable is identified as dependent or independent), and it produces a statistic between –1 and 1. The closer the absolute value is to 1, the stronger the relationship.

The reason correlation follows the visual display of the data is that you want to verify visually that the data appear to have a relationship and try to put a measure on it; in this case the correlation between income and purchases is 89.64 percent. In statistics this is referred to as *correlation* (or sometimes the *coefficient of correlation*), abbreviated as *r*. But we emphasize that in practice you should check correlation before performing detailed regression analysis. It is wasted effort to do the regression analysis and then find out that the data, in fact, did not possess a strong relationship.

 Creating the Estimating Function

The correlation is strong and the scatter chart definitely shows a somewhat linear pattern linking household income and weekly wine purchases. The problem now becomes, how do you determine the coefficients α and β of the linear function that will become your estimating function or *regression equation?* The whole idea here is not only to determine a function that is a good estimator, but, in fact, to find the line that is the best estimator of this relationship. Now, how should you do this? This will take a few moments, but the process will ensure that you understand exactly what regression analysis really means. So grab your pencil and pay attention!

First, you construct a line that will be a candidate for your solution. Then, you use it to determine the characteristics that will make a line the best estimator of the relationship. Once you understand the key factors that make a good estimator, you can use technology and a little math to generate the best estimator. We show why it is the best and then use it to generate estimation. So, first you need a line for a candidate. Suppose you were to construct a line from the last two points in the data, (140, 8) and (160, 9), and derive its equation. Use this as your candidate. Determine the slope and then the Y intercept.

$$\text{Slope} = \frac{\Delta Y}{\Delta X} = \frac{9 - 8}{160 - 140} = \frac{1}{20} = .05$$

yields the equation:

$$Y_g = .05X + b$$

By substituting either of the points (140, 8) or (160, 9) into the general equation, you will get 1 as the Y intercept, which results in your candidate for the estimator Y_g.

$$Y_g = .05X + 1$$

Figure 12.5 shows the line that is generated by those two points on the data set of the survey sample. But, you ask, is it a good estimator of this relationship? To answer that question, you can use the equation to generate its corresponding values of Y as shown in Table 12.3. Looking at Table 12.3 and Figure 12.5, you would probably agree it is a good estimate; hence, we refer to it as Y_g (for good). But here is the important question: Is it the best estimator, that is, the regression line? You need some criteria to help you make this decision.

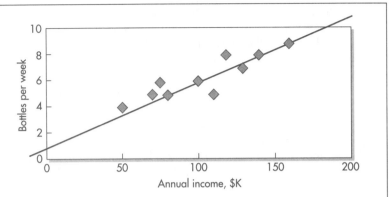

FIGURE 12.5 Y_g graphed on the survey set of points plotting wine purchases by annual income.

Goodness of Fit for Line Y_g

Just how good is the fit for the line $Y_g = .05X + 1$? If this were a perfect fit, then you would observe that each purchase value would be defined by the function, and, as a result, each point in your data collection would be on that line. In a perfect fit, the last column in Table 12.3 would read "Exact match" for each point. But as you can see, some of the points are above or below the estimating line Y_g. And you should suspect that the greater these distances are from the estimating line, the poorer the associated linear estimate.

So what should be the criteria for a line that will be the best fit? Look at what has been done in Table 12.3. One criterion to assess the goodness of fit to the data is to measure for each x_i, the difference between the estimating function's Y value and the actual Y value of one of the data points. This difference is termed a *residual*

TABLE 12.3 COMPARING Y_g WITH THE SURVEY POINTS

Income, $K	Purchases	Estimate, $Y_g = .05X + 1$	How Well Y_g Hits Points
50	4	3.50	A little below
70	5	4.50	A little below
75	6	4.75	A little below
80	5	5.00	Exact match
100	6	6.00	Exact match
110	5	6.50	A little above
120	8	7.00	A little below
130	7	7.50	A little above
140	8	8.00	Exact match
160	9	9.00	Exact match

and the process is known as *residual analysis.* And once again, the concept of variation enters the model.

The method for determining the amount of deviation is to compare each point on the line with the actual value from the data, and record that difference. The sum of these deviations is defined as the *total residual value* for this estimator. Your intuition should loudly proclaim that the best estimator will, in fact, be the function that yields the smallest total residual value. As an example, suppose you calculate in Table 12.4 the deviations with respect to the guess estimator, the line Y_g.

 Criteria for the Best Estimator

There are two deviations that are summed, the error or residual values, and the squares of these errors. The squares of the deviations are included because they give a more accurate sense of the actual differences because they will not get cancelled out due to sign. It stands to reason that the best estimator Y_b would be an equation that produces a sum of zero for the residuals, and the sum of the squares would be the least.

The following two equations say in mathematics what was just stated in the previous sentence. That is, for all (x_i, y_i) of data and points (x_i, y_b) belonging to the line Y_b, the following equations must be true. This hopefully makes logical as well as mathematical sense up to this point.

$$\sum_{i=1}^{\mu} (Y_i - Y_b) = 0 \quad \text{and} \quad \sum_{i=1}^{\mu} (Y_i - Y_b)^2 \quad \text{is a minimum}$$

TABLE 12.4 RESIDUAL ANALYSIS FOR Y_g

Income X	Purchases Y	Predicted Y_g $Y_g = .05X + 1$	Residual $(Y - Y_g)$	Residual^2 $(Y - Y_g)^2$
50	4	3.50	0.50	0.2500
70	5	4.50	0.50	0.2500
75	6	4.75	1.25	1.5625
80	5	5.00	0	0
100	6	6.00	0	0
110	5	6.50	−1.50	2.2500
120	8	7.00	1.00	1.0000
130	7	7.50	−0.50	0.2500
140	8	8.00	0	0
160	9	9.00	0	0
		Sums	1.25	5.5625

REGRESSION AND THE COMPUTER

There are numerous calculations required to obtain the optimum solution. Most of you will admit that such an extensive use of numerical calculations brings with it an opportunity for error, itself an interesting statistical problem.

When we encountered intensive calculations in the time value of money in Part 1, we employed the calculator to ease the burden of arithmetic calculations. Correspondingly, in the case for statistics we use spreadsheet software to demonstrate solutions to these problems. We do not explain the keystrokes required to perform this analysis due to the various versions of the software available. The example employs Microsoft Excel. To help you perform the same analysis, we describe the key steps required for doing this with a microcomputer.

Step 1. Enter the data in sequential rows and columns. At this point you can run a very quick scatter chart or *XY* graph to just check how the data look, if you have not already done so. What is important is that you visually check the relationship before doing regression. See Figure 12.4 for an example.

Income, $K	Purchases
50	4
70	5
75	6
80	5
100	6
110	5
120	8
130	7
140	8
160	9

Step 2. Test for how well the data are correlated. Use the CORREL function, highlight the two ranges, and determine the correlation to be 89.64 percent, which is a strong indicator that the variables are correlated. Again, see Figure 12.4.

Step 3. Select the Regression option from the Analytical Tools menu. Highlight the ranges specified in Table 12.5.

Step 4. Do a quick check. Interpret your output, graphically and analytically. See Figure 12.6 as an example of rather generic output.

TABLE 12.5 EXCEL RANGE SETTINGS FOR REGRESSION

Range	Setting
X	Highlight the column of cells that represent the independent variable, in this case, the 10 cells containing the income data.
Y	Highlight the column of cells that represent the dependent variable, in this case, the 10 corresponding cells containing the wine-purchase data.
Output	Highlight a section of the sheet for the output of the regression analysis. Key point here is to know that about 20 rows and 10 columns of results will be displayed, so select a range that has nothing in its cells, or you can specify a new sheet.

Step 5. Interpret your output numerically. See Figure 12.7.

Step 6. Be thankful for microcomputers!

In the next sections, we demonstrate that the derived estimator is better than Y_b and explain the key statistics from the Excel output. The labels "R Square" and "Multiple R" are measures of correlation, but most important, on the lower part of the output you will find β and α beside the "X Variable" and "Intercept" cells. Yes, you have found the coefficients of the best estimator Y_b:

$$Y_b = .0421\ x + 1.938$$

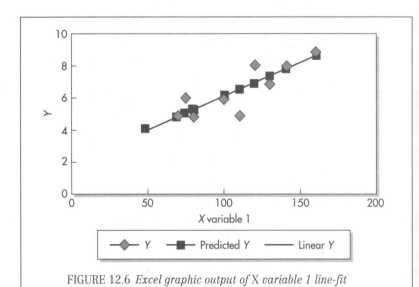

FIGURE 12.6 *Excel graphic output of* X *variable 1 line-fit plot.*

How This Equation Is the Best Fit

Figure 12.8 shows the fit for Y_b. But how do you know if this equation is better then the equation you used earlier? Recall that the sum of the squared deviations of the line Y_g, which you thought was actually a pretty good estimate, was 5.5625. Upon examining Table 12.6, it is clear that the line Y_b is better than Y_g and, further, that the requirements set forth earlier have been satisfied. Compare—the summation of the deviations is indeed 0, and you have minimized the squared residuals, 4.733.

$$\sum_{i=1}^{\mu} (Y_i - Y_b) = 0 \quad \text{and} \quad \sum_{i=1}^{\mu} (Y_i - Y_b)^2 \quad \text{is a minimum}$$

Measuring the Strength of the Estimator

In beginning your research you set a clear goal: Is there a relationship between family income as indicated by the survey participants and the amount of wine they purchase in a week? As a result, you have the following equation Y_b as the best predictor of wine-purchasing behavior as a function of family income. The next part of your analysis is to determine how good an estimate the derived equation Y_b is, and this brings us to the concept of the coefficient of determination.

$$Y_b = \beta_b X + \alpha_b = .0421x + 1.938$$

The *coefficient of determination* is a measure of how close the linear estimator fits the data—more technically, the degree to which the line defines or explains

Regression data		Summary Output	
Income, SK	Consumption	Regression statistics	
50	4	Multiple R	0.896425
70	5	R Square	0.803578
75	6	Adjusted R Square	0.779025
80	5	Standard Error	0.769235
100	6	Observations	10
110	5		
120	8	Coefficients	
130	7	Intercept	1.937858
140	8	X Variable 1	0.042146
160	9		

FIGURE 12.7 *Excel numeric output.*

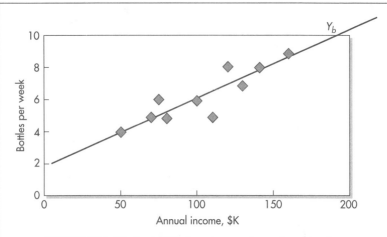

FIGURE 12.8 *The best fit* Y_b *for wine purchases by annual income (*$Y = .0421x + 1.938$*).*

the relationship between the dependent and independent variables. The most common statistic that measures what is called "goodness of fit" is the coefficient of determination (referred to as r^2 in statistical presentations or R Square on the Excel output [Figure 12.7]). The r^2 for this analysis is 0.803578.

Look at the solution for Y_b in Figure 12.8 and suppose it was a perfect fit—then, wouldn't every data point be on that line? There would be no deviation between the y_i value of the data (x_i, y_i) and the y_b value derived from the equation of the estimating line. But in truth, these points are not on the line; therefore, this number grows larger as the points are farther from the

TABLE 12.6 DERIVING THE BEST LINEAR ESTIMATE

Income x	Purchase y	Predicted Y_b $.042146x + 1.9378$	Residual $(y - y_b)$	Residual^2 $(y - y_b)^2$
50	4	4.0452	−0.0452	0.0020
70	5	4.8881	0.1119	0.0125
75	6	5.0988	0.9012	0.8121
80	5	5.3096	−0.3096	0.0958
100	6	6.1525	−0.1525	0.0233
110	5	6.5740	−1.5740	2.4773
120	8	6.9954	1.0046	1.0092
130	7	7.4169	−0.4169	0.1738
140	8	7.8383	0.1617	0.0261
160	9	8.6813	0.3188	0.1016
		Sums	0.0000	4.733

best estimator Y_b. Just because you generate an equation, it does not mean that it is a good predictor. The coefficient of determination measures the degree to which this deviation $(y_i - y_b)$ exists. Figure 12.9 shows the comparison between a set of data for which the best estimator is a good fit and a set for which it is not. To show the nature of poor fit, the second figure shows two lines that could possibly satisfy the data points. The closer the value of r^2 is to 1, the better the fit. A perfect fit would yield $r^2 = 1$. The closer the value of r^2 is to 0, the poorer the fit.

 Determining the Strength of the Relationship

Now we can explain correlation r, the strength of the relationship between the variables, in a little more depth. The range of values for correlation is $-1 \leq r \leq 1$, the measure of strength being: The closer to 1, the better the two variables behave together. Correlation takes its sign from the coefficient β from the regression estimator; hence, it indicates direct (positive slope) and inverse relationships (negative slope).

Since the coefficient β of the estimator is positive, then the correlation is positive and the strength is quite good at .896 (Multiple R on the Excel report).

The Power of Inference

So what has all this got you? The reason you undertook this study was to determine if there is a relationship between annual income and wine-purchasing behavior. Not only is there a positive relationship (the slope is positive), it is reasonably strong, as judged by the coefficient of determination, $r^2 = .80357$. Now that you have the equation, how do you use it to infer wine

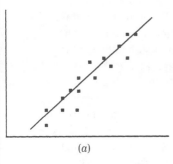 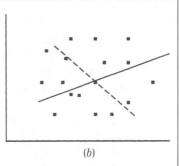

(a) (b)

FIGURE 12.9 *Coefficient of determination and goodness of fit: (a) good linear fit, correlation close to 1; and (b) poor fit, correlation close to 0.*

consumption behavior? For example, if somebody has an annual income of $200,000, how much wine would you expect them to purchase on a weekly basis?

$$Y = .0421x + 1.938$$

$$Y = .0421(200) + 1.938$$

$$Y = 10.358$$

A Note on Standard Error

One last point—what does the standard error from the Excel output tell you? Standard error is very similar to the standard error of the mean that you used in hypothesis testing. That is, you can build a confidence level of 95 percent by determining points ± 2 standard deviations from the derived answer from the estimator. You estimated that a customer who makes a salary of $200,000 will purchase 10.38 bottles of wine per week. You can estimate with 95 percent certainty that this customer will purchase between $10.38 - 2(.77)$ and $10.38 + 2(.77)$ bottles. Which translates to approximately 9 to 12 bottles of wine a week. So, you have made it! This equation allows you to infer purchasing based upon income, and you have built a confidence interval around it. Only the applications can make this better!

APPLICATIONS OF REGRESSION ANALYSIS

This section demonstrates how the material in this chapter can be applied to predicting annual maintenance costs and future expenses and revenues.

 Predicting Annual Machinery Maintenance Costs

Although some machinery has been bought by you, most of the machinery was purchased by the original owner of the vineyard. You can tell by examining the data that there is a definite relationship between the age of a machine and the annual repair costs to maintain it. You have selected 10 random machines and compiled their annual repair costs in order to determine a relationship that will allow you to predict repair costs given the age of the machine.

Given the following data, use a spreadsheet program or a calculator to prepare a scattergram to assess if the data looks like it is suitable for a regression model, use the CORREL function to determine the degree of correlation, and determine the linear regression equation.

As Figure 12.10 shows, there is a high correlation, indicating that the two variables do behave well together. The graph also shows that they move together, confirming the correlation of .96. They appear to be a good fit for a linear model.

Figure 12.11 presents the Excel solution, along with the data.

From the data on the right side of the figure you can see the coefficients for the line that is the best predictor. As well, the coefficient of determination r^2 is 0.928, indicating that this equation is a very good estimator of maintenance costs based upon this sample.

$$Y = \beta x + \alpha = 212x - 287.33$$

You now can answer such questions as what the expected annual repair cost is for a machine that is 15 years old.

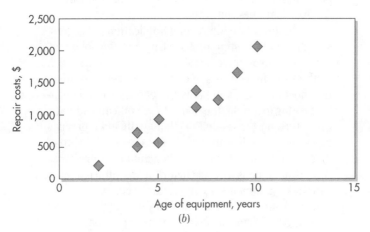

Age of equipment	Repair costs, $
2	200
4	680
5	900
7	1350
8	1200
4	490
9	1600
10	2000
5	540
7	1100
Correlation:	0.96330

(a)

(b)

FIGURE 12.10 *A good scatterplot:* (a) *table of values, and* (b) *plot of repair costs to years of age.*

Machinery Data		Summary Output	
Age of		Regression statistics	
equipment	Repair costs, $	Multiple R	0.96333354
2	200	R Square	0.928115
4	680	Adjusted R Square	0.91901294
5	900	Standard Error	157.487132
7	1350	Observations	10
8	1200		
4	490	Coefficients	
9	1600	Intercept	−287.328647
10	2000	X Variable 1	212.02109
5	540		
7	1100		

FIGURE 12.11 *The Excel solution.*

$$Y = \beta x + \alpha = 212x - 287.33$$
$$Y = 212(15) - 287.33$$
$$Y = 2,892.67$$

 Forecasting Security Performance

You have just completed an excellent analysis of the performance of the three portfolios from Chapters 7 and 8, to the point where you examined risk versus reward and even explored the efficient frontier. Based upon your recommendation, the firm has selected portfolio manager B to manage the retirement account. But the question has come up regarding performance— what kind of returns can you expect based upon the return of the S&P? Specifically, if the S&P goes up 15 percent, how will portfolio B perform in response? An excellent question, you observe.

One of the more interesting applications of regression is found in estimating security and portfolio performance based upon some market benchmark, such as the Dow Jones average or the S&P 500. Essentially, the theory goes, if you know the behavior of a benchmark—for example, the S&P—then you can estimate the return on the related portfolio with some precision by studying the line that describes the relationship of its return to the return of the benchmark over time. And, if the past is any predictor for the future, then you can make judgments about certain securities relative to your investment strategy. Are they strongly correlated to the S&P—either positively, in the sense that they move together, or negatively, in the sense that they go down as the S&P goes up (or vice versa, to act as a hedge for the portfolio)—and are they aggressive or safe compared to the S&P? The answers are found in the concept of slope, your friend β. Enough with the theory, let's get to the problem.

To answer the performance question, you will analyze the performance of portfolio manager B with respect to the S&P over the same time periods. As you did before, first make sure there is a correlation, graphically as well as quantitatively, then perform regression to see what β tell you about this relationship. Figure 12.12 shows the data and the *XY* plot.

Since the scatter chart definitely shows a linear pattern, indicating that the S&P can be used as a predictor of fund performance, the problem now becomes to determine how well these two variables are related. This brings you to the coefficient of correlation. The CORREL function shows .9432, indicating a very strong

Year	S&P 500	Port. B
1	0.060	0.050
2	0.050	0.080
3	0.040	0.050
4	0.020	0.020
5	0.060	0.070
6	0.070	0.070
7	0.090	0.110
8	0.110	0.100
9	0.110	0.110
10	0.120	0.140
11	0.130	0.110
12	0.170	0.170

	Port. B
Correlation with S&P	0.9432124

(*a*)

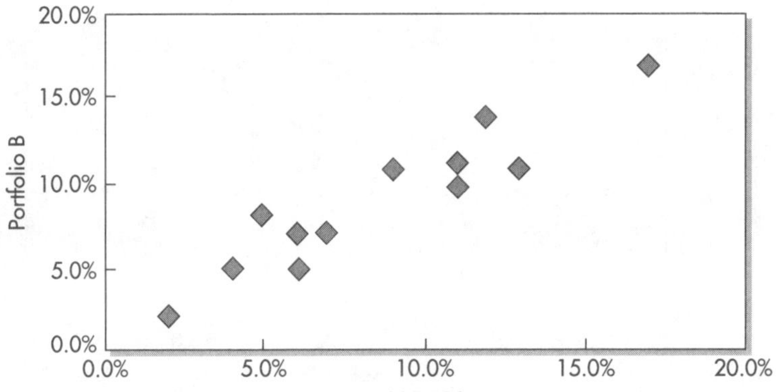

(*b*)

FIGURE 12.12 *Portfolio manager B versus the S&P 500: (a) table of values, and (b) plot of the data.*

relationship between the variables. Recall that the closer the absolute value is to 1, the stronger the relationship.

Next, determine the linear estimator from the regression function. It is important to know which variable is the independent variable (the x range for Excel) so that you can employ the right relationship. Since you are estimating portfolio B as a function of the S&P, the S&P must be the independent variable, and portfolio B is therefore the dependent variable. After performing the regression analysis, you will get the output from Excel shown in Figure 12.13. Again, the entire output is not produced in the figure.

The equation that describes the relationship between the variables is derived from the last two lines of the output.

$$y = \alpha + \beta x \qquad \text{becomes} \qquad y = .012 + .9086x$$

The result of this equation is that if you make a judgment on the performance of the S&P for the next

Regression Statistics	
Multiple R	0.94321239
R Square	0.88964962
Adjusted R Square	0.87861458
Standard Error	0.01455585
Observations	12

Coefficients	
Intercept	0.01201369
X Variable 1	0.90857833

(a)

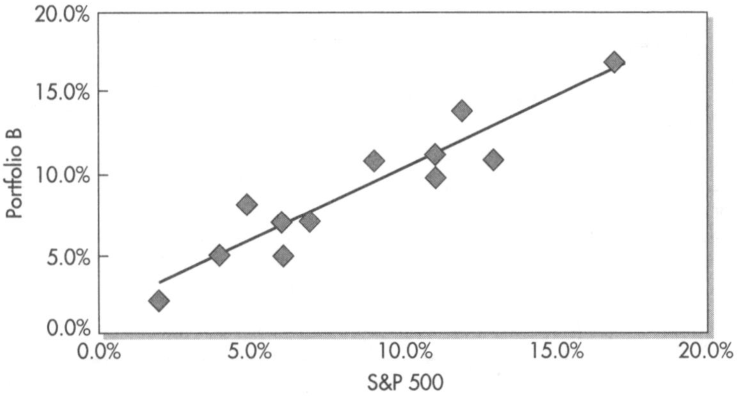

(b)

FIGURE 12.13 *Excel output and chart for beta analysis of portfolio B versus the S&P 500: (a) Excel output, and (b) chart.*

period, you can use the equation to predict the corresponding performance of the portfolio.

So what does the β value of .908 tell you? First, because the slope is positive, you can infer a direct positive relationship—that is, as the S&P goes up, so will the performance of portfolio B. As well, if the S&P goes down, so will portfolio B. But there is even a more subtle point to this analysis. Consider the relationship of β in Figure 12.14.

In this case the value of β is very close to 1, indicating that portfolio B will move in tandem with the S&P benchmark. Is there significance to values either greater or less than 1? Relatively speaking, you might consider an aggressive investor to seek those securities or portfolios where $\beta > 1$. What $\beta > 1$ indicates is that the security will, on average, outperform the benchmark. For example, if $\beta = 2$ then you could infer that the selected security will, on average, perform twice as well as the given benchmark. On the other hand, the defensive investor will seek opportunities where $0 < \beta < 1$. All this from your friend, β.

Finally, what kind of confidence do you have in your estimator? By looking at the Excel output you can build a 95 percent confidence interval on your estimate by using the standard error, 0.01455. The question is, what kind of return would you anticipate from portfolio B if the S&P were to go up 15 percent this period?

$$y = 0.012 + 0.9086x$$
$$\text{becomes} \quad y = 0.012 + 0.9086(0.15) = 0.1483$$

You can expect a return of 14.83 percent if the S&P were to go up 15 percent. And for your confidence interval:

$$\text{Upper limit} = 0.1483 + 2(0.01455) = 0.1483 + 0.0291$$
$$= 0.1774 \quad \text{or 17.74 percent}$$

$$\text{Lower limit} = 0.1483 - 2(0.01455) = 0.1483 - 0.0291$$
$$= 0.1192 \quad \text{or 11.92 percent}$$

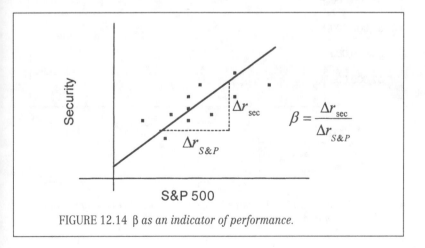

FIGURE 12.14 *β as an indicator of performance.*

Logarithmic Scales in Regression

Suppose your company has undergone rapid growth, and sales have grown exponentially over the past few years. Your job is to forecast the next few years of sales based on some compounding rate. Someone has told you about generating your data on a logarithmic scale to assess its appropriateness. But how will that help?

The key to the observation is the relationship between exponential functions, logarithms, and the linear equation. That is, by taking the logarithms of the exponential data, and plotting the points, do you see a good linear fit? If so, the original data can be estimated with an exponential model. Figure 12.15 shows the annual sales data and the related exponential-like graph, meaning that the data appears to be exponential in nature.

Upon examination of the data it is clear that there is some exponential relationship. The next step is to take the natural log of the sales data and plot it to see if

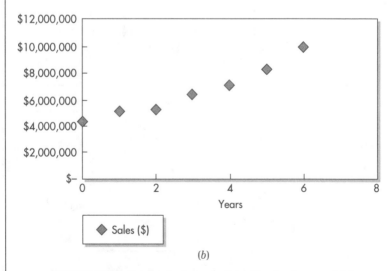

Year	Sales $
0	4,350,000
1	5,000,000
2	5,200,000
3	6,720,000
4	7,150,000
5	8,259,000
6	9,900,000

(a)

(b)

FIGURE 12.15 *Total sales by year: (a) table of values, and (b) plot of annual sales.*

there is a linear fit. Now why would that be? Consider the following relationship with logarithms. Yes, finally there is a place where you can use all those logarithmic relationships. The following equations attempt to define the rationale for this activity.

Take the general exponential equation.

$$y = ab^x$$

Take the natural log of both sides.

$$\ln y = \ln ab^x$$

Log of a product is the sum of the logs.

$$\ln y = \ln a + \ln b^x$$

Log of a power creates a product relationship between the base and power. The result is a linear equation.

$$\ln y = \ln a + x \ln b$$

So, based on this beautiful exploitation of logarithms, you are now ready to assess the quality of making an exponential regression based upon what the linear case tells you. A close examination of Figure 12.16 shows just how good the log-scaled data fits a linear model. You might want to take ln $4,350,000 to verify the value of 15.285686.

As you examine the linear trend line on the natural logs of the sales data, it would certainly seem that it is a very good estimator. But the linear case is used as a test for how good a fit this can be. Now take the regression analysis from Figure 12.17 and determine the actual equation. Here is how it is done. Logarithms just don't get any better than this.

So, based on the derivation you use the regression data, which is in a logarithmic scale, to translate to the exponential function that represents total sales. Again start with the logarithmic equation you used to create the linear relationship.

$$\ln y = \ln a + x \ln b$$

Make the substitutions from the Excel printout.

$$\ln y = 15.26 + x \,(0.13533)$$

The sum of logs is the product of the numbers.

$$y = (e^{15.26})(e^{x(0.13533)})$$

Determine the base (1.145) by solving $e^{0.13533}$. The coefficient will be $e^{15.26}$, which is 4,239,686.

$$y = (e^{15.26})(e^{(0.13533)x})$$

$$y = 4,239,686(1.145^x)$$

Nirvana!

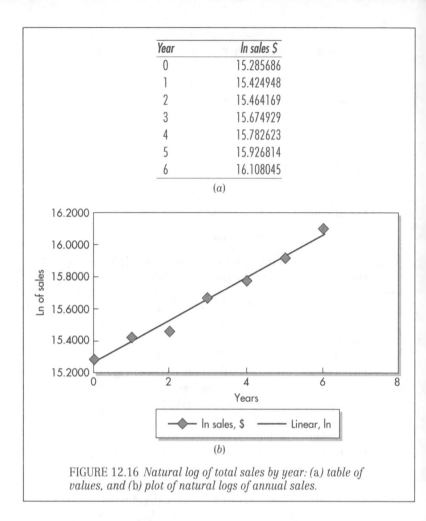

Year	ln sales $
0	15.285686
1	15.424948
2	15.464169
3	15.674929
4	15.782623
5	15.926814
6	16.108045

(a)

(b)

FIGURE 12.16 *Natural log of total sales by year: (a) table of values, and (b) plot of natural logs of annual sales.*

So, what can you project as the total sales for the next few years? You now have an equation that is a very good estimator based on linear analysis. Check out the r^2. The following table uses the equation just developed to project the next few years of sales. The sixth year is included to compare with the last year given in

Regression Statistics	
Multiple R	0.992498512
R Square	0.985053313
Adjusted R Square	0.982063976
Standard Error	0.039448744
Observations	12

	Coefficients
Intercept	15.26075268
X Variable 1	0.135330774

FIGURE 12.17 *Excel regression output.*

the data. As you can see, this is an excellent estimator, and a wonderful use of logarithms.

Year	Sales
6	9,556,550
7	10,941,441
8	12,527,025
9	14,342,384

Multiple Regression

This is an optional section that really requires that you have a computer, because the next step is certainly never to be done manually, or even with a calculator. Now that you have determined a wonderful relationship, a strong one, between income and wine consumption, is there a relationship with the monthly amount spent on food as well?

Multiple regression differs from the original examples in that two or more independent variables X_1 and X_2 are used to explain the relationship with Y. We continue to examine a linear model, but the equation changes to adapt to another independent variable; that is, there are two betas, one for annual income and one for monthly food expenditure. Most likely, if you are doing multiple regression you will be employing a spreadsheet program of some sort. We explain how to perform this analysis with Microsoft Excel.

$$Y = \beta_1 X_1 + \beta_2 X_2 + \alpha$$

The data are amended to include a third column for monthly food bill, placed between the income and consumption columns.

Step 1. Enter the data in sequential rows and columns.

Income, $K	Monthly Food Bill	Consumption
50	65	4
70	80	5
75	85	6
80	90	5
100	100	6
110	95	5
120	110	8
130	110	7
140	120	8
160	160	9

Step 2. Here is where we make a strong case for performing the correlation analysis. Which variable has the strongest relationship with purchasing behavior? Whichever one it is, maybe it is sufficient to explain the behavior all on its own, thereby making it a simple model.

	Income	Food Bill	Purchases
Corr to income	100.000%	94.291%	89.642%
Corr to food bill	94.291	100.000	91.024
Corr to purchases	89.642	91.024	100.000

The matrix shows that the strongest correlation is with the food bill, and if only one variable were to be used, then that would be the one, not income. Interesting.

Step 3. Select the Regression option from the Analytical Tools menu. Highlight the ranges specified in Table 12.7.

Step 4. Interpret your output numerically. See Figure 12.18.

This produces a very interesting result: The second independent variable, the monthly food bill, proves to be a bigger contributor to explaining the wine-purchasing behavior. How is this the case? Examine the data for both independent variables—they are basically the same measures, yet the coefficient of Variable 2 (monthly food expenditure) is more than twice that of Variable 1.

The equation expressing the weekly wine purchases as a function of annual income and monthly food

TABLE 12.7 EXCEL RANGE SETTINGS FOR REGRESSION

Range	Setting
X	Highlight the columns of cells that represent the independent variables, in this case, the 10 cells containing the income data and the monthly food bill. Do not include the name of the data in the range.
Y	Highlight the column of cells that represent the dependent variable, in this case, the 10 corresponding cells containing the purchase data.
Output	Highlight a section of the sheet for the output of the regression analysis.

	Regression Data		Summary Output	
Income	Food bill	Purchases	Regression statistics	
50	65	4	Multiple R	0.917417
70	80	5	R Square	0.841654
75	85	6	Adjusted R Square	0.796412
80	90	5	Standard Error	0.738351
100	100	6	Observations	10
110	95	5		
120	110	8	Coefficients	
130	110	7	Intercept	0.904225
140	120	8	X Variable 1	0.016173
160	160	9	X Variable 2	0.036669

FIGURE 12.18 *Multiple regression output.*

expenditure is defined here as a result of the associated spreadsheet output. When performing multiple regression, r^2, the coefficient of determination, gets inflated as additional variables attempt to explain the change in the dependent variable. To correct for this inaccuracy, statisticians use an adjusted r^2 to indicate the strength of the estimator.

$$Y = \beta_1 X_1 + \beta_2 X_2 + \alpha = .0162X_1 + .0367X_2 + .904$$

Inference

If a family has an annual income of $200,000 and has a weekly food bill of $160, then based on the analysis, how many bottles of wine will you predict they will purchase?

$$Y = .0162(200) + .0367(160) + .904$$

$$Y = 3.24 + 5.872 + .904$$

$$Y = 10.016 \quad \text{or 10 bottles per week}$$

Sounds like a cheerful house!

END POINT

Regression analysis is the one of the most important and useful tools from statistics. It is absolutely one that any person in business must know how to perform. The process relies on understanding the goal, carefully determining the data to collect, identifying dependent and independent relationships, and performing the calculations. The results help you to then estimate behavior based upon values of the independent variable. And how much faith you put in this estimator is a function of your correlation analysis. But the power of this process is the ability to predict what will happen based on data as opposed to a gut feeling.

It is certainly true that using technology makes this process much easier. So which technique you should use is really not the question. Most likely you will employ a spreadsheet, or some other automated way to perform this analysis. What is important is that you understand how these coefficients are determined and the methods by which you have to assess the strength of the relationship between the variables. Once you are using an automated method, a clear understanding of the assumptions behind your estimator will lead you to proper usage and understanding of the degree of correlation.

All the Algebra and High School Math You Need for Business

13

Algebra Redux

The purpose of this review is to examine those core concepts from high school math that you will need to successfully understand the topics in time value of money and statistics. It is short, topically driven to make it easy to use, and stuffed with examples to demonstrate the topic. In fact, this section is probably better referred to as *learning by example*. Because most of you have seen this material in a classroom in your distant past, this approach should allow you to get only that which you need in the most efficient manner for your relearning or refreshing.

RECOMMENDED METHOD OF PROCEEDING

If it has been a long time since you have done math or you did not do very well in math classes, work your way through this section topic by topic. Think of this section as a prerequisite review to help make sure the basics are in place to ensure understanding of the math steps employed in the financial and statistical topics.

If your skills are in reasonable shape then you might want to skim through the section and work only on those areas that are not familiar to you.

- *Standards in presentation.* Each topic is explained briefly, and then demonstrated by examples. In many of the examples you will find comments to explain what occurred at that stage of the problem. Hopefully, this brief comment will answer the question that is in your mind at that point in doing the problem. It's an attempt at offline help.

- *What you need.* The three *P*s would help immensely—paper, pencil, and patience. Have pencil and paper nearby so you can perform the exercises to verify your understanding. On some sections, such as the exponents, the calculator will certainly help.

OPERATIONS WITH NUMERICAL AND ALGEBRAIC EXPRESSIONS

Addition and Subtraction

$$(2x - 5) + (6x + 5) = \qquad x^2y + xy^2 =$$

When working with signed numbers—for example, 4, −3, 0, 15—it is important to be attentive to the signs before performing the operation. When *adding* two numerals or algebraic expressions, the following rules apply:

- If the signs are the same, keep the sign and add the quantities (the absolute values or the "pure" number).

- The *absolute value* of a number is defined as the distance that number is from 0, or simply, the number without its sign. Notationally, it is identified by $|4| = 4$ or $|−5| = 5$.

- You can only add or subtract *like terms* (expressions with the same variables to the same power—$3xy$ and $−6xy$, but not $7x^2y$.) Don't be fooled if two or more expressions have the same variables—the only thing you can add to an x is another x, $5x$ or $−3x$, but not an x^2 or an xy.

Examples

$$4 + 8 = 12 \qquad −4 + −8 = −12 \qquad −6x + −8x = −14x$$

- If the signs are the not the same, take the difference of the quantities and apply the sign of the larger quantity.

Examples

$$4 + −8 = −4 \qquad 5x^2 + (−4x^2) = x^2 \qquad 6y + −8y = −2y$$

$$−4 + 8 = 4 \qquad (2x − 5) + (6x + 5) = 8x \qquad x^2y + xy^2 = \text{as is}$$

When *subtracting,* the rule is pretty simple: Change the sign(s) of the expression you are subtracting and then follow the rules set forth in addition—that is, you make the problem a two-step problem, change the sign of the subtrahend, and then proceed as in addition.

Examples

$$4 - (-8) = 4 + (+8) = 12$$
$$-4 - (8) = -4 + (-8) = -12$$
$$-6y - (-8y) = -6y + (8y) = 2y$$
$$-6ab - (4ab) = -6ab + (-4ab) = -10ab$$

Order of Operations

$$33 - 32/4 = \qquad 8 + 4(2) =$$

This problem presents a procedural issue: Do you subtract 32 from 33 and divide, or do you divide 32 by 4 and then subtract from 33? As a result, one of the first things we must address when proceeding into multiplication and division is which of the four operations has priority. Here's the rule:

The ORDER OF OPERATIONS *(My Dear Aunt Sally)*

1. Moving from left to right, do multiplication and division first.
2. Then, perform addition and subtraction (collect like terms).

Examples

Multiplication first, then add like terms.

$$3(-4) - 7 = -12 - 7 = -12 + (-7) = -19$$

Division first, then add like terms.

$$33 - 32/4 = 33 - 8 = 25$$

Multiplication first, then add like terms.

$$4(5) - 3(6) = 20 - 18 = 2$$

Multiplication and Division

When working with the product and ratio of algebraic terms, you have to be attentive to exponents. The numerical coefficients are easy, just divide or multiply. It's the powers of the variable that require your attention. The following definitions and rules will help:

- When *multiplying or dividing* two numerals, or algebraic terms, if the signs are alike, then the answer is positive. If the signs are opposite, the answer is negative. When multiplying expressions with variables, you must pay attention to exponents.

An *exponent* is the power to which a given base is raised. You have heard of squaring a number, for example 5^2. In this case, 2 is the exponent and 5 is the base. The key to solving an exponential expression like 5^2 is to remember that the exponent indicates how many times the base will be taken as a factor with itself. For this example, 5^2 means 5×5, which is 25. If a negative number is being squared, it should be in parenthesis; for example, $(-5)^2 = 25$. In this way it is clear that the base is -5.

When working with *exponents* remember the following rules:

- By definition, $x^n = x \cdot x \cdot \ldots \cdot x$ (n times or factors).
- By definition, anything to the zero power is 1; that is, $x^0 = 1$.
- Exponential product rule: $x^a \cdot x^b = x^{a+b}$.
- Exponential division rule: $\dfrac{x^a}{x^b} = x^{a-b}$

Examples

$$(4)(-8) = -32 \qquad (-6)(-8) = 48$$

$$(4xy)(-6x^2z^2) = -24x^3yz^2 \qquad (-3x^2)^3 = -27x^6$$

$$(2^3)(2^2) = 2^5 = 32 \qquad (-2)^4 = 16$$

$$\frac{-36}{-9} = 4 \qquad \frac{-72x^2y^4}{-9xy^2} = 8xy^2$$

When dividing, be sure to subtract the exponents and do not cancel out the base. Often students cancel the fives in that last problem. Don't do it. Just translate it to 5^{4-2}, which equals 5^2.

Products of Binomials and Polynomials

$$(x + 4)^2 = (x + 2)(x - 5)$$

This was the point where, for many people, algebra started to make no sense, and if it weren't for FOIL and memorization, most people would have retired and gone no further into the land of mathematics. There are two types of problems you need to be able to perform. The first is *multiplication by a single term*.

Example

Single term products (monomials with polynomials):

$$2x(3x - 6) =$$

Distribute $2x$ into each term of the binomial and multiply. Then collect like terms.

$$2x(3x - 6) = (2x)3x - (2x)6$$

$$= 6x^2 - 12x$$

$$4ab^2(a^2 - 2b + ab) = 4a^3b^2 - 8ab^3 + 4a^2b^3$$

When *multiplying a polynomial by a binomial,* the general method is to distribute the binomial into the other expression, perform the multiplication, and collect like terms, as demonstrated in the following. For the *product of two binomials,* you can use the old FOIL method as a special case.

Example

Binomial products (binomials with polynomials):

$$(x + 1)(x + 4) =$$

Distribute $(x + 1)$ into each term.

$$(x + 1)(x + 4) = (x + 1)x + (x + 1)4$$

Now multiply and collect like terms.

$$= x^2 + x + 4x + 4$$
$$= x^2 + 5x + 4$$

Example

Binomial with polynomial:

$$(x + 2)(x^2 - 5x - 5) =$$

Trick: Be careful of that minus sign. The minus sign requires that you change the signs in $(x + 2)$.

$$(x + 2)x^2 - (x + 2)5x - (x + 2)5$$
$$x^3 + 2x^2 - 5x^2 - 10x - 5x - 10$$
$$x^3 - 3x^2 - 15x - 10$$

Everyone remembers FOIL. FOIL refers to the old trick for multiplying binomials. To do this method, perform the product of the first terms, the outer terms, the inner terms, and the last terms, and then add like terms.

$$(x - 3)(x + 3) =$$

First	Outer	Inner	Last	Now add
x^2 +	$3x$ −	$3x$ −	9 =	$x^2 - 9$

$$(x + 1)(x - 4) = x^2 - 3x + 4$$

Operating with Exponents

$$(1.08)^0 = \qquad (1.08)^{-1} =$$

When working with the product and ratio of algebraic terms, you have to be attentive to exponents. The numerical coefficients are easy; it's the power of the variable that requires your attention. The additional definitions and rules will help in operating with exponents:

- By definition, $x^{1/n} = \sqrt[n]{x}$ $\qquad x^{-n} = \dfrac{1}{x^n}$

- The power of ratios:

$$\left(\frac{x}{y}\right)^{a} = \frac{x^{a}}{y^{a}} \qquad \text{or} \qquad \left(\frac{x}{y}\right)^{-a} = \frac{x^{-a}}{y^{-a}} = \frac{y^{a}}{x^{a}}$$

Examples

$$\frac{1}{3^{-2}} = 9 \qquad \frac{-24x^{6}y^{8}}{4x^{-2}y^{2}} = -6x^{8}y^{6} \qquad \frac{-48x^{-4}y^{6}z^{-2}}{-6x^{2}y^{2}z^{-4}} = 8x^{-6}y^{4}z^{2}$$

$$\left(\frac{4}{3}\right)^{2} = \frac{16}{9} \qquad \frac{54x^{4}y^{6}}{(-3x^{2}y)^{2}} = 6y^{4} \qquad \left(\frac{9x^{2}}{16y^{4}}\right)^{-1/2} = \frac{4y^{2}}{3x}$$

$$8^{1/3} = \sqrt[3]{8} = 2 \qquad \left(\frac{9}{4}\right)^{1/2} = \frac{3}{2} \qquad 27^{2/3} = (\sqrt[3]{27})^{2} = (3)^{2} = 9$$

$$(1.08)^{0} = 1 \qquad (1.08)^{1} = 1.08 \qquad (1.08)^{-1} = \frac{1}{1.08} = .9259$$

CALC TIP
Using Fractional Exponents

Well, the problems in that last row might have had a few of you running to the calculator (which is exactly what you should have done). These three problems are important because they determine the financial multipliers that determine the future worth of an investment or its discounted value. These are explained in Part 1, on the time value of money. If you have a Power key (^) on your calculator, see the Calc Tip in Chapter 1 on how to use it.

Now we'll examine the use of the calculator with these problems and look at a revision of the order of operations. When doing root or power problems with the calculator, use the y^{x} key, where y is the base and is entered first. Then enter the exponent value for x. If x is fractional in nature, use parentheses around the x entry. The reason you want to use parentheses is because sometimes you can't enter the real value—entering .5 for 1/2 is fine, but entering .33 for 1/3 will lead to an incorrect value.

$$9^{1/2} = \sqrt{9} = 3$$

On the calculator this becomes:

Type 9 and press Enter.

Type (1 ÷ 2) and type =.

Your answer should be 3.

$$125^{1/3} = \qquad 15^{2/3} = 6.0822$$

More on Order of Operations

Consider the solution for:

$$-8^{2} + 4 =$$

This problem exhibits a major source of misunderstanding: What is being squared, 8 or –8? Or the question could be rephrased as, What is the base related to the exponent 2? In a nonmathematical answer, suppose you are the exponent. To determine the base, all you need do is look down. If you see a number, like 8, it is the base. If you see parentheses, then what is inside the parentheses is the base. The convention is that when the sign is to be part of the base, then it must be in parentheses.

Therefore, to solve problems like this one, you need to make a revision to the order of operations and have an understanding of which operation has priority. Unless parentheses are used, the base associated with the exponent is the value 8, not –8. This may be disturbing, but with the convention defined it should no longer be questionable.

Revised ORDER OF OPERATIONS *(Please Excuse My Dear Aunt Sally)*

1. Expressions inside parenthesis must be performed first.
2. Then, perform any exponential operations.
3. Then My Dear Aunt Sally will apply.

Examples

$$-4^{1/2} =$$

Since the base is 4, the problem becomes taking the negative root of 4.

$$-4^{1/2} = -\sqrt{4} = -2$$

But let's be careful. Suppose the base actually was –4.

$$(-4)^{1/2} = \sqrt{-4}$$

This root has no solution since there is no real number that when squared will equal –4. The imaginary solution $\pm 2i$ has no immediate application in this business orientation.

$$-8^2 + 4 =$$

Be careful, remember what the base is. Answer is –60.

 ## THE IMPORTANCE OF FACTORING

$$5x + 5y \qquad x^2 + 12x + 20$$

Factoring is like a puzzle—you try to find the factors that yield the given expression; for example, the factors of 35 are 5 and 7. When you get to solving equations, the ability to factor is a critical skill because it is the first technique you employ to find roots. There are a few general steps to follow:

- From the expression, factor out any common term—for example, a constant or a combination of the variable and a constant.

- If the remaining expression is of a degree higher than 1, then try to factor it into the product of binomials and/or polynomials.

Examples

$$5x + 5y = 5(x + y)$$

Since the 5 is in common it can become a factor.

$$40x^2y - 32xy^2 =$$

Recognize that a factor of 8 is in common and then you'll see that an xy is also in common.

$$40x^2y - 32xy^2 = 8(5x^2y - 4xy^2)$$

$$40x^2y - 32xy^2 = 8xy(5x - 4y)$$

When factoring trinomials (3 terms in a single variable), you're doing the opposite of FOIL. Set up two sets of parentheses and assume that you can factor the trinomial. When the lead term is x^2, then the two factors x and x can be placed as the first terms in the parentheses. Then try to find the factors of the constant term such that, when added, they will equal the middle term. Here are some quick rules:

- If the constant term is positive, then both signs in the binomials must be the same. And it will be the sign of the middle term.

- If the constant term is negative, then both signs in the binomials are opposite. In this situation, look for roots whose sum is the middle term, but be careful, because opposite signs will actually be a difference. See the second example for this type of factoring.

- If there is no middle term, look for the difference of perfect squares. $(a^2 - b^2)$ is factored into $(a - b)(a + b)$.

Examples

$$x^2 + 12x + 20 = (x + \ )(x + \ )$$

Both factor signs are plus because of the first rule. Although 4 and 5 are factors of 20, they do not sum to 12; hence, they are not the correct solution. The answer is

$$(x + 2)(x + 10)$$

$$x^2 - 3x - 40 = (x - \ )(x + \ )$$

Factor signs are plus and minus because of second rule.

The factors of –40, –8 and 5, add up to –3. There are other factors of –40, but they do not sum to –3. If you get the right number but opposite sign, just change the signs in your factors. The answer is

$$= (x - 8)(x + 5)$$

$$x^2 - 25 = (x - \quad)(x + \quad)$$

Signs are plus and minus because of the second rule. Now look for factors that are the same, hence dropping out. The answer is

$$(x - 5)(x + 5)$$

Try these:

$$x^2 + 13x + 22 = \qquad x^2 + 13x - 30 =$$

$$3x^2 - 48b^2 = \qquad 3x^2 - 18x + 27 =$$

 SOLVING FIRST-DEGREE EQUATIONS

The Basics

$$5x + 8 = 2x + 14 \qquad 3(x + 1) = 5(x - 3) + 2$$

Some basics about equations before starting. First, you must recognize the difference between a variable and a constant. *Variables* are placeholders for values to be determined or substituted for at a later point in your analysis—for example, your old friends x and y. A *constant* is a value that is unchanged for a given relationship, such as 8, 14, π, .7, or 1/2. When combined in a relationship of equality, the objective is to solve the equation for that variable—for example, $y = 5x + 12$, or $2x - 2 = 22$.

Relationships or equations may involve a single variable, where the objective is to solve for it, or more than one variable, in which case the objective is to solve for one variable in terms of the others.

Equations are classified by their *degree,* that is, the highest power of the variable that appears in the equation. Degree is important in that it is an indication of the maximum number of solutions (*roots*) that may solve the equation.

Examples

First-degree equation in a single variable:

$$5x + 8 = 2x + 14$$

Second-degree equation in a single variable:

$$3x^2 = 12$$

First-degree equation in two variables:

$$2x + 3y = 12$$

When solving equations with a single variable, the basic strategy is to isolate the variable—that is, put all terms containing the variable on one side of the equation and all the constants on the other side—then simplify to solve. Use the following rules for solving equations:

- What you do to one side of an equation, you must do to the other—that is, if you add 5 to one side, you must add 5 to the other.
- Simplify by adding or subtracting like terms.
- When you have combined all the terms with the variable, solve for it by dividing both sides by the numerical coefficient of the variable.

Example

$$5x + 8 = 2x + 14$$

Use the first rule to subtract 8 from both sides, and use the second rule to simplify.

$$5x + 8 - 8 = 2x + 14 - 8$$
$$5x = 2x + 6$$

Use the first rule to subtract $2x$ from both sides, simplify, and use the third rule to divide both sides by 3.

$$5x - 2x = 2x - 2x + 6$$
$$3x = 6$$
$$\frac{3x}{3} = \frac{6}{3}$$
$$x = 2$$

First-Degree Equations in a Single Variable

Solve the following equations by applying the rules from the preceding section. And remember, My Dear Aunt Sally would warn you to remove parentheses before applying the rules. The last problem is not a trick, the x^2 terms subtract out.

$$-5x = 30 \qquad\qquad 3x = x - 4$$
$$5(x - 8) = 2 - x \qquad 3(x + 1) = 5(x - 3) + 2$$
$$(x - 2)(x + 3) = x^2 + 2x - 10$$

Equations with Denominators

When there are denominators in an equation, the trick is to multiply both sides by the lowest common denominator (LCD). What this will do is clear the denominators from all terms in the equation, thereby making it easier to solve. Be careful when subtracting a term if the term contains a polynomial—the minus goes into the whole term (see following example).

Example

$$\frac{4x}{2} - \frac{(x-2)}{3} = 4$$

Multiply both sides (each term) by 6, the LCD. Simplify and be careful about the minus sign on the second term. Here's where the minus will get you if you are not careful.

$$\frac{(6)4x}{2} - \frac{(6)(x-2)}{3} = 4(6)$$

$$12x - 2(x-2) = 24$$

$$12x - 2x + 4 = 24$$

$$x = 2$$

A few more:

$$\frac{3(x-4)}{2} = 9 \qquad \frac{2x-1}{3} - \frac{1+x}{5} = -1$$

There are times when you are asked to solve equations for a variable when alphabetic constants are given. The trick is to treat these alphabetic constants just like a numeral and solve for x in terms of them.

Example

$$3x + K = 2(75 - M)$$

Solve for x by clearing the parenthesis, then isolate the variable.

$$3x + K = 150 - 2M$$

$$3x = 150 - 2M - K$$

Now divide by the coefficient and solve for x.

$$x = \frac{150 - 2M - K}{3}$$

Try this

$$\frac{a}{x} - \frac{1}{a} = 2$$

 **FUNCTIONS**

Independent and Dependent Variables

$$5y - 2x = 6 \qquad \text{Revenue} = 100q$$

Some equations are relationships between two variables, such as x and y, or projected sales revenue related to the number of units sold. In the second equation it is clear that revenue is a function of q—for every unit sold q, revenue increases by $100. It is also clear that the more units sold, the greater the revenue. Although the selection may seem arbitrary, the trick in these relationships is to determine which variable will be the *independent variable* (a variable that you can control—for example, number of units sold or number of hours worked). The other variable will be the *dependent variable* (a variable that responds to changes in the independent variable—for example, sales revenue as a function of the number of units sold). Once determined, solve for the dependent variable in terms of the independent variable plus any constants. When the relationship is of the form $y =$ or revenue $=$, you can clearly see the dependent relationship. A *function* is a special relationship, whereby any selected value of x yields a unique value of the dependent variable. You might remember this association as *ordered pairs*. To indicate this defined relationship, we say that y is a function of x, noted as $y = f(x)$.

There are two ways to display the association defined by a function: as a table of values or as a graph. In business the best way to understand the behavior of a relationship is to graph it—projected sales units, cost of units sold, and so on. To construct a visual representation of the function, the first step is to make a table of ordered pairs, then plot them on an axis. A few basic rules will guide you.

- The basic strategy is to isolate the dependent variable, put everything else on the other side, and then simplify. Use the same rules as in solving equations with a single variable.

- Select values for x and then find their corresponding values of y by substituting the selected x value into the function and solving.

- Generate a table of values. The left column will show the value of x; the right column will show the corresponding value of y.

Example

$$4y - 2x = 8$$

Isolate the y term, rule 1, and solve for y, not $4y$.

$$4y - 2x + 2x = 2x + 8$$

$$4y = 2x + 8$$

$$\frac{4y}{4} = \frac{2x + 8}{4}$$

$$y = \frac{2x}{4} + \frac{8}{4}$$

$$y = .5x + 2$$

Making a Table and Graph

$$4y - 2x = 8 \qquad \text{Revenue} = 100q$$

Once the dependent variable of the relationship has been solved for in terms of the independent variable, you are ready to determine points. A point, of the form (x, y), assigns to the given x the corresponding value of y. This basically means that you should choose a value for x, plug it into the equation, and determine the resultant value of y.

First, select values for the independent variable. When selecting, always select 0 as the first value for x, and then any values that will make solving for y easy. For example, in the current problem, you should select even values for x (e.g., 0, 2, 4, –2, –4), because they will yield integer values, thus making graphing (as well as the calculation) easier. In each case, substitute the value for x and solve for y. Verify the following values for $y = .5x + 2$:

x	$y = .5x + 2$
0	2
2	3
4	4
10	7
–2	1
–4	0

Whenever a value of x returns 0, as does –4 in the example, that value is termed a root of the equation. A *root* is any value that makes the dependent variable 0. As you will see in a moment, the root is also where the graph will intersect the axis of the independent variable.

Functions can be classified as *increasing* in an interval of x if it is true that whenever $x_1 < x_2$ for any values in the interval, then $f(x_1) < f(x_2)$. If just the opposite is true—that is, $f(x_1) > f(x_2)$—then the function is *decreasing*. The graph is often the main indicator of these properties, and can be important when inferring behavior of a dependent variable (for example, family income) with respect to the independent variable (years of education). See the examples in Figure 13.1. Some functions can be everywhere increasing or decreasing, such as linear and exponential functions.

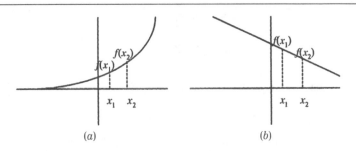

FIGURE 13.1 *Increasing and decreasing functions.*
(a) Increasing function: when $x_2 > x_1$ then $f(x_2) > f(x_1)$.
(b) Decreasing function: When $x_2 > x_1$ then $f(x_2) < f(x_1)$.

To put it simply, an increasing function would be moving upward to the right; a decreasing function would move downward to the right. This is an important observation when looking at regression trend lines (see Chapter 12).

The Value of Functional Notation

$$f(x) = .5x + 2 \qquad R(q) = 100q$$

To emphasize that y is a function of x, the equation is often presented in the form $y = f(x)$. For us in algebra it permits a very clear dependent association by use of this notation. Consider the example $y = .5x + 2$. Using functional notation this becomes $f(x) = .5x + 2$. Now substitute whatever value is in the parenthesis for x in the equation.

x	$f(x) = .5x + 2$
0	$f(0) = .5(0) + 2 = 2$
2	$f(2) = .5(2) + 2 = 3$

More important, the value of this notation in business is that it allows you to name a function like revenue as $R(q)$, or costs as $C(q)$, so that when many relationships are graphed they can be displayed on the same axis for comparative value and labeled for their identification—for example, cost versus revenue.

q	$R(q) = 100q$
0	$R(0) = 100(0) = 0$
25	$R(25) = 100(25) = 2,500$
100	$R(100) = 100(100) = 10,000$

Making the Graph

$$y = .5x + 2 \qquad \text{Revenue} = 100q$$

A graph is a pictorial view of the points you determined on the table. When creating a graph, the axes (the rulers upon which you measure the variables) are mutually perpendicular: Positive directions go to the right and up, and negative measures go to the left and down. Once the table of values has been determined, creating the graph requires attention to only a few conventions.

- The horizontal axis measures the independent variable.

- The vertical axis measures the corresponding dependent variable.

- Units may be of different size than that of the independent variable to support the measures of the dependent variable—for example, total sales, which could be a much larger number relative to the number of units sold. Scale is not a problem as long as it is consistent within each axis.

The fact that the points in Figure 13.2 are on a line is taken up in the next section. The points are graphed in the following way: (0, 2) is 0 units left or right and 2 units up; (–2, 1) is 2 units to the left and 1 unit up. And remember, you always start with the value of $x = 0$; this will return the *y intercept,* which is where the line crosses the *y* axis.

Behavior of the Linear Function

$$y = .5x + 2 \qquad R(q) = 100q$$

The *linear function* is one of the most important functions in business because it describes trend relationships, where the change factor is a constant. It is a first-degree function in two variables of the form $y = mx + b$ and is named *linear* because it produces a line

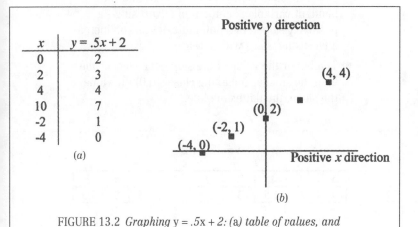

x	$y = .5x + 2$
0	2
2	3
4	4
10	7
-2	1
-4	0

(a)

FIGURE 13.2 *Graphing* y = .5x + 2: *(a) table of values, and (b) plot of the points.*

when graphed. The line clearly conveys the trend—steep, flat, positively directed, or negative. Sometimes it is referred to as an *arithmetic progression,* which means that the values of the dependent variable increase (or decrease) in a constant proportion. This proportion, or change in y with respect to change in x, is defined as the *slope* of the line, which defines the direct variation, if you will, between x and y. In Figure 13.3 the table is flipped and a standard unit is used to demonstrate this point.

There are two important tasks you must be able to perform with respect to linear functions: graph the function and determine the slope. The good news is that if you have the equation in its functional form $y = mx + b$, the coefficient m of x is the slope, and the constant b is the y intercept. But suppose you had to find the slope, and it is not apparent that the coefficient of x is the slope. Given any two points $P_1(x_1, y_1)$ and $P_2(x_2, y_2)$ on the line, slope can be determined by substituting the x and y coordinates into the ratio shown in Figure 13.4. Since slope is unique to any line, any selection of points will always return the unique slope. Take any two points on the line and try it, you'll get the value .5. See the steps in slope in Figure 13.4.

 THE IMPORTANCE OF SLOPE

By knowing the slope you know the intimate behavior between the dependent and independent variable. The β of your regression analysis is nothing more than the slope of the line. Translating the concept of change to the graph, you can quickly determine the behavior of the function strictly by knowing the slope.

- A line with positive slope goes upward to the right in a northeast direction; negatively sloped lines will go upward to the left in the northwest direction. Suppose the dependent variable is sales and the independent variable is amount of advertising—a positively sloped function indicates as you increase advertising, sales will increase.

- The larger the value of the slope, the steeper the line; the smaller (meaning closer to 0) the value of the slope, the flatter the line.

$$y = .5\,x + 2$$

x	0	1	2	3	4	5	6	7
y	2	2.5	3	3.5	4	4.5	5	5.5

FIGURE 13.3 *Analyzing the arithmetic progression of* y: *As* x *increases a unit,* y *responds by increasing .5 units.*

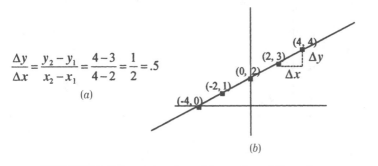

FIGURE 13.4 *Determining slope:* (a) *equation of the ratio,
and* (b) *plot of the line.*

An easy way to remember this concept is to consider
the graph $y = x$. What does it look like? It is a graph
through the origin bisecting quadrants 1 and 3, making
a 45-degree angle with the positive x axis. These slopes
are displayed in Figure 13.5. Lines with slopes greater
than 1 are steeper than that 45-degree angle. Likewise
lines with slope less than 1, for example, 1/2 or
smaller, would be flatter.

So, the easiest way to sketch a linear function is to
find its slope, determine the y intercept, and then estimate how the line will behave from that point. Figure
13.6 demonstrates this technique with two equations,
$y = -2x + 5$ and $y = x + 3$.

- Because the equations are in the slope intercept
  form $y = mx + b$, then the y intercept of the first
  equation is (0, 5).

- The slope is –2, indicating that the line will go northwest somewhat steeply. To mark off another point go
  1 unit to the right and 2 units down, to the point (1, 3).

- The graph in Figure 13.6b shows the process with
  a positive slope of 1. Note that you start at the y

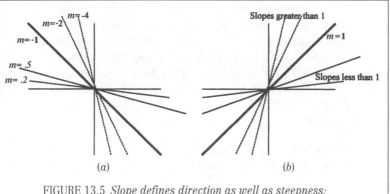

FIGURE 13.5 *Slope defines direction as well as steepness:*
(a) *negative slopes, and* (b) *positive slopes.*

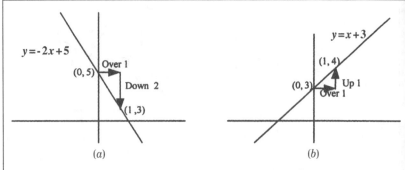

FIGURE 13.6 *Sketching using the slope and y intercept: (a)
slope of –2, y intercept (0, 5); and (b) slope of 1, y intercept
(0, 3).*

intercept, walk over 1 unit, up 1 unit and arrive at
(1, 4). Now connect the points and you have the
sketch. This graph is not as steep as the other, and
it goes upward to the right, an indication of positive
slope.

 **BEHAVIOR OF
THE QUADRATIC FUNCTION**

The Basics

Analyze:

$$y = x^2 - 2x - 8 \quad \text{or} \quad y = -x^2 + 16$$

The beauty of the quadratic function is that it is the
first function you encounter that exhibits optimality.
Unlike the line that has the constant trend relationship
(slope) and continues forever in a direction, the quadratic function produces a parabola—it changes direction at its turning point, thereby yielding a maximum or
minimum. You get a parabola because the quadratic is
a second-degree equation in a single variable, the general form of which is $y = ax^2 + bx + c$. To describe the
behavior of this function, you need to know the turning
point, whether it is a maximum or minimum point, and
the roots of the equation (who can forget the quadratic
formula?). Figure 13.7 shows the table of values that
were used for $y = x^2 - 2x - 8$ and $y = -x^2 + 16$, to graph
their related parabolas.

Process for Sketching
the Quadratic Function

When analyzing the behavior of the quadratic, your
first step is to get it into the *general form* $y = ax^2 +$

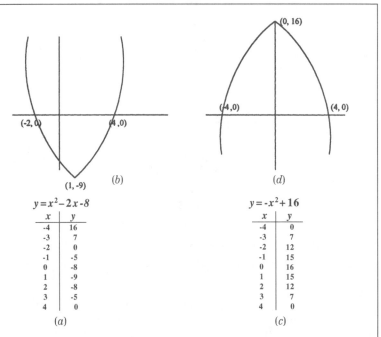

FIGURE 13.7 *A tale of two quadratics. (a) Table of values for* $y = x^2 + 2x - 8$, *and (b) graph of the parabola. (c) Table of values for* $y = x^2 + 16$, *and (d) graph of the parabola.*

$bx + c$. Just as the general form told you so much in the linear case, so it does with the quadratic. Note in the two examples that when the coefficient a of x^2 is positive the parabola is a minimum shape—that is, there is a lowest point—and when it is negative it produces the shape of a maximum. Therefore:

If $a < 0$ then $ax^2 + bx + c$ will be a maximum.

If $a > 0$ then $ax^2 + bx + c$ will be a minimum.

Now that you recognize the shape as a maximum or minimum, you need to determine the actual turning point—the maximum or minimum—and along the way this will also show you how to sketch the curve. The answer lies in appreciating the symmetry of the parabola. As you examine both examples, the curve is symmetrical around a line that happens to go through the turning point. Hence, if you knew that line you would know the turning point and could sketch the curve (remember you already know the general shape from the a term.) We take advantage of a result from calculus to state that the equation of this very special line, called the *axis of symmetry*, is:

$$x = -\frac{b}{2a}$$

Show that this works for the example $y = x^2 - 2x - 8$ (see Figure 13.8). In this quadratic, $a = 1$, $b = -2$, and

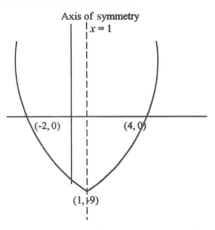

Axis of symmetry
$x = 1$

(-2, 0)   (4, 0)

(1, -9)

FIGURE 13.8 *The axis of symmetry for* y = x² – 2x – 8.

$c = -8$. Since the value of $a > 0$, then this function will be a minimum. Now determine the axis of symmetry.

$$x = -\frac{b}{2a} = -\frac{-2}{2(1)} = 1$$

So the function is symmetrical around $x = 1$.

Now the turning point is found by substituting the value found for the axis of symmetry into the original function, $y = f(x)$.

$$f\left(-\frac{b}{2a}\right) = f(1) = (1)2 - 2(1) - 8 = 1 - 2 - 8 = -9$$

So the method for sketching a quadratic comes down to a few easy steps:

• Recognize the type (look to the a value).
• Determine axis of symmetry (to help you sketch as well as giving the x value of the turning point).
• Determine the y value of the turning point by solving $f(-b/2a)$.

Note that we do not make use of the roots to sketch this function. Roots, if available, will certainly help (see the next section), but because they may not always exist, they should not be relied on for graphing and sketching purposes. For a little practice, show that the axis of symmetry for the second example, $y = -x^2 + 16$, is $x = 0$, and that the turning point is (0, 16).

Analyzing the Roots of a Quadratic Function

Analyze

$$y = x^2 - 2x - 8 \quad \text{or} \quad y = -x^2 + 16$$

Roots are important for two reasons: First, they are the values of the independent variable that make the equation yield 0; and second, they may help in sketching the curve. The problem is that the roots of a quadratic may not exist, and if they do, they may not be easily found. This is the reason root analysis is not included as a part of the sketching procedure. The reason sketching is important is that to sketch means understanding the behavior, which is the most important part of the analysis. So with respect to finding roots, a quadratic will have at most two real roots, which means (reading into the word *most*) that there could be no, one, or two roots.

As an example, determine the roots of $y = x^2 - 2x - 8$. Here are two methods of finding the roots, from the easiest technique, factoring, to the dreadful quadratic formula. And as a piece of advice, always assume the trinomial can be factored—exhaust the potential roots before going to the method of last resort.

Using Factoring (The Easy Way)

$$y = x^2 - 2x - 8$$

To find roots, set the equation to 0, then find the factors (remember factoring?). Now set the factors equal to 0, and solve each factor.

$$x^2 - 2x - 8 = 0$$

$$(x - 4)(x + 2) = 0$$

$$x - 4 = 0 \qquad x + 2 = 0$$

$$x = 4 \qquad x = -2$$

Using the Quadratic Formula

With direct substitution you can determine the roots, albeit with great pain.

$$y = ax^2 + bx + c = x^2 - 2x - 8$$

Therefore $a = 1$, $b = -2$ and $c = -8$.

$$x = \frac{-b \pm \sqrt{b^2 - 4ac}}{2a} = \frac{-(-2) \pm \sqrt{(-2)^2 - 4(1)(-8)}}{2(1)}$$

$$x = \frac{2 \pm \sqrt{(-2)^2 - 4(1)(-8)}}{2(1)} = \frac{2 \pm \sqrt{36}}{2}$$

$$x = \frac{2 \pm 6}{2} = 1 \pm 3 = -2 \text{ and } 4$$

This last relationship yields the two roots, $x = -2$ and $x = 4$. The first way is certainly the easier method, so why is this painful formula with us? Why do you go to a dentist? Because you need them both. There will be times when the roots (no pun on root canal, please) can't be found by factoring, or they may not even exist. Even an X-ray wouldn't help! Consider the analysis of the equation $y = -x^2 + 2x - 2$ as a demonstration of this point. You may try, but you can't factor the equation the easy way. So you have no choice but to either skip this section or try the old reliable quadratic formula. Before you try the quadratic formula, it would serve as an excellent review to sketch the function using the method discussed earlier, because it will help explain the results of the quadratic formula (see Figure 13.9).

Now this may be a treat for those of you who remember something called *imaginary* or *complex* numbers. But in the world of business there is nothing imaginary (this is an awful pun, but the message is important), "for our down and dirty math in business, this has no value to us beyond what it tells us about the graph." If an equation yields complex roots, then simply, its graph will not intersect the x axis. What is important is that the graph must make sense with the algebra. That is, if there are no real roots, meaning that there is a negative value under the radical, then this graph can't have any intersection points on the axis, as when you got two roots in the original example. Figure 13.10 shows the three variations based upon the analysis of roots.

You might remember something called the test for roots using the quadratic discriminant (the underside of the radical) and the determination of the type of root. When a root is graphed it is termed the x *intercept,* because it represents a point where the line crosses the x axis.

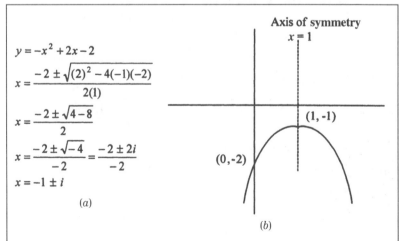

$$y = -x^2 + 2x - 2$$

$$x = \frac{-2 \pm \sqrt{(2)^2 - 4(-1)(-2)}}{2(1)}$$

$$x = \frac{-2 \pm \sqrt{4 - 8}}{2}$$

$$x = \frac{-2 \pm \sqrt{-4}}{-2} = \frac{-2 \pm 2i}{-2}$$

$$x = -1 \pm i$$

(a)

Axis of symmetry
$x = 1$

(1, -1)

(0, -2)

(b)

FIGURE 13.9 *A quadratic with imaginary roots: (a) solution of* y = -x² + 2x - 2, *and (b) graph of the parabola.*

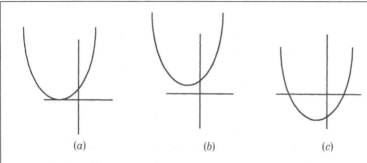

FIGURE 13.10 *Graphical implications of the roots: (a) if* $b^2 - 4ac = 0$, *then one real root; (b) if* $b^2 - 4ac < 0$, *then no real roots; and (c) if* $b^2 - 4ac > 0$, *then two real roots.*

Discriminant	Roots	Graphically
$b^2 - 4ac = 0$	1 real root	1 x intercept
$b^2 - 4ac > 0$	2 real roots	2 x intercepts
$b^2 - 4ac < 0$	0 real roots	0 x intercepts

So you can ask, what is important in this analysis of quadratics? As a model you want to find that maximum or minimum. Given the following two equations, determine whether they are a max or a min, sketch the curve, and determine the turning point.

Analyze:

$$y = -x^2 + x + 6 \qquad 0 = y - x^2 - 4x - 5$$

Type	Max	Min
Axis of symmetry	$x = 1/2$	$x = -2$
Turning point	(1/2, 6.25)	(−2, 1)
Roots (x intercepts)	(−2, 0) and (3, 0)	None

SOLVING SYSTEMS OF EQUATIONS

Two Linear Equations

$$\begin{aligned} x + 2y &= 12 & 5x + 2y &= 11 \\ x - y &= -3 & 6x + 3y &= 15 \end{aligned}$$

Back in school these systems were called *simultaneous equations*—that is, given two equations find the point or points that satisfy both equations at the same time. There are a number of examples in business where this technique is necessary—break-even analysis and equilibrium of supply and demand, to name two. There are two elimination methods used to solve these problems, the method of substitution and gaussian elimination. Both techniques have you reduce the system of two equations with two variables down to one equation with one variable.

Use the method of *elimination by substitution* when one of the variables has 1 as its coefficient, thereby making it easy to solve for, and then substitute in the other equation. The first set of equations is ideal for this method. Although both equations have coefficients equal to 1, use the second equation to solve for x in terms of y.

$$x + 2y = 12$$
$$\underline{x - y = -3}$$
$$x = y - 3$$

Once you have x in terms of y in the second equation, you can substitute for x in the first equation, the expression for x you solved for in the second. Simplify and solve.

$$x + 2y = 12$$
$$(y - 3) + 2y = 12$$
$$3y - 3 = 12$$
$$3y = 15$$
$$y = 5$$

Once you have found the solution for one variable, go back to the substitution and replace the variable with the solved value.

$$x = y - 3$$
$$x = 5 - 3 = 2$$

In these equations it is arbitrary as to which substitution you use since both equations have variables with coefficients equal to 1. You could just as easily have solved the first equation for x ($x = -2y + 12$) and substituted into the second equation. But the substitution technique will be very cumbersome in the second system of equations because the characteristics of the coefficients are different—that is, no coefficients are 1. When systems are more complicated, use the gaussian elimination technique.

What has actually been solved for in these situations? When you get an answer such as $x = 2$ and $y = 5$, what does it mean? These values are actually coordinates—they represent a point that is the intersection of these two lines. Incidentally, if you get a solution 0 = 0, then the system has produced the same line. In this situation one equation is a multiple of the other. If you get a solution 0 = k where k is a constant other than 0, then the system is two parallel lines. Figure 13.11 displays the graph of the system just analyzed. If these two equations do not look familiar to you, take a moment to put both of the original equations into their slope intercept form. You will then see the connection.

The *gaussian elimination method* (named after the same person who gave us the equation for the normal curve, Carl Friedrich Gauss) uses the following technique: Multiply the entire equation by a quantity such that when added to the other equation, one of the variables can be subtracted or added out. You may have to multiply the equations by different quantities such that the lead coefficients will be the same. The main thing to remember about this process is that you must multiply both sides by whatever quantity you select. Follow this example.

$$5x + 2y = 11$$

$$6x + 3y = 15$$

First step is to look at the coefficients for the easiest situation. In this case, 2 and 3 are less difficult than 5 and 6. One easy trick is to multiply each equation by the coefficients from the other equation. In this case, multiply the first equation by 3 and the second equation by 2.

$$(3) \ (5x + 2y = 11)$$

$$(2) \ (6x + 3y = 15)$$

Once the multiplication has been performed, the coefficients of one of the variables will be the same. Then add or subtract to clear out one of the variables.

$$15x + 6y = 33$$
$$12x + 6y = 30$$

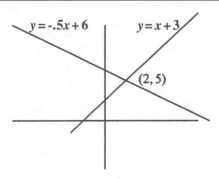

FIGURE 13.11 *Graphical view of a system of equations.*

Because the signs of the y terms are the same, subtract the two equations. Now you are left with one equation in one variable, hence the term *elimination* method.

$$3x + 0y = 3$$

$$x = 1$$

After solving for one variable, substitute that value in one of the equations to solve for the remaining variable.

$$15 (1) + 6y = 33$$

$$6y = 18$$

$$y = 3$$

The beauty of the gaussian elimination method is that it is easily applied to three equations with three unknowns, and so on. Here are two examples to try by any method you like. The first set you could solve either way, but the second prefers Gauss.

$$4x + 5y = 18 \qquad 2x - 3y = 12$$
$$x - 3y = -4 \qquad 5x + 4y = 7$$

The Classic Mixture Problem

There is one classic mixture-type problem that is seen in business frequently and is a variation of simultaneous equations.

$60,000 is invested in two funds—one fund averages an 8 percent yield, the other a 6 percent yield. If at the end of 1 year the total interest earned on the two investments is $4,320, how much was invested in each fund?

In this problem you create two equations: The first equation sums the funds to the total, $60,000, and the second sums the interest amounts to $4,320. Let the variables A and B be the amounts invested in each fund. A is the 8 percent fund and B is the 6 percent fund.

$$A + B = 60,000$$

$$0.08A + 0.06B = 4,320$$

In this type of problem the best tool is eliminating the variable by substitution. Solve for A in the first equation. Then substitute for A, the expression $(60,000 - B)$ in the second. Simplify and solve.

$$A = 60,000 - B$$

$$0.08(60,000 - B) + 0.06B = 4,320$$

$$4,800 - 0.08B + 0.06B = 4,320$$

$$-0.02B = -480$$

$$B = 24,000$$

Once you have found the solution for one fund, go back to the substitution and replace the variable with the solved value.

$$A = 60,000 - B$$

$$A = 60,000 - 24,000$$

$$A = 36,000$$

One Linear and One Quadratic Equation

$$y = -3x + 3$$
$$y = x^2 + 4x - 5$$

The other type of problem you should be prepared for is how to solve a system in which not all equations are linear. The trick in doing these problems is to try to sketch the two functions, and to be careful that there may be one, two, or no solutions to the problem. That is why a sketch will help. Consider the example.

$$y = -3x + 3$$
$$y = x^2 + 4x - 5$$

The key to starting this problem is to note that both equations are functions of x, and in the "$y =$" format. Therefore, set both equations equal to each other, and solve.

$$-3x + 3 = x^2 + 4x - 5$$

$$0 = x^2 + 7x - 8$$

Now you can see why, given a linear function and a quadratic, there may be no, one, or two solutions by the nature of the roots, when solving for x.

$$0 = x^2 + 7x - 8$$

$$0 = (x - 1)(x + 8)$$

$$x = 1 \quad \text{and} \quad x = -8$$

Now go back to either equation (preferably the linear case because it will be easier), and solve for the corresponding values of y. The solutions are $(1, 0)$ and $(-8, 27)$.

How does the graph reinforce this solution? There must be two points of intersection. Examine Figure 13.12 to see how the graph reflects what was just solved in the system of equations.

Now, based upon the type of equation you could have no roots, or even one root, as well as the two shown in the example. In the following two problems you encounter each situation. Graphically, if there is

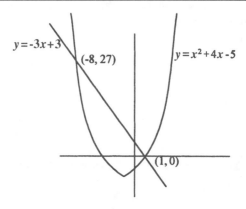

FIGURE 13.12 *Linear and quadratic systems: points of inter-section of the line y = –3x + 3 and the parabola y = x² + 4x – 5.*

one solution to the equations, then you have only one point of intersection. If you get a negative under the radical, then there are no real roots, and therefore no points of intersection. Try the following:

$$y = -2x - 14 \qquad y = -2x - 15$$
$$y = x^2 + 4x - 5 \qquad y = x^2 + 4x - 5$$

BEHAVIOR OF THE EXPONENTIAL FUNCTION

The Basics

Analyze:

$$y = 2^x \qquad y = e^x$$

The beauty of the exponential function is that it is the soul of the financial functions. Basically, all of the time value of money calculations evolve from exponential functions. Exponential functions are also models for population growth and any relationship where the dependent variable grows geometrically.

Suppose you take as your first task, that you should be able to sketch these functions as you did with the linear and quadratic cases. As you examine the two examples, they differ from quadratics inasmuch as the variable and constant are reversed. Figure 13.13 shows the table of values for the function 2^x and its corresponding graph. If you are not sure of the values, use the calculator to verify the entries. The graph in Figure 13.13 shows it is a forever-increasing function.

The function $y = 2^x$ represents very nicely the nature of an exponential function whose base is greater than 1. There are two important components of this graph, that part for which $x > 0$ and the part for which $x < 0$.

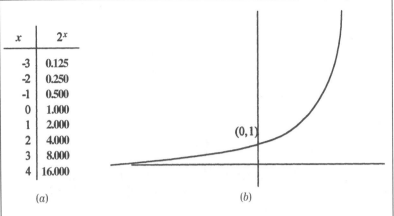

FIGURE 13.13 *The exponential function 2^x: (a) table of values, and (b) graph of the curve.*

The curve for values of x greater than 0 shows an extremely dramatic increasing function. Each successive integral value of x results in a doubling of the preceding value of y. This is the characteristic of what is termed a *geometric* progression—each term in the sequence is a multiple of the preceding term (see the table of values in Figure 13.13). It is reasonable to assume that any base greater than 2 will have an even steeper curve. (If you're not sure, take a few examples such as $y = 3^x$ or $y = 5^x$ and see what happens as x takes on values such as 2, 3, and 4. Then compare.)

So how does $y = 2^x$ behave for values of x in the negative direction? This is an important observation: As x gets smaller—that is, as x takes on values –1, –2, –3— what does the curve look like? The key is to examine the values of y as x goes farther into the negative direction.

$$y = 2^x$$

becomes

$$y = 2^0 = 1 \qquad y = 2^{-1} = \frac{1}{2} = 0.5 \qquad y = 2^{-2} = \frac{1}{4} = 0.25$$

So, as x decreases—that is, as the value of x keeps getting smaller—it becomes so small that the values of $y = 2^x$ become insignificant (or approach 0 in the limiting sense). If you are not sure of this principle, keep substituting values for x such as –3, –4, or –5, and see that the resulting value of y is getting very small, and that there is no way that this progression is going to change.

What does your intuition say regarding the shape of an exponential function whose base value is between 1 and 2—for example, 1.5^x, 1.1^x, or 1.05^x? As shown in Figure 13.14, as the base increases, the curve gets steeper, so in this case, the closer the base gets to

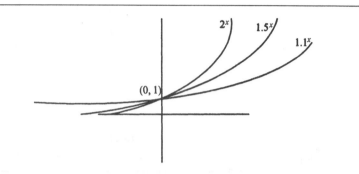

FIGURE 13.14 *Changing the base of exponential functions.*

1—that is, $y = 1^x$—the flatter the curve will be. In fact, $y = 1^x$ is a line parallel to the x axis through $(0, 1)$.

The curves in Figure 13.14 represent the financial multipliers for the future value of a cash amount. For example, if you get 10 percent on your money, you can determine its future value by making a calculation of the function $y = 1.1^x$, where x is the number of years the money will be invested. For an investment of $100 for 6 years at 10 percent compounded annually, the formula is as follows. For more on this turn to Chapter 1.

$$FV = 100(1 + 0.10)^6 = 100(1.1)^6 = 100(1.77156) = 177.16$$

The value 1.77156 is found on the curve $y = 1.1^x$ for $x = 6$.

The Behavior behind Present Value

Analyze:

$$y = 2^{-x}$$

How does the behavior of the exponential function change if the exponent is a negative value, for example, $y = 2^{-x}$? This is the significance as to why present value behaves the way it does; that is, why does it decrease in value as time increases? Here is the reason. As you examine the function $y = 2^{-x}$, what can you say is true as the values of x increase from 0? Examine the table and graph in Figure 13.15. As the value of x gets larger, the value of the function $y = 2^{-x}$ decreases. Again, it is the significance of the negative of the power of the independent variable. So, as the graph shows, as time increases the value of the dependent variable decreases. In fact, this is a forever-decreasing function.

So what is the point of knowing or appreciating the behavior of these functions? Simply that the numbers you find for these exponential functions become the multipliers that help you determine the future or present values. Consider $y = 1.1^{-x}$, and the value of the function when $x = 2$. The result of the equation is the

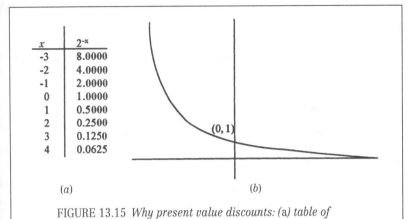

x	2^{-x}
-3	8.0000
-2	4.0000
-1	2.0000
0	1.0000
1	0.5000
2	0.2500
3	0.1250
4	0.0625

(0, 1)

(a)   (b)

FIGURE 13.15 *Why present value discounts: (a) table of values, and (b) graph of the curve* $y = 2^{-x}$.

value $y = 0.8264$. This is the multiplier that you use to find the present value of an amount discounted at 10 percent in 2 years.

Each of these functions produces the required multiplier used in the present or future value to calculate the actual amount. So when you look at the curve $y = 1.1^x$ or 1.05^x, as before, you are seeing the multipliers used for producing the future value. You can also see that the 1.1^x curve is steeper than the 1.05^x curve, which is exactly what you would expect, that a greater rate would yield a greater future value. The beauty of these curves is that they represent the origin of how money grows or discounts.

BEHAVIOR OF e^x AND CONTINUOUS COMPOUNDING

Analyze:

$$y = e^x$$

There are two relationships you need to explore to better understand the significance of e to time value of money. First, what does the function e^x look like, and then how is e defined? The preceding section graphed a general exponential function 2^x. Knowing that e is approximated by the value 2.718, it should be very similar to 2^x, but just a bit steeper, as shown in Figure 13.16.

CALC TIP
Finding Values of e^x

Your calculator should have an e^x key or a menu in which EXP is an option. Both of these keys will return the value of e^x for a given entry for x. For example, from the table in Figure 13.16 you can see that when $x = 3$, the corresponding value of $y = e^x$ is 20.086. With

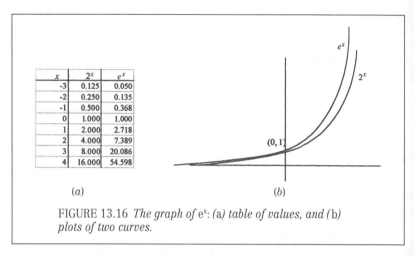

FIGURE 13.16 *The graph of* e^x: *(a) table of values, and (b) plots of two curves.*

the calculator, enter 3 and press either the e^x or the EXP key to get a return of 20.086.

Where did the value of e come from? As shown in the text, the value of e is found by increasing the number of conversion periods in the compounding of future or present value. Suppose you do a slight variation of the compounding formula to show the convergence to e itself. Examine the second equation, which contains the essence of the observation: What is the value of this expression as n gets large? A little algebra for the second version might make these calculations a little easier. What is the value of the last expression as n gets large? Check out the table.

$$FV = PV\left(1 + \frac{r}{n}\right)^{nt} \quad \text{becomes} \quad \left(1 + \frac{1}{n}\right)^n$$

n	$\left(1 + \dfrac{1}{n}\right)^n$
2	2.25
10	2.59374
20	2.65329
100	2.70481
500	2.71556
1,000	2.71692
10,000	2.71814

As the table shows, the expression is converging to 2.718. These results are good enough to believe that this relationship is yielding e. In higher levels of mathematics, the concept of a limit—that is, letting n get as large as you want—is used to define e. From the following definition, you can let n get as large as you want as in the preceding table. As you let n get very large (read "as n goes to infinity"), the value of the expression converges to a number, and that number is e.

$$e = \lim_{n \to \infty} \left(1 + \frac{1}{n}\right)^n$$

This special limit defines e.

CALC TIP

The Continuous Compounding Multiplier e^{rt}

If you can accept the preceding definition for e then it is very easy to show how it became the equation for continuous compounding. Although beyond the scope of this introduction to finance, with a few substitutions and letting the number of periods go into infinity, you will arrive at the desired relationship.

$$FV = PV\left(1 + \frac{r}{n}\right)^{nt}$$

The periodic case becomes e for the continous case:

$$FV = PVe^{rt}$$

 USING SUMMATION NOTATION

$$FV = \sum_{n=0}^{2} 100(1 + 0.08)^n \qquad PV = \sum_{n=0}^{2} 100(1 + 0.08)^{-n}$$

Summation or sigma notation $\sum$ defines a way to express the sum of a series of values. You encounter this notation while studying annuities or in statistics, where it is used to convey adding all the elements in a distribution, as in calculating the mean. Here's an example:

The sequential sum of $1 + 2 + 3 + 4 + 5 = 15$ can be written as a summation, where the symbol $\sum$ is shorthand for a sum. Using this notation, the sum can be written as follows, where i is the index and 1, 5 are the limits of summation.

$$1 + 2 + 3 + 4 + 5 = \sum_{i=1}^{5} i = 15$$

Examples

$$\sum_{i=2}^{7} ix = 2x + 3x + 4x + 5x + 6x + 7x = 27x$$

$$\sum_{j=1}^{5} j^2 = 1^2 + 2^2 + 3^2 + 4^2 + 5^2 = 1 + 4 + 9 + 16 + 25 = 55$$

Now that you have seen a few examples let's go to the topic for which you will need this notation, annuities. The following summation equation defines 3 annuity payments of $100 for an ordinary, end-of-term annuity. This equation is equal to the sum of 3 terms with increasing exponential values beginning at 1 and ending at 3. The 100 is treated as a constant and belongs to each term.

$$FV = \sum_{n=0}^{2} 100(1 + 0.08)^n$$

$$= 100(1 + 0.08)^0 + 100(1 + 0.08)^1 + 100(1 + 0.08)^2$$

$$= 100 + 108 + 116.64 = 324.64$$

If an annuity is up-front or beginning-of-term then the annuity has the advantage of an additional term for gathering interest. Its cash flow is slightly different, and affects the limits of the summation.

$$FV = \sum_{n=1}^{3} 100(1 + 0.08)^n$$

$$= 100(1 + 0.08)^1 + 100(1 + 0.08)^2 + 100(1 + 0.08)^3$$

$$= 108 + 116.64 + 125.97 = 350.61$$

From what you learned before, negative exponents produce discounting, which defines the present value. The summation still works the same way, but in this case you are dealing with the inverse of the compounding factor. For example, what is the present value of 3 $100 payments made at the beginning of each year at a rate of 8 percent?

$$PV = \sum_{n=0}^{2} 100(1 + 0.08)^{-n}$$

$$= 100(1 + 0.08)^0 + 100(1 + 0.08)^{-1} + 100(1 + 0.08)^{-2}$$

$$= \frac{100}{(1 + 0.08)^0} + \frac{100}{(1 + 0.08)^1} + \frac{100}{(1 + 0.08)^2}$$

$$= 100 + 92.59 + 85.73 = 278.32$$

 **USING LOGARITHMS**
Definition and Base

$$\ln 6 = \qquad \ln 200 = \qquad \ln 2{,}048 =$$

Although in high school you were taught logarithms to the base 10, in college and in business the preferred base is the constant $e = 2.718$. Quite honestly, the benefits of using logs have long been surpassed by the calculator in much the same way as the horse was replaced by the automobile. Just as there is occasional excitement about riding a horse, so there is the occasional need for logarithms.

The easiest way to understand logs is to interpret them as exponents but working from one agreed-upon base, such as 10 or e. The logarithm of a number N is the power to which the chosen base must be raised to equal that number. A few examples:

Definition: $\text{Log}_b N = x$ means $b^x = N$

Logarithms			
Number	Base 2	Base e	Base 10
1	0.000	0.000	0.0000
2	1.000	0.693	0.3010
10	3.322	2.302	1.0000
100	6.643	4.605	2.0000

Examples from the table:

$\text{Log}_2 2 = 1$ because by definition $2^1 = 2$

$\text{Log}_{10} 2 = 0.3010$ because by definition $10^{0.3010} = 2$

But when dealing with e you have to use the calculator or resort to log tables, which we will not do here. Look up natural logarithms in your manual and find the calculator keys that allow you to find the ln of a number. In most calculators it is an assigned key. To find the log of a number, you usually type it in and then press the Ln key to find the natural logarithm.

To find the natural logarithm of 20, or ln 20, type 20 and press the Ln key. ln 20 = 2.996, which means that $e^{2.996} = 20$.

As practice you can verify the following:

$\ln 6 = 1.79175$ $\ln 200 = 5.29832$ $\ln 2,048 = 7.62462$

We do not review the operations with logarithms because you are accustomed to working with the calculator for dealing with multiplication, division, and roots. But there are a couple of worthwhile observations.

Relationship with Exponential Functions

The inverse of an exponential function is a logarithmic function. But first, what are logarithmic functions? Sim-

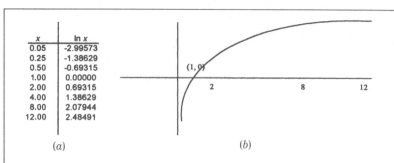

FIGURE 13.17 *Graph of ln x: (a) table of values, and (b) plot of the curve.*

ply, a logarithmic function is when the variable is part of a logarithm. Consider the graph of $y = \ln x$.

As you can see in Figure 13.17, the log curve displays very slow growth, with negative values of y for values of x less than 1. Also, once x is greater than 1, the values of y are all positive. Data that groups like this in a scattergram suggests a logarithmic model for regression.

Exponential functions and logarithms of the same base are inverse relationships, that is, they undo each other. Graphically, as displayed in Table 13.1, the relationship is symmetrical around the line $y = x$.

To see the inverse nature of the functions, perform the following operations with any value of x: Take $f(x)$, then $g(f(x))$, and you should get x. The expression $g(f(x))$ refers to a two-step operation in which you determine $f(x)$, then take g of that value. The graphs appear in Figure 13.18. This relationship has symmetry around the line $y = x$ as a demonstration of the inverse nature of the functions.

TABLE 13.1 THE INVERSE RELATIONSHIP BETWEEN e^x AND $\ln x$

x	$f(x) = e^x$	x	$g(x) = \ln x$
0	1	1.00	0
1	2.72	2.72	1
2	7.39	7.39	2
3	20.09	20.09	3
4	54.60	54.60	4
5	148.41	148.41	5
6	403.43	403.43	6
7	1,096.63	1,096.63	7
8	2,980.96	2,980.96	8
9	8,103.08	8,103.08	9
10	22,026.47	22,026.47	10

Select: $x = 2$

Solve for $f(2) = 7.39$

Now solve for $g(7.39) = 2$

FACTORIALS AND THEIR APPLICATIONS

Factorials make their appearance in probability as a way to count the number of arrangements or combinations of objects. *Factorials* themselves represent a shorthand for a series of products defined by all the natural numbers less than or equal to the given factorial. This is best explained by some examples.

$n!$ (read as "n factorial") $= n \times (n-1) \times (n-2) \times \cdots 1$

$5! = 5 \times 4 \times 3 \times 2 \times 1 = 120$　　$7! = 7 \times 6 \times 5 \times 4 \times 3 \times 2 \times 1$

$$7! = 7 \times 6 \times 5!$$

$$7! = 5{,}040$$

Permutations

How many different ways can 4 books be arranged on a shelf?　A *permutation* is defined as the number of different ways n objects can be arranged. Sometimes you are looking for the number of arrangements for all the objects, and other times you are looking for partial arrangements, such as 6 objects taken 3 at a time. Order is very important in permutations; each different order of the objects represents a different event. We demonstrate how factorials get involved.

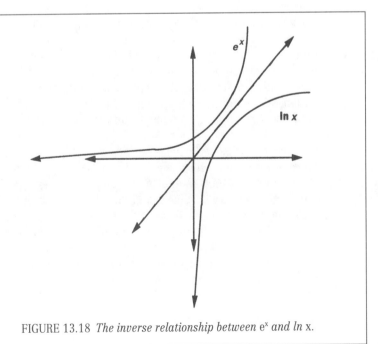

FIGURE 13.18 *The inverse relationship between* e^x *and ln* x.

How many ways can A B C *be arranged?* How many letters could be in the first position? Right, any of the three. But once a choice is made how many letters could go in the second position? Right, only two. And then the last is determined, so there is only one selection. This results in a multiplicative relationship of $3 \times 2 \times 1$ or 6 different arrangements. Hence, the use of factorials, in this case 3!

When trying to determine arrangements for all n objects, taken n at a time, the answer is $n!$ So, for example, there are 26! arrangements of a 26-book encyclopedia set, using all 26 books. But what if only 2 books were to be selected from all 26 books?

How many ways can 26 books be arranged 2 at a time? There are 26 choices for the first selection. But once one is selected, there are only 25 for the second. Answer: $26 \times 25 = 650$ arrangements.

Notationally, problems like this one are written as $_nP_r$, and understood as n objects taken r at a time. Mathematically, this is calculated as the following equation:

$$_nP_r = \frac{n!}{(n-r)!}$$

For example

$$_{26}P_2 = \frac{26!}{(26-2)!} = \frac{26!}{24!} = \frac{26 \times 25 \times 24!}{24!} = 650$$

Combinations

How many different combinations of 4 books can be arranged on a shelf? A *combination* is defined as the number of different ways n objects can be selected or grouped, and differs from a permutation in that order is not considered. Since there is no regard for order, n objects taken n at a time will result in only one combination. We demonstrate how combinations are different from permutations and how factorials get involved.

How many groups of 3 can be made from A B C? Since order is no longer a consideration—that is, *ABC* is the same as *BAC, CAB* and so on—then all six permutations present the same group. In calculating the combination you use the formula for solving for the permutation but divide by the number of objects taken at a time, since that represents the number of groups that will be alike. In the situation of *ABC* you have 3! divided by 3!, resulting in 1. As the following problem requires, define 0! = 1.

$$_nC_r = \frac{_nP_r}{r!} = \frac{n!}{r!(n-r)!}$$

For example

$$_3C_3 = \frac{3!}{3!(3-3)!} = \frac{6}{6} = 1$$

Now consider the encyclopedia set. How many different 2-book combinations can be made using all 26 books? The key to doing these problems is to remember that the arrangement A and B is the same as the arrangement B and A; hence, you divide by the number of items being taken at a time.

$$_nC_r = \frac{n!}{r!(n-r)!} = \frac{26!}{2!(26-2)!} = \frac{26!}{2! \times 24!}$$

$$= \frac{26 \times 25 \times 24!}{2 \times 24!} = \frac{650}{2} = 325$$

Time Value of Money and Standard Normal Distribution Tables

TABLE A.1 FUTURE VALUE OF $1

Periods	0.50%	0.75%	1.00%	1.50%	2.00%	3.00%	4.00%	5.00%	6.00%	7.00%	8.00%
1	1.00500	1.00750	1.01000	1.01500	1.02000	1.03000	1.04000	1.05000	1.06000	1.07000	1.08000
2	1.01003	1.01506	1.02010	1.03023	1.04040	1.06090	1.08160	1.10250	1.12360	1.14490	1.16640
3	1.01508	1.02267	1.03030	1.04568	1.06121	1.09273	1.12486	1.15763	1.19102	1.22504	1.25971
4	1.02015	1.03034	1.04060	1.06136	1.08243	1.12551	1.16986	1.21551	1.26248	1.31080	1.36049
5	1.02525	1.03807	1.05101	1.07728	1.10408	1.15927	1.21665	1.27628	1.33823	1.40255	1.46933
6	1.03038	1.04585	1.06152	1.09344	1.12616	1.19405	1.26532	1.34010	1.41852	1.50073	1.58687
7	1.03553	1.05370	1.07214	1.10984	1.14869	1.22987	1.31593	1.40710	1.50363	1.60578	1.71382
8	1.04071	1.06160	1.08286	1.12649	1.17166	1.26677	1.36857	1.47746	1.59385	1.71819	1.85093
9	1.04591	1.06956	1.09369	1.14339	1.19509	1.30477	1.42331	1.55133	1.68948	1.83846	1.99900
10	1.05114	1.07758	1.10462	1.16054	1.21899	1.34392	1.48024	1.62889	1.79085	1.96715	2.15892
11	1.05640	1.08566	1.11567	1.17795	1.24337	1.38423	1.53945	1.71034	1.89830	2.10485	2.33164
12	1.06168	1.09381	1.12683	1.19562	1.26824	1.42576	1.60103	1.79586	2.01220	2.25219	2.51817
13	1.06699	1.10201	1.13809	1.21355	1.29361	1.46853	1.66507	1.88565	2.13293	2.40985	2.71962
14	1.07232	1.11028	1.14947	1.23176	1.31948	1.51259	1.73168	1.97993	2.26090	2.57853	2.93719
15	1.07768	1.11860	1.16097	1.25023	1.34587	1.55797	1.80094	2.07893	2.39656	2.75903	3.17217

TABLE A.2 PRESENT VALUE OF $1

Periods	0.50%	0.75%	1.00%	1.50%	2.00%	3.00%	4.00%	5.00%	6.00%	7.00%	8.00%
1	0.99502	0.99256	0.99010	0.98522	0.98039	0.97087	0.96154	0.95238	0.94340	0.93458	0.92593
2	0.99007	0.98517	0.98030	0.97066	0.96117	0.94260	0.92456	0.90703	0.89000	0.87344	0.85734
3	0.98515	0.97783	0.97059	0.95632	0.94232	0.91514	0.88900	0.86384	0.83962	0.81630	0.79383
4	0.98025	0.97055	0.96098	0.94218	0.92385	0.88849	0.85480	0.82270	0.79209	0.76290	0.73503
5	0.97537	0.96333	0.95147	0.92826	0.90573	0.86261	0.82193	0.78353	0.74726	0.71299	0.68058
6	0.97052	0.95616	0.94205	0.91454	0.88797	0.83748	0.79031	0.74622	0.70496	0.66634	0.63107
7	0.96569	0.94904	0.93272	0.90103	0.87056	0.81309	0.75992	0.71068	0.66506	0.62275	0.58349
8	0.96089	0.94198	0.92348	0.88771	0.85349	0.78941	0.73069	0.67684	0.62741	0.58201	0.54027
9	0.95610	0.93496	0.91434	0.87459	0.83676	0.76642	0.70259	0.64461	0.59190	0.54393	0.50025
10	0.95135	0.92800	0.90529	0.86167	0.82035	0.74409	0.67556	0.61391	0.55839	0.50835	0.46319
11	0.94661	0.92109	0.89632	0.84893	0.80426	0.72242	0.64958	0.58468	0.52679	0.47509	0.42888
12	0.94191	0.91424	0.88745	0.83639	0.78849	0.70138	0.62460	0.55684	0.49697	0.44401	0.39711
13	0.93722	0.90743	0.87866	0.82403	0.77303	0.68095	0.60057	0.53032	0.46884	0.41496	0.36770
14	0.93256	0.90068	0.86996	0.81185	0.75788	0.66112	0.57748	0.50507	0.44230	0.38782	0.34046
15	0.92792	0.89397	0.86135	0.79985	0.74301	0.64186	0.55526	0.48102	0.41727	0.36245	0.31524

TABLE A.3 FUTURE VALUE OF AN ANNUITY IN ARREARS

Periods	0.50%	0.75%	1.00%	1.50%	2.00%	3.00%	4.00%	5.00%	6.00%	7.00%	8.00%
1	1.00000	1.00000	1.00000	1.00000	1.00000	1.00000	1.00000	1.00000	1.00000	1.00000	1.00000
2	2.00500	2.00750	2.01000	2.01500	2.02000	2.03000	2.04000	2.05000	2.06000	2.07000	2.08000
3	3.01502	3.02256	3.03010	3.04522	3.06040	3.09090	3.12160	3.15250	3.18360	3.21490	3.24640
4	4.03010	4.04523	4.06040	4.09090	4.12161	4.18363	4.24646	4.31013	4.37462	4.43994	4.50611
5	5.05025	5.07556	5.10101	5.15227	5.20404	5.30914	5.41632	5.52563	5.63709	5.75074	5.86660
6	6.07550	6.11363	6.15202	6.22955	6.30812	6.46841	6.63298	6.80191	6.97532	7.15329	7.33593
7	7.10588	7.15948	7.21354	7.32299	7.43428	7.66246	7.89829	8.14201	8.39384	8.65402	8.92280
8	8.14141	8.21318	8.28567	8.43284	8.58297	8.89234	9.21423	9.54911	9.89747	10.25980	10.63663
9	9.18212	9.27478	9.36853	9.55933	9.75463	10.15911	10.58280	11.02656	11.49132	11.97799	12.48756
10	10.22803	10.34434	10.46221	10.70272	10.94972	11.46388	12.00611	12.57789	13.18079	13.81645	14.48656
11	11.27917	11.42192	11.56683	11.86326	12.16872	12.80780	13.48635	14.20679	14.97164	15.78360	16.64549
12	12.33556	12.50759	12.68250	13.04121	13.41209	14.19203	15.02581	15.91713	16.86994	17.88845	18.97713
13	13.39724	13.60139	13.80933	14.23683	14.68033	15.61779	16.62684	17.71298	18.88214	20.14064	21.49530
14	14.46423	14.70340	14.94742	15.45038	15.97394	17.08632	18.29191	19.59863	21.01507	22.55049	24.21492
15	15.53655	15.81368	16.09690	16.68214	17.29342	18.59891	20.02359	21.57856	23.27597	25.12902	27.15211
16	16.61423	16.93228	17.25786	17.93237	18.63929	20.15688	21.82453	23.65749	25.67253	27.88805	30.32428
17	17.69730	18.05927	18.43044	19.20136	20.01207	21.76159	23.69751	25.84037	28.21888	30.84022	33.75023
18	18.78579	19.19472	19.61475	20.48938	21.41231	23.41444	25.64541	28.13238	30.90565	33.99903	37.45024
19	19.87972	20.33868	20.81090	21.79672	22.84056	25.11687	27.67123	30.53900	33.75999	37.37896	41.44626
20	20.97912	21.49122	22.01900	23.12367	24.29737	26.87037	29.77808	33.06595	36.78559	40.99549	45.76196

TABLE A.4 PRESENT VALUE OF AN ANNUITY IN ARREARS

Periods	0.50%	0.75%	1.00%	1.50%	2.00%	3.00%	4.00%	5.00%	6.00%	7.00%	8.00%
1	0.99502	0.99256	0.99010	0.98522	0.98039	0.97087	0.96154	0.95238	0.94340	0.93458	0.92593
2	1.98510	1.97772	1.97040	1.95588	1.94156	1.91347	1.88609	1.85941	1.83339	1.80802	1.78326
3	2.97025	2.95556	2.94099	2.91220	2.88388	2.82861	2.77509	2.72325	2.67301	2.62432	2.57710
4	3.95050	3.92611	3.90197	3.85438	3.80773	3.71710	3.62990	3.54595	3.46511	3.38721	3.31213
5	4.92587	4.88944	4.85343	4.78264	4.71346	4.57971	4.45182	4.32948	4.21236	4.10020	3.99271
6	5.89638	5.84560	5.79548	5.69719	5.60143	5.41719	5.24214	5.07569	4.91732	4.76654	4.62288
7	6.86207	6.79464	6.72819	6.59821	6.47199	6.23028	6.00205	5.78637	5.58238	5.38929	5.20637
8	7.82296	7.73661	7.65168	7.48593	7.32548	7.01969	6.73274	6.46321	6.20979	5.97130	5.74664
9	8.77906	8.67158	8.56602	8.36052	8.16224	7.78611	7.43533	7.10782	6.80169	6.51523	6.24689
10	9.73041	9.59958	9.47130	9.22218	8.98259	8.53020	8.11090	7.72173	7.36009	7.02358	6.71008
11	10.67703	10.52067	10.36763	10.07112	9.78685	9.25262	8.76048	8.30641	7.88687	7.49867	7.13896
12	11.61893	11.43491	11.25508	10.90751	10.57534	9.95400	9.38507	8.86325	8.38384	7.94269	7.53608
13	12.44615	12.34235	12.13374	11.73153	11.34837	10.63496	9.98565	9.39357	8.85268	8.35765	7.90378
14	13.48871	13.24302	13.00370	12.54338	12.10625	11.29607	10.56312	9.89864	9.29498	8.74547	8.24424
15	14.41662	14.13699	13.86505	13.34323	12.84926	11.93794	11.11839	10.37966	9.71225	9.10791	8.55948
16	15.33993	15.02431	14.71787	14.13126	13.57771	12.56110	11.65230	10.83777	10.10590	9.44665	8.85137
17	16.25863	15.90502	15.56225	14.90765	14.29187	13.16612	12.16567	11.27407	10.47726	9.76322	9.12164
18	17.17277	16.77918	16.39827	15.67256	14.99203	13.75351	12.65930	11.68959	10.82760	10.05909	9.37189
19	18.08236	17.64683	17.22601	16.42617	15.67846	14.32380	13.13394	12.08532	11.15812	10.33560	9.60360
20	18.98742	18.50802	18.04555	17.16864	16.35143	14.87747	13.59033	12.46221	11.46992	10.59401	9.81815

TABLE A.5 AREA UNDER THE CURVE: STANDARD NORMAL DISTRIBUTION

The entries in the table give the areas under
the standard normal curve from 0 to z.

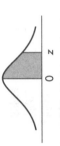

z	.00	.01	.02	.03	.04	.05	.06	.07	.08	.09
0.0	.0000	.0040	.0080	.0120	.0160	.0199	.0239	.0279	.0319	.0359
0.1	.0398	.0438	.0478	.0517	.0557	.0596	.0636	.0675	.0714	.0753
0.2	.0793	.0832	.0871	.0910	.0948	.0987	.1026	.1064	.1103	.1141
0.3	.1179	.1217	.1255	.1293	.1331	.1368	.1406	.1443	.1480	.1517
0.4	.1554	.1591	.1628	.1664	.1700	.1736	.1772	.1808	.1844	.1879
0.5	.1915	.1950	.1985	.2019	.2054	.2088	.2123	.2157	.2190	.2224
0.6	.2257	.2291	.2324	.2357	.2389	.2422	.2454	.2486	.2517	.2549
0.7	.2580	.2611	.2642	.2673	.2704	.2734	.2764	.2794	.2823	.2852
0.8	.2881	.2910	.2939	.2967	.2995	.3023	.3051	.3078	.3106	.3133
0.9	.3159	.3186	.3212	.3238	.3264	.3289	.3315	.3340	.3365	.3389
1.0	.3413	.3438	.3461	.3485	.3508	.3531	.3554	.3577	.3599	.3621
1.1	.3643	.3665	.3686	.3708	.3729	.3749	.3770	.3790	.3810	.3830
1.2	.3849	.3869	.3888	.3907	.3925	.3944	.3962	.3980	.3997	.4015

z										
1.4	.4192	.4207	.4222	.4236	.4251	.4265	.4279	.4292	.4306	.4319
1.5	.4332	.4345	.4357	.4370	.4382	.4394	.4406	.4418	.4429	.4441
1.6	.4452	.4463	.4474	.4484	.4495	.4505	.4515	.4525	.4535	.4545
1.7	.4554	.4564	.4573	.4582	.4591	.4599	.4608	.4616	.4625	.4633
1.8	.4641	.4649	.4656	.4664	.4671	.4678	.4686	.4693	.4699	.4706
1.9	.4713	.4719	.4726	.4732	.4738	.4744	.4750	.4756	.4761	.4767
2.0	.4772	.4778	.4783	.4788	.4793	.4798	.4803	.4808	.4812	.4817
2.1	.4821	.4826	.4830	.4834	.4838	.4842	.4846	.4850	.4854	.4857
2.2	.4861	.4864	.4868	.4871	.4875	.4878	.4881	.4884	.4887	.4890
2.3	.4893	.4896	.4898	.4901	.4904	.4906	.4909	.4911	.4913	.4916
2.4	.4918	.4920	.4922	.4925	.4927	.4929	.4931	.4932	.4934	.4936
2.5	.4938	.4940	.4941	.4943	.4945	.4946	.4948	.4949	.4951	.4952
2.6	.4953	.4955	.4956	.4957	.4959	.4960	.4961	.4962	.4963	.4964
2.7	.4965	.4966	.4967	.4968	.4969	.4970	.4971	.4972	.4973	.4974
2.8	.4974	.4975	.4976	.4977	.4977	.4978	.4979	.4979	.4980	.4981
2.9	.4981	.4982	.4982	.4983	.4984	.4984	.4985	.4985	.4986	.4986
3.0	.4987	.4987	.4987	.4988	.4988	.4989	.4989	.4989	.4990	.4990

SOURCE: Prem S. Mann, Statistics for Business and Economics, John Wiley & Sons, 1994.

INDEX

α, 243, 244
  determining, 247–249
Action points, 246
Algebra review, 291–329
Alternative hypothesis, 240, 241
Annuities:
  beginning-of-term, 67–69
  defining, 66–76
  end-of-term, 69–70
  future value of, 68–70
  influences on, 67, 76
  present value of, 73–76
  rate of, 67
  time period of, 67
  timing in, 67
Average deviation, 178–180

β, 243, 244
  determining, 249–251
  significance of, 251–252
Bernoulli, Jakob, 198
Bernoulli trials, 198–199
Best estimator, 270
Best fit, 273
Binomial distribution:
  applications of, 206–208
  approximating with normal distribution, 233–234
  finding mean/standard deviation for, 233–234
  shortcuts for, 205–206
Binomial probability function, 201–202
Bins, 150–151, 171
Bivariate analysis, 260
  steps in conducting, 262–264
Bonds, 89–115
  coupon, 89, 90–93, 99–100, 109

determining price of, 106–107, 109–110
discount, 104–106
factors affecting, 107
as investments, 90, 97–99, 115
parity of market for, 104
premium, 102–104
pricing with NPV, 139–140
purpose of, 89–90
rate of return, 107–108
workings of, 89–91
yield to maturity, 111–114
zero-coupon, 89, 93–97, 114–115
Buying versus leasing, 78–79

Calculators:
  benefits of using, 13
  mistakes in use of, 14–15, 72
  registers in, 15, 29–30, 49
Cash flows, 65–87
  applications of, 78–87
  comparing, 133–134
  conventions in analyzing, 119
  diagramming, 50, 121
  negative/zero, 134–136, 138–139
  types of, 117
Causation versus correlation, 260
Central limit theorem, 228
Central tendency, 156–159, 203
  methods of identifying, 156–157
Chebyshev, P.L., 184–185
Chebyshev's rule, 184–185, 214
Class marks, 185